The Compassionate Conservative

SEEKING RESPONSIBILITY AND HUMAN DIGNITY

by Joseph J. Jacobs, Ph.D.

Huntington House Publishers

Huntington House Publishers
P.O. Box 53788
Lafayette, Louisiana 70505

Library of Congress Card Catalog Number 95-78181
Hardback 1-56384-108-8
Tradepaper 1-56384-106-1

Printed in the U.S.A.

Dedication

To my daughters, Meg, Linda, and Val,
their hearts full of liberal compassion, who express
their affection and love by calling me
"the compassionate conservative."

Contents

Part Three
Toward Solutions

Foreword

After half a century of watching the proliferation of government programs, the American people are questioning whether government truly has, as liberal politicians claim, the wherewithal to provide the cure for society's ills. That questioning has afforded conservatives a prime opportunity to dispel a myth that has been perpetrated across the national political spectrum for decades: the myth that liberal political policy is inherently more compassionate and altruistic than conservative social and economic policy.

The purveyors of that myth have taken advantage of a common presupposition that cultural values are somehow antithetical to economic achievement. This opposition is, in fact, quite false. Democratic capitalism has been history's best weapon against poverty, oppression, and tyranny. Free markets have generated an environment in which an unrivaled number of men and women have been able to attain for themselves an unparalleled standard of living. As economist Joseph Schumpeter once observed, "The capitalists' achievement does not consist in providing silk stockings for queens, but in bringing them within reach of factory girls."

Compassion administered through the state on the other hand, though it may provide basic needs to many, can eventually become an obstacle to escaping poverty. For example, if a single mother qualifying for assistance under our current welfare system were to take a job, she would be faced with the highest effective marginal tax rates on the books; thus her net income would total less than her welfare check. Such policy penalizes personal initiative, fosters dependence, and illustrates why the truer measure of compassion is not how many are receiving assistance but how few.

Some conservatives think there is a better way for the state to provide for the disadvantaged: by creating opportunity—opportunity for ownership, jobs, entrepreneurship, innovation, savings, and investment. The principle at work here is that expressed by Maimonides, the Jewish philosopher, that the highest level of charity is finding a person a job so that he or she will no longer have to rely on charity. In pursuing a policy of opportunity, conservatives can demonstrate a compassionate spirit that considers the welfare of the whole person, not just those needs that can be fed with a little bit of cash. Compassionate conservatives, like Dr. Joseph Jacobs and me, believe it is time to reinvent government programs in such a way as to remove the incentives to failure and replace them with opportunities (and thereby motivations) to succeed.

While America was fully under the sway of the compassion myth, liberals successfully misconstrued this conservative message of opportunity vs. handouts—especially when applied to issues such as funding for education, affirmative action, nationalized health care, welfare reform, and progressive taxation—as an unsympathetic one. If conservatives are to succeed, therefore, in completing the revolution which began with the 1994 elections, the burden is upon them to demonstrate that their motives are equally benevolent as those of the liberals though the reasoning behind their proposals may differ.

In other words, in order to create the kind of opportunity that will uplift the nation's downtrodden, conservatism must be accompanied by high ideals and strong moral values. Conservatives can seem cold and calculating when they disregard the moral, social, and cultural corollaries of their precepts. In so doing, they lose the enthusiasm that can transform an election into a cause. As the late historian Russell Kirk said, when economic conservatism is separated from moral values, both rot separately, in separate tombs.

It was Abraham Lincoln who argued that both components of the conservative ideology, the economic and the moral, are essential and that abandoning either would cause the Republican party to "go to pieces." This combination of economic opportunity and moral passion proved unbeatable. It was the real explanation for decades of Republican dominance. When it was abandoned, that dominance abruptly ended. Frederick Douglass wrote, "The life of the Republican Party lay in its devotion to justice, liberty and humanity. When it abandoned or slighted those great moral ideas and devoted itself to materialistic measures, it no longer appealed to the heart of the nation."

That debate from the last century could have been taken from this morning's newspaper. The feelings are just as strong and the response must be the same. It should be our goal to create a coalition of conscience that will inspire both moral and economic hope and build a culture worthy of freedom.

Dr. Joseph Jacobs' timely work, *The Compassionate Conservative*, is a great contribution to that cause. Because of his lifetime of accomplishment in business and philanthropy, he recognizes that the achievements of capitalism depend on the achievement of the human spirit. I applaud Dr. Jacobs for setting the record straight—for redefining conservatism, and for challenging the myth that capitalists and those who believe in the marketplace are by nature greedy and unsympathetic. The truth is, as compassionate conservatives, we are believers in the power and promise of free markets, free minds, and free nations. We are also believers in fostering the values—and the opportunities—that make that promise possible.

—JACK KEMP

Preface

For many of us, the phrase *compassionate conservative* is an oxymoron. But, as you'll see from reading this book, one can learn a lot by peering beneath the labels. The Jacobs family has spent a lifetime doing just that.

Ours isn't an atypical story. As third generation Americans—the affluent children of a successful entrepreneur born of immigrant parents—the three of us have all been political liberals, and feminists. From our point of view, we have seen our father become more conservative through the years, increasingly voting for Republican and often (in our view) right-wing candidates. Because we are all outspoken, we rarely agreed with each other on political issues. At times, our discussions became loud and heated, with him calling us irrational and us calling him insensitive. During one such battle, he accused us of being opinionated, and we responded, "Where do you think we learned it?" We ended laughing. (A few years later, we gave him a plaque inscribed with a quote from Jonathan Swift, "We love each other because our ailments are the same," which he has hung proudly on the wall of the kitchen.)

With his growing success, Dad also became familiar with the power and destructive potential of inherited wealth. Although less experienced, we intuitively agreed with him. In 1989, to make this conviction concrete, Dad established the Jacobs Family Foundation, to allow us to participate in giving away the money that we would have inherited. Cooperation was difficult at first, as the three of us were used to the shorthand equation of: conservative = evil. To us, conservatives were selfish (i.e., rich) people who were insensitive in dealing with the problems of minorities and the poor. Yet, here were our parents, wanting to give the best part of their fortune away to these very poor, and including us in the process.

The three of us wanted to have input into the way the money was given away. So, it behooved us to jump feet-first into the debate and try to outvote him whenever our views came into direct conflict.

The power to outvote him led inevitably to the specter of his money going to the causes he found most odious. Yet, the fact that he willingly gave up that power was a testament to his willingness to consider our point of view.

We began to realize that the foundation was not a contest; that is, that we were not pitting our liberal views against his conservative ones. In fact, it was clear that the compassion which we had to ascribe to our parents in the beginning just to get along, actually existed! We became cautious about what we brought to the table, and began to feel our way through the process of what would bring consensus and what wouldn't. When one of us began to show interest in a micro-enterprise group that funded small banks in Mexico, we agreed unanimously to give them a small grant. Here was something that both liberals and conservatives could get behind! It was pure capitalism, yet it targeted the poorest of the poor, particularly women, which appealed to the liberal sensibilities of the three of us.

That we could reach a common goal by agreed-upon means was a revelation to all of us—parents and daughters alike. This thin thread of commonality grew into the vision we now share: our deep-felt commitment to self-help programs and the self-esteem they bring. We try to express our compassion in concrete ways and are able to achieve consensus on almost every issue.

The terms *liberal* and *conservative* mean less to us now and we resist almost instinctively the labeling we used to do so readily. It is a tribute to our parents, though, that we have all had the freedom to voice our opinions and, at the same time, the capacity to change them.

—Margaret, Linda, and Valerie Jacobs

Acknowledgments

Where do ideas come from? Few, if any, are truly original. That incredible computer we call a brain receives and stores innumerable bits of data—in my case for close to eight decades. The sources of those data and how they got integrated into the thoughts in this book are lost in time and dim memory. Tens of thousands of written words I've read and listened to, from conversations and observations in my ethnic neighborhood in Brooklyn; from family, friends, and business associates; from heads of state, leading political figures, Nobel laureates, and intellectuals at whose feet I worshipped—all are there.

Though tracing the origin of ideas is difficult, if not impossible, I was helped immensely by Rick Henderson of the Reason Foundation, who ferreted out obscure references that had helped form my thoughts. He also provided many new references that reinforced these ideas. He and his staff did a monumental job in providing authoritative support for the ideas I promulgated.

Heather Wood Ion, author and intellectual, provided coherence, innumerable pertinent references, and a critical viewpoint during the preparation of the manuscript that was a firm and welcome guiding hand to my efforts.

Ron Cummings and Jennifer Vanica, my colleagues in the Jacobs Family Foundation, were my "loyal opposition"— along with my daughters. I defended *and* modified these ideas in good-natured Socratic dialogue with all of them.

Pat Sangster translated my mostly illegible scribblings (I never learned to type) to that mysterious and fearsome device called a word processor, which produced, as though by magic, something I could read and edit—innumerable times I might add. A heartfelt thanks for her patience and good humor.

I have had the good fortune to be able to test these ideas in practice—in the real world. I acknowledge and pay tribute to my colleagues in Jacobs Engineering Group who have demonstrated repeatedly that compassion need not condone indulgence and that high standards of ethics, honesty, and performance are the ultimate acknowledgment of human dignity and the only certain path to success. They have demonstrated beyond question that pride is the ultimate reward for constructive and demanding compassion. As a proud "teacher," I acknowledge that my pupils have surpassed me and do honor to my name.

To many friends like Michael Novak, Joe Alibrandi, Bob Barton, Joe Farah, Clay LaForce, David Dreier, Peter Tanous, and many others who have read the manuscript—I thank all of them for their enthusiastic encouragement.

Finally, to my family, the center of my life, the arboretum of open discussion in which the synthesis of this book was made possible, I express my great love and devotion.

Introduction

We must dream of an aristocracy of achievement arising out of a democracy of opportunity.

—Thomas Jefferson

The need to command the "high ground" is an instinct from our prehistoric origins: To be on the hill in order to spot the game which will provide food; to be able to see your enemies approach; above all, to have the advantage in attacking. In one way or another, command of the high ground is a prize we all seek.

While in war, real estate, or hunting, the instinct for the high ground has a plausible derivation, its transposition to the realm of ideas, morals, or ethics is less obvious, but no less real. Earthen hills have easily defined boundaries, but in the world of ideas, those boundaries are less clearly delineated because the coordinates are in language and in words—not in meters or feet. For ages, scholars have explored the imprecision, the subtle nuances, and, above all, the shifting meanings of words. Because words appeal to the emotions, form ideas, and inspire action, they are the tools used to command the intellectual and moral high ground.

Words and language have been a passion with me for a long time. For an engineer to be in love with language may seem out of character. Anyone who has had any dealings with engineers knows what I mean. As the founder and chairman of a company that employs thousands of engineers, I have found the struggle to cut through the turgid wall of ponderous clichés to be endless. I know why this is so. We engineers are taught to be precise, to look at things objectively, to observe physical phenomena dispassionately. Yet, words do have passion and all sorts of human feelings embedded within them. One of the writing habits of scientists and engineers that irritates me is the repetitive use of the passive voice—"It was determined," "It was observed," "The following conclusions were drawn," and on and on. By using that dull, stultifying style, scientists imply an objectivity that they are afraid does not really exist. They try to deny their own humanity.

Nevertheless, I understand, because along with my reverence for language, my engineering training cries out for more precision, more accuracy, and above all, for timeless consistency in the words we use. Sadly, none of these is attainable. An inch, or a foot, or a mile is always the same, carefully defined by an inscribed bar of metal in the Bureau of Standards in Washington. One of the beauties of language, and yet one of its most disturbing features, is the ever-changing nuances and gradual shifts in meaning as a language lives, grows, and breathes.

This discussion of words and my interest in them has direct bearing upon the examination of efforts by those who claim to own the "high ground" of moral rectitude. I wish to challenge these claims.

While an inch is always an inch, words shift in meaning. A Socialist today is not the same as a Socialist of yesteryear—nor is a liberal or a conservative, and on and on, through every nuance of moral and social thought. I have struggled with those two words, *liberal* and *conservative*, for years. They defy precise description. My own progression from the radical activism of my college days to my more conservative positions of today has led me to wonder whether I have undergone a drastic change over the intervening years. Indeed, in many ways I have, but when I probe my inner feelings and the emotions that motivate me, I find very little difference from the youth of fifty years ago. My desire to do good, to help people, to alleviate suffering, to cry against injustice, to care, in the broadest sense, is undiminished. Has the transposition from liberal to conservative been the result of a diminishment in my desire to "do good"? Unequivocally not! Then, perhaps something about those two labels, liberal and conservative, has changed.

I can and shall mount arguments to show that today's liberals are, by any classical definition, really conservative, for isn't the prime characteristic of a conservative the reliance upon old-fashioned methodology—a reluctance to innovate? The techniques advocated by present-day liberals to solve social problems are merely a repetition of the same old prescriptions devised during Franklin D. Roosevelt's presidency more than fifty years ago. So, have the labels or the content changed?

Franklin Roosevelt's era was one of desperate, dark days, and I was there—in my high-school and college years. Whatever the reasons, laissez-faire capitalism and rugged individualism were simply not able to cope with the enormous dislocation in our economy. The only organizable force strong enough was a political one—the government.

The traditional stronghold of voluntary control in our democracy was local government. Unfortunately, it too was helpless. FDR was visionary enough, or demagogic enough—it matters not which—to use the central government effectively. Government action, much of it of dubious legal validity, played an important psychological role in calming and helping desperate, unhappy people. Liberal leaders of today still look to government to implement their compassion. However, the conditions of the thirties were vastly different from those of today. Why stick to rigid repetition and such so-called conservative solutions for today's social problems? Liberals are bound by their tradition, even more so than conservatives.

To the extent that conservatives are willing to resist methods which restrict freedom, and to rely more on the people to devise their own remedies, they are, in fact, really more liberal. Their objective is clearly to liberate the people in this case from an overbearing government. The individualism of the early twentieth century failed in a time of extraordinary need. But, isn't it clear that the big-government approach Roosevelt employed in the thirties has grown into an oppressive force? To the extent that a conservative seeks to liberate the common man from his dependence upon the goodwill of government, he is by root definition a liberal. Thus, the traditional guardian of order, the conservative, rejects too much order—a paradox.

So, to whom am I referring when I use the word *liberal*? I mean those who believe that they have a monopoly upon compassion or that their compassion is deeper or stronger than that of others. I mean those who believe that their solutions to society's problems are superior to others' because their motives are stronger or purer than the motives of those offering alternative solutions. These, then, are the liberals with whom I take issue.

On the other hand, we conservatives have a tendency to characterize liberals as fuzzy-headed or too idealistic or lacking practicality. These characterizations, however, really only speak to their solutions and not to their motives. We readily accept that their desire to do good is unimpeachable. We merely ask that we be accorded the same status.

As much as I'd like to use labels that describe the way people actually think, I cannot avoid using the shorthand words liberal and conservative. Still, labels are treacherous because people are not frozen in immobile patterns. We can only talk about average or typical attitudes, though we know we invite attack by comparison with specific contradictions, which are inevitable.

In the nineteenth century, liberals placed their faith in individual citizens rather than in bureaucrats or social elites as they do today. (The contemporary term *empowerment* could appropriately be applied to the liberals of that day.) Conservatives, by contrast, sought to maintain a stratified society with order imposed from above.

The struggle to reconcile these labels, liberal and conservative, has troubled me for some time. I've given many speeches where I used the term *Jeffersonian Conservative*. Since most liberals take Jefferson to be their patron saint, that too seems to be an oxymoron. In fact, Jefferson almost wholly supported the real conservative agenda of today, as the quotations used throughout this book demonstrate.

If one were to make a public free association test describing liberals, words like *caring, sensitive, sympathetic, passionate,* and *unselfish* would have a very high correlation. Though most conservatives would vigorously deny the truth of it, we would reluctantly accept that among the broad population, the antonyms of those same words would have a similar correlation with the word conservative.

The best word I can think of to describe all the admired adjectives above is *compassion,* a word of Judeo-Christian ethic which denotes so many praiseworthy and highly regarded emotions that almost all aspire to it. It is the high ground of social and moral thought—and the liberals have captured it in their own minds and in the minds of the general populace. This is a false assumption and a shaky high ground. Nevertheless, by assuming virtually exclusive command of the high ground of morality, and the lofty motive of compassion, the liberals' solutions to human problems gain an extra gravitational force. It is that position that conservatives challenge.

It is this assumption that they have a special capacity for compassion that defines the liberal. Having made that assumption, then by their definition, those they deem to have less compassion are classified as conservatives. Were we able to convince them that we have compassion equal to theirs, it would shake the very roots of the liberal ethic.

What we observe is that compassion is so highly regarded that people go to desperate ends to seek objects for their compassion, attempting to validate their goodness for themselves and to others. What else can explain the passion for the snail darter or the desert tortoise, and the elevation of endangered species to almost divine status? The liberals, in their zeal to validate their compassion, create whole classes of poor, homeless, abused, sexually harassed, and stressed, by grouping all of the so-called victims in our society. When they run out of human pain, they go to animals or insects or forests.

Michael Novak, the religious philosopher, says, "Compassion is the lure of the left!" The basic reasoning goes like this: Their motives are pure and compassionate; therefore, their solutions to problems are blessed, whereas the solutions offered by conservatives are suspect. Most liberal arguments attempt to discredit conservative solutions by discrediting motives instead of methodology.

One might legitimately ask, "Why is it so important to establish a stake in the compassionate high ground?" It is important because the wish for validation of one's compassion is one of the powerful motivations of man.* The conservative view is sorely needed to prevent, or at least to temper, the headlong rush into destructive actions often advocated by liberals in the name of compassion. But, conflicting methodologies will never be considered objectively or on their merits conservative as long as the liberals claim moral superiority over conservatives.

Once the question of motivation is bypassed, once it is conceded that compassion is not the sole domain of liberals, once it is accepted that conservatives may be driven by compassion as intense as that of liberals, then the true differences between conservative and liberal methodology can be delineated. We can then debate the real question, which is "Will Route A be more likely to attain compassionate ends than Route B?" Attributing impure motives to Route B is a tactic that results in an emotional, rather than a rational, response to issues. Yet, it is done every day.

The true measure of the value of compassion does not reside in the intensity of the emotion, but rather in the public good created when the compassion is put into practice. Most importantly, in the desire to help others, we must first ensure that we do no harm.

After examining my own transition over the years, I decisively rejected the idea that I have lost my compassion. What, then, are the differences between what I was then and what I am now? Out of experience, the solutions I gravitate

---

*I use the generic term *man* in this book for convenience, and not because I want to avoid being politically correct.

to now are more attuned to the real world that I have lived in for almost eight decades. I do not argue that my solutions are implicitly better than less pragmatic ones. Many great actions have sprung from idealistic, impulsive, and emotional acts, born out of passionate conviction—but many tragic ones have, too. As we get experience, we learn that life is infinitely more complex than our innocent dreams. We learn that what appear to be easy and simple solutions often have secondary and tertiary effects which can pervert the ends we had sought. Thus, many liberal solutions often tend to produce undesirable side effects.

I have observed that liberals use the theoretical concept of compassion as their ultimate value; they view the motive as an end in itself. I do not diminish the great accomplishments of liberal zeal, fueled by indignation and impatience at the rate at which social injustice is rectified. Nor do I pretend that conservative compassion and caution are necessarily superior to that of the liberals. But, if the compassion of the conservatives is considered *equal* to that of liberals, then we can, together, build a better world.

What is the essential delineation between liberal and conservative compassion? In the early days of the church, the word *Agape* was often translated as *love*, or *charity*. Yet, it really denotes compassion, as I use it—the kind of honest and often disciplining love a classical teacher, coach, or religious leader would have for a student—helping him to grow up, do it on his own, take responsibility, and, in turn, pass these values on to the next generation. That is the compassion that I seek and that most conservatives share with me.

Why am I writing this book? I make no pretense at being a scholar. On the other hand, I consider myself a thoughtful man. I have a sense of social responsibility, and in my reading I have been exposed to social and philosophic theories that have intrigued and stimulated me. My training as an engineer leads me impulsively to put theories to the test.

In a fifty-year career in business, I have been surprised at how many correlations, as well as contradictions, I have been able to observe in how these theoretical ideas work in practice. In particular, I have been struck by the difficulties involved in putting compassion into practice benignly. Time after time, this noble force has been degraded to something not so noble.

Not having been able to live my life as a laboratory experiment, collecting and comparing data, I confess that the value of my observations is not scientific. But, it is my hope that the events and observations which made me evolve from the liberal views of my college days will help others understand what impels us conservatives, our compassion intact, to seek our place in influencing and realizing individual, societal, governmental, and even global goals and visions.

Hopefully, this book can clarify the words that separate us. Then, conservatives can make their arguments from the same moral heights as the liberals—for we, too, search for self-validation through compassion. Together, whatever the labels we use, we desperately seek nothing less than a better world.

Part One

Roots of the Problem

1. The Tyranny of Words

I have sworn upon the altar of God eternal hostility against every tyranny over the mind of man.

—Thomas Jefferson

This chapter heading is borrowed from the title of a book by Stuart Chase published more than fifty years ago. It was not a new idea then, nor is it now, that words can tyrannize us; that they can take on special meanings that make our emotions surge, that impel us to action, that build up or tear down our self-esteem. From Socrates to Marshall McLuhan, the best minds have remarked upon and studied the power of words to persuade, to move men and mountains, to cause immense good—or immense harm.

I read Chase at an early age when my mind was awakening, and it started me on a lifelong addiction to words. For one embarking upon an engineering education, this was difficult to accommodate. Engineering requires precision, immutable physical laws, and constancy. The "other" language is diffuse, constantly changing and, most difficult of all to accept, quite capable of being interpreted in a myriad of ways. Yet, that is precisely what hooked me on words. Language emanates from the heart and engineering from the brain, so to speak. The "left brain" dominates in one case and the "right brain" dominates in the other. Just as engineering can help create an airplane, a computer, an automobile, and so many other things to improve our lives, so words can impel men to die, to exult, to love, to hate, to sacrifice, and to envy. Words have the power to do these things with the same force as the great machines the engineers design.

As I gradually recognized that both the precision of engineering and science, and the constant mutation of language, together represented what we really are and what we are moved by, I accepted and embraced this ambivalence. The world of unrepealable physical laws binds our lives within defined limits. But, the world of emotion frees our minds and spirits from those constraints. Either can impel action or mobilize energy.

Take the word *compassion*. Can one think of a word with more inherent moral force? Isn't it the central moral imperative of the Judeo-Christian ethic? But, *think* about it. Doesn't it also imply a certain lack of humility on the part of those who are compassionate? And, isn't humility itself often trumpeted as one of the great virtues by that same ethic? One can slide very easily from compassion to feeling sorry for, and from there to pity. To equate compassion with pity is certainly troublesome, but who is wise enough to know where the line is? For with pity, that assumption of superiority is laid naked, and for the pitied, the degradation is palpable.

Charity may be secretly resented by those who receive it, though public gratitude is expected. Coming from a proud family and a proud culture, I've learned that compassion can be devastatingly destructive because it can so easily become denigrating. Sensitivity to this by-product is often a missing ingredient in liberal compassion. The temptation to use compassion as an agent to increase one's own self-esteem, at the expense of the receiver of that compassion, is difficult to resist.

Take another derivative line from compassionate to *indulgent*. This is equally troubling because being indulgent is not nearly as virtuous as being compassionate. Again, who is wise enough to know when compassion insidiously moves to indulgence and finally—even worse—to dependency?

A simplistic and homely analogy is a thoroughly spoiled child who grows up into an unhappy, maladjusted man-child who cannot function adequately in the world. What starts out as compassion and love gradually turns to indulgence by the unwise parents, and finally to spoiled rotten. Compassion thus becomes corrosive.

Corrosive compassion—what a chilling combination of words! It signals that the dignity of any abstract concept can be defiled when reduced to practice—as we will see repeatedly throughout this book.

Perhaps that is the essential point which distinguishes the conservative view from the liberal one. Liberals often regard their virtues in absolute, unimpeachable terms. But, compassion must eventually be translated into action before its impact can be enjoyed by society—otherwise, it's only a self-indulgent dream. Therein lies the paradox, because the action too often degrades the purity of the motive. How many aphorisms do we have to convey this? We say, "He meant well" and "The road to hell is paved with good intentions." It seems to me that the vulnerability of the liberals' exclusive claim to this moral high ground is the quicksand upon which it rests—reduction to practice.

The words *reduction to practice* have a special derivation from patent law. It is an underlying principle that an idea, no matter how exquisite or brilliant, is not patentable. An absolute requirement for an idea to be patentable is that it must be demonstrated to work. This pragmatic (and essentially conservative) idea must be applied to social theory to accord it the virtue it claims when it's just a theoretical construct. Compassion, untested, is a highly virtuous and prized emotion. It is in the implementation, or reduction to practice, that conservative compassion and liberal compassion differ. Because the emotion is pure, liberals tend to bestow upon their methodology a special virtue. The conservative, on the other hand, regards the implementation and the effects produced therefrom as the primary criteria for judging the value of the compassionate thought.

My late friend Sidney Hook, in his transition from a Marxist to one of Marxism's most vociferous and effective critics, stated this eloquently: "I was guilty of judging capitalism by its operations and socialism by its hopes and aspirations; capitalism by its works and socialism by its literature."

I was fortunate to have known Sidney Hook well enough

to have had a number of discussions and arguments with him. I rarely prevailed in these arguments. The only time I came close was when I asked him to define his then-current politics. He said, "I suppose I would call myself a democratic socialist," which reflected, I thought, his reluctance to go all the way to "conservative." The word oxymoron had not been invented then, so I said, "But Sidney, that's internally self-contradictory." His terse reply, "You may be right," was as close to winning a point with him as I ever came.

The Socialist theoreticians are so used to comparing their theory to other theories that they cannot bring themselves to evaluate their theories in light of the reality of socialism. Ask the convinced Socialist or the passionate advocate of central planning why he persists in advocating a system that has been demonstrated to be a failure and the likely answer will be, "If only the right people had been involved it could have worked. There is nothing wrong with the system proposed if only the right people implemented it!" That is the whole point. Men are imperfect—even those who construct the theory.

The Realm of Emotion

We need the untrammeled, uninhibited emotions to integrate ourselves from childhood to adulthood. Having reached adulthood, must we lose all of our wonderment and surrender to cynicism? True maturity is, in my view, the best balance between the restrictive obligations of the real world and the lack of restraint of our youthful yearnings. In philosophic jargon, internally we have the classic conflict between freedom and order.

That segment of society which nourishes the childhood yearning in us, I choose to call the "art world," for want of a better term. Let me enumerate those I include in this realm and let the reader choose a better one: Of course, the artists, the sculptors, the painters, the composers, and the craftsmen, but also those who write—newspapers, books, poetry, plays. Include as well the performers, screen and television actors, the sportsmen, the musicians, the magicians, the jugglers, and the comedians—in short, those who successfully stimulate our emotions.

All of these appeal primarily to our childlike and primal instincts—those parts of our childhood and youth that were uninhibited by the restrictions of the civilized society. They are constructive parts of our adult life only when filtering out the dark, destructive sides of our instinctual youthful behavior, the childishness, if you will. Along with our maturity and sense of responsibility, we accept with joy and gratitude what these wonderful people have to offer us, for they nourish our emotions without any boundaries of inhibition.

It is not a surprising observation that many creative people, perhaps the majority, tend to be politically liberal. Of course, there are conservative creative people, too. I cannot use a slide rule to calibrate maturity, liberalism, or conservatism. I, therefore, leap unashamedly to the observation that liberalism and liberal thought are less inhibited and conservatives are the opposite. Neither can claim moral superiority. The creative see the world as they yearn for it to be; conservatives picture the world as it is. But, neither group has a monopoly upon wishing it were better.

I revert to Thomas Sowell's much more elegant analysis and description of these opposing ways of perceiving social problems. He describes what I might label uninhibited as "unconstrained vision." In contrast, the "constrained visions," which can be categorized as mature, recognize that human beings and human nature are imperfect. They respect history and do not let their hopefulness for the perfectibility of man blind them to the reality of what we really are. It's a curious anomaly that unconstrained vision focuses upon objectives, whereas constrained vision focuses on the process, because, according to the conservative argument, the objectives cannot be reached if the process is faulty.

The Power of Words

There are many words of great power. One burned in my mind as a particularly egregious example of a fine word that has been totally corrupted in the present-day lexicon is the word *discrimination*. I am a scarred veteran of the bruising fight over forced busing in the early sixties. Our three daughters were of high-school age at the time and the Pasadena/Altadena area in California where we lived was indeed segregated—not by any legal process, but by natural gravitational force—an all too human instinct to be comfortable with people who are most like us.

I remember attending a meeting supporting forced busing, presided over by a liberal white minister who urged the audience to expiate its guilt over the discrimination prevalent in our society by supporting busing as the only means of overcoming segregation. I got up and said something like this:

> I think your choice of words is bad. I am proud to be a discriminating man. I teach my children to be discriminating—to discriminate between good behavior and bad, between good literature and bad, and the good and bad of social behavior. It is only the bigot who will ascribe good or bad characteristics to a person based solely on skin color, ethnic origin, or any other visible characteristic that is in no way connected to his thought processes and especially to his actions. That is not discrimination; that is a lack of discrimination—that is generalization of the worst kind. And generalization is the antonym of discrimination. It is those who generalize without discrimination who should be censured.

I then went on to warn that in the zeal to eliminate involuntary segregation and prejudice, we could be introducing harmful secondary effects. I questioned whether the impact upon children being literally forced away from their neighborhoods and friends, to mix with strangers with whom they had few common interests, might defeat the well-intentioned objectives. I worried about the emotional impact upon small children being used to assuage the guilt of their parents. I stressed that this emotional impact existed as much for the black children as for the white.

When done, I was subjected to a scathing denunciation

by the minister, who ridiculed me and accused me of out-right prejudice, saying it was obvious that I was against busing because of personal antipathy toward "colored people." I was portrayed as a bigoted redneck to be scorned by all right thinking people.

I remember being suffused with anger at this knee-jerk liberal who inferred that if I didn't agree with the solutions he supported, my motives were impure and suspect—not that my criticisms were good or bad.

After this incident, I became more aware of the liberal tendency to impugn the motives of those who criticize their solutions to social problems. I began to note the liberal propensity to believe that their motives were purer than mine or those of other conservatives. This belief leads them to ascribe extra virtue to their prescriptions.

There are two words used recurrently in any discussion of race relations: *desegregation* and *integration*. They are often used interchangeably, yet they are quite different.

Desegregation is an action to remove any political acts which force segregation or separation of one group of citizens from another because of color. Thus, when the Supreme Court in *Brown vs. Board of Education* denied the concept of "separate but equal," that was a proper constitutional decision.

Not satisfied with its proper function of striking down segregation, the court then ventured into prescribing what the end results of desegregation should be. Though integration may be a desirable end to desegregation, it is by no means a proper arena for lawmaking—yet that's what the Supreme Court unwittingly tried to do.

Desegregation and integration are not the same thing. They differ in many ways. For instance, the question of time is a substantial differentiator. Segregation can be wiped out very quickly by passing laws that ban it. Integration, though, may take generations to accomplish and probably can never be done completely—and why should it?

To force integration requires one to make sociological judgments and sociology is, at best, imperfect. However, that's what the Supreme Court injected into what should have been a straightforward legal judgment. In 1968, when the Court ruled against de facto segregation, it opened a Pandora's box of sociological time bombs that led to bureaucracy and to the perversion of the Civil Rights Act of 1964 in order to legitimize quotas. These derivatives are based upon bad social doctrine and are producing unintended tragic results. The recent movement of some college students to form all-black fraternities says something about the dignity of individual choice in social matters.

Segregation was outlawed, but integration will result only from intelligent choice. Let the people decide if they want to integrate and how quickly they want it to happen. If we recognize that time is a factor, I am confident that the people, both black and white, will choose wisely. Forced integration is an affront to the dignity of everyone, including blacks.

I am constantly troubled by the demagoguery of black leaders who stake their claim to a piece of the economic pie based upon guilt. There is no recognition that the pointing of blame is also in itself racist and tribal. I have enough trouble avoiding being unfair or insensitive in my everyday actions without accepting guilt for deeds perpetrated by men now dead. As Thomas Sowell says, "Live people are being sacrificed because of what dead people did."

I am a devoted admirer of Thomas Sowell. A black economist of keen intellect, he has been a perpetual gadfly not only to the black political leadership, but to all the stereotypical white liberal social attitudes.

In one column, he addressed this question of guilt from a novel angle. He pointed out that slavery has existed in the world for thousands of years. The derivation of the word *slave* is from the ethnic origin of the "Slavs," who were sold into slavery over a much longer period than the Africans who were enslaved here. For thousands of years, the merchant class in many regions bought and sold slaves like any other commodity. Indeed, in Africa the taking of slaves between tribes was the norm. In the Western Hemisphere, the United States was not the primary user of African slaves. Brazil, for instance, had six times as many as we did.

What Sowell points out is that Western civilization, and

Americans in particular, were the first people in centuries of institutionalized slavery whose moral standards rejected servitude. He says:

> Despite the universality of this hideous institution and its victims, books and articles on slavery are overwhelmingly about slavery in the United States or at most, about slavery in the Western Hemisphere. Many use this as a moral indictment, selectively applied to Western Civilization.

> Ironically, it was Western civilization which eventually destroyed slavery around the world, during the era when European imperialism reached every continent. (*Forbes*, 11 April 1994)

The clear implication here is that, rather than be bogged down with a burden of unremitting guilt for this unsavory period in our history, we should take some solace in the fact that our forefathers were the moral leaders who caused the virtual elimination of slavery around the world. No wonder Thomas Sowell is viewed as so threatening by the liberal black political leadership. The idea that our historical guilt should be attenuated by some measure of pride at having been the leaders in overturning slavery does not serve the political agenda. The Civil War was a bloody testament to our moral position.

I freely acknowledge that the civil rights movement, inspired and led by liberals, was a great step forward for this country. To break the cycle of legal and institutional segregation required forceful measures, and for that the liberals are to be applauded. There have been, undoubtedly, many undesirable by-products, but on balance, the accomplishment was praiseworthy.

One bad by-product was the busing program. It was not desegregation; it was forced integration. The busing movement arose from a study by James G. Coleman, a sociologist from Johns Hopkins University. The report from a committee he headed, financed by the U.S. Office of Education, was entitled "Equality of Educational Opportunity" and published in July 1966.

The tyranny of words is illustrated nowhere better than

in this instance. According to *U.S. News and World Report*, the Office of Education "hailed [the report] as evidence that only through racial integration could Negroes be brought up to educational equality with whites. The U.S. Commission on Civil Rights cited the Coleman Report as a basis for recommending a federal law that would ban predominantly Negro schools."

But, Coleman never advocated forced integration. He wrote an article in the fall of 1967, making two clear observations:

1) The amount of money spent on schooling has very little to do with how well students perform, and

2) A child's home background plays a much more important role in his accomplishments in school than the racial composition of the classes he attends.

"Some observers have inferred from the report," Coleman wrote, "that only through racial integration will Negroes' educational achievement begin to match that of whites. . . . I believe such inferences are mistaken and that the recommendations following from them are self-defeating. Racial integration of the schools is important," he continued, "[but] the task of increasing achievement of lower-class children cannot be fully implemented by school integration even if integration were wholly achieved. Integration is not the only means, nor even necessarily the most efficient means for increasing lower-class achievement."

In later articles, Coleman wrote that the government, "using the courts if necessary, has an affirmative duty to end forced segregation in public schools, or to abolish two-track racial education." However, he also wrote that "it is not the place of the judicial system to forcibly integrate schools or housing. The democratic process must deal with these problems."

It seems to be generally acknowledged now, even by the original proponents of school busing, that it has been relatively ineffective and may have had damaging by-products. In the confrontation with that liberal minister, I asked only that the possibility of these bad by-products be considered.

None of the critics of busing has called for a return to

separate school systems for black and white youngsters. But, they do point out that the legitimate concerns of black parents and students were overshadowed by the desire of liberal reformers to do good, and thus, to validate their compassion. Though a hidden reason may have been to deflect envy or jealousy of middle-class whites by the underprivileged blacks, the image of doing good was a psychological payoff for the reformer.

Recent headlines have revealed that black college students are voluntarily and proudly resegregating themselves. What a startling turnabout! But, the pull for people with common interests, common problems, and common standards to gravitate toward each other is an all too human trait. Why liberals consider this sinful or insidious is beyond me. Though the exclusion of others from their closed circle can be cruel, the real losers are those who confine their lives in this way, excluding the richness of diversity. Those blacks who are cruelly excluding whites from their secret society should be cautioned that the comfort derived from speaking their special language and sharing their common pain may be less than it could be if diversity were accepted. I would not for a moment accuse these black students of immoral actions, as white fraternities and clubs were so accused in the sixties. I would, on the other hand, warn them that their lives may be much less complete.

Other programs of forced integration, as opposed to desegregation, are harmful, as well. Quota systems based upon the same racist factors—color or other arbitrarily determined minority characteristics—are in this category. Can anyone define a minority? It is an absolutely indefinable term. For example, why aren't we two million children of Lebanese immigrants a certifiable minority? Quotas based upon color, it seems to me, commit the same sin that the bigots did in the sixties. They generalize and do not discriminate based upon merit which, after all, is the only measure that can enhance self-worth.

To discriminate, in the form of quotas based upon color, is terribly demeaning to those who supposedly benefit from the quotas. To use color to discriminate *for* is as reprehensible as discriminating *against*. The late Arthur Ashe, a much admired black tennis player, eloquently articulated this point in his autobiography: "To use quotas as a means of rectifying past sins of prejudice is the most demeaning thing you can do to a minority." The black or Latino who believes that he was selected because the WASP society wanted to assuage its guilt cannot derive much self-esteem or satisfaction from being selected. Cynicism is the inevitable result.

Frankly, very few of us are willing to accept guilt foisted upon us by the liberal elite for what somebody else's forebears did. Indeed, most of us are descendants of immigrants who suffered similar oppression within recent memory. My father, for instance, came to this country from Lebanon in 1886, fleeing the cruel oppression of the Ottoman Empire which lasted for over four hundred years.

The final point here, however, is the stark illustration of how a great and wonderful word, discrimination, can be demeaned and corrupted. It may seem a trivial by-product, but the perversion of the great word discrimination from a virtue to one of opprobrium saddens me. But, it's done. It's finished. Anyone who discriminates is bad. However, like a good entrepreneur and risk-taker, I'll continue to try to rescue that fine word. All I ask is that we be fair.

But wait—*fair* is another word that is consistently misused, or more correctly, one that lacks any consistent meaning.

A common childhood memory flashes: "But, Mother, you're not being fair!" It is a very subjective word, isn't it? Fairness is purely in the eye of the beholder. Any situation in which we don't get what we think we deserve is labeled "unfair."

In the great demagoguery of income tax policy debate, fairness is the key word. "Everybody should be asked to pay their 'fair share' (of taxes)," the liberals trumpet. From that, the next leap is to "The rich should pay their 'fair share.'" Get that word *rich* in there—isn't that an attention grabber? Now we introduce the villain who ratifies the word fair, for is there any imagery about the word *rich* that bestows virtue? One must return to the early twentieth century, the Horatio Alger fables, for such associations. Fairness will get worked over pretty thoroughly in this book because it's such an inherent part of liberal rhetoric. Like compassion, it's a word of such implied virtue that the claim of being fair can be used to cover an enormous array of sins against society and to rationalize destructive actions that turn out to be anything but compassionate—or fair. The coupling of the word *fair* with *rich* makes a clear implication, doesn't it? It says quite clearly that the rich (perceived to be "Anyone who earns $100 a week more than I do") are not fair. They must be forced (by the liberals) to be fair. What arrogant demagoguery.

As alluded to in the Introduction—the very terms conservative and liberal can be easily turned on their heads. It's not very difficult for a conservative to argue convincingly that he truly is a liberal—wanting to "liberate" the people from the oppressive power of government—for we can classify the power of the bureaucracy over the disadvantaged as just another form of slavery. Listen in on the conversations of those in the welfare culture in the ghetto and you will find that the simultaneous fear and resentment of the "man"—or the bureaucrat upon whose goodwill they depend—is palpable. What must be avoided is that a new form of slavery, i.e., a dependency upon an ostensibly compassionate government or bureaucracy, does not turn out to be the social equivalent of the compassionate plantation owner. Above all, conservatives express their compassion by trying to free the underclass or the oppressed from their dependency upon big government and its oppressive straw bosses, the bureaucracy.

Another word that has thundered into modern discourse like the fourth horse of the Apocalypse is *entitlement*. What is the derivation of that word? I suppose a person is "entitled" to a reward for having done something. It seems clear that one must earn an entitlement by doing something useful that deserves to be rewarded. But, what are the requirements for entitlements in today's political dialogue? Unfortunately, the only requirement seems to be an established "need." A need becomes a right, and a right becomes an entitlement. The recipients rarely have done anything that entitles them to receive these benefits.

The use of the word *entitlement* reflects the inherent power of words to affect emotions. To illustrate the impact of word selection, in private industry, added payments given on top of straight salary are called "benefits." Benefits are given, but entitlements, on the other hand, are a collection of obligations. The emotional imagery of this word is important since entitlements are the fastest growing and, unfortunately, the most refractory part of our budget—a budget that is leading us into ruinous debt.

What do all of these words we've discussed have in common? They do not have what Stuart Chase (borrowing from the semanticists Ogden and Richards) calls a *referent*. There is no concrete object or thing in the real world to which they can be referred or compared. Even with a referent, there are no absolutes, only relative consistency. Using the words I have highlighted as though they had a consistent or agreed-upon meaning, is what makes the liberal rhetoric most damaging to society.

The media has helped institutionalize the corruption of the meaning of words that are now skewed substantially from their original intent. We are in danger of entering an era of Orwellian "new speak," with political correctness creating a hideous contradiction of our coveted right to free speech.

According to Joseph H. Berke in *Tyranny of Malice*, "Conformity is a further way of avoiding recognition and hostility for having or doing anything outstanding. It is a capitulation to the fear of being successful, which may be fed by strong social as well as internal pressures."

The current liberal conformity and the whole concept of political correctness is evidence of a corrosive fear of excellence and may also be a way of deflecting envy. We are basing social policy on a fear which expresses not only the politics of guilt, but also the politics of victimization. Political correctness was formerly only a term applicable to totalitarian states, but now it has pervaded our society like a virulent infection. It is an attempt to give rigid meanings to nonreferent words.

Those who have command of words, who know how to arouse our emotions, can not only make our hearts sing with joy, but they can also frighten us into self-destructive actions. The power to tyrannize us by selecting the words and pictures we see is an awesome one. We scientists, who can manipulate physical things, stand in awe and fear of the tyranny of words that can enslave us.

It should be quite apparent that I have no training or stature in semantics. Yet, I have unashamedly taken on a task that scholars have labored over for centuries—trying to explain or analyze words with other words! Nevertheless, I shall risk it, for I am an entrepreneur, and for most of my life I have courted failure and taken risk. The prospect of one more failure does not daunt me. On the other hand, the prospect of expressing to thoughtful people the danger inherent in words is worth undertaking. We must resist indoctrination. We do not want our emotions manipulated in order to have us support someone else's compassion.

Perhaps liberals are jealous because we judge our compassion to be as worthy as those who attempt to sway us to the liberal agenda. We must learn that the power of words to tyrannize us can also be used by conservatives to implement noncorrosive compassion.

2. The Arrogant Elitists

Men by their constitutions are naturally divided into two parties: 1) Those who fear and distrust the people, and wish to draw all powers from them into the hands of the higher classes; 2) Those who identify themselves with the people, have confidence in them, cherish and consider them as the most honest and safe, though not the most wise depository of the public interests.
—Thomas Jefferson

Elitism is a natural condition. It is an expression of the natural order of things. All men are created equal, but in any field they will display unequal talents. Yet, some who wish to deny this self-evident truth pursue political means to punish or neutralize the skillful and successful.

The unrealistic, falsely compassionate wish that inequality could be eliminated leads many liberals astray. They seek to avoid the dilemma of selecting the superior performers, or the elite. Ironically, these same people easily accept an intellectual elite. The liberals have trouble seeing the contradiction between their assumption of their own unequal (and superior) intellectual capacity and their desire for a political system that produces equal benefits for all.

Acceptance of differing capabilities comes easily when there are quantitative measures available, but acceptance decreases as the elite is selected by less and less precise measurements. The sports elite is a prime example of the former. Batting averages in baseball or handicaps in golf give us a precise measure and define an elite performance. In sports, especially, membership in this elite is so tenuous and short-lived that arrogance is self-limiting, except when athletes use their celebrity to draw public attention to their political views, which usually are unexceptional. Publicity given to the performance of sports figures has recently led several to try to place themselves outside the law and the moral norms of society. Witness the reported problems of Pete Rose, the charge against Mike Tyson, and, of recent note, the massive press coverage of O. J. Simpson's apparent fall from grace.

Certainly, in the business world there is an elite—again measured by a multiplicity of criteria. One example is the so-called bottom line. Business magazines are always publishing tables measuring the performance of companies in various ways—sales volume, return on investment, earnings per share, rate of increasing earnings, and on and on. These are attempts to define the elite in business with an objective, repeatable measurement.

It is in the areas of morality, philosophy, emotions, storytelling, and other nondeterminant functions that selection of the elite becomes most difficult, however. There are quantitative measures in terms of box office or gold records or popularity charts that rate those in the arts. But, these are not necessarily repeatable because they measure reaction to a reaction, rather than the action itself—popularity, if you will. Today's chart toppers can become tomorrow's dismal failures.

It is a common practice to use popularity as a measure of worth. Political activists of all kinds strive for popular support and use all kinds of outrageous maneuvers to attract it. Causes become popular with no objective evaluation of their worth. Yet, massive program after massive program has been enacted by Congress, thoughtlessly based on the popularity of a cause! The shameless pursuit of press and media exposure is the major weapon of an activist seeking popularity to validate his agenda.

The arts are areas in which some of the elite tend to transfer their celebrity to social issues. Consider, for instance, Vice President Al Gore's posing as an environmental expert.

Although his book on the subject is shot through with questionable science, it is accepted as unquestioned truth.

Elitism would be of no great moment if we were considering only the positive virtues of the elite—what they contribute to society, to our standard of living, our entertainment, and our emotional fulfillment. But, elitism has its dark side, too. As human beings, it is too easy for those who are members of the elite—or profess to be—to become arrogant, and becoming arrogant can be dangerous.

The term *arrogant elitist*, which is often used today, carries with it a warning sign in the powerful word arrogant. Despite all the positive values emanating from an elite, the negative connotation of the adjective *arrogant* dominates the imagery. The arrogant elite is with us everywhere: In business, in the arts, in politics, in philosophy—the whole gamut of human activity. But, each of these is judged in different ways. Arrogance is more self-correcting when the results of that arrogance have a measurable effect. That's one of the great advantages of the free market system where, as individuals and consumers, we can express our approval or disapproval of arrogance in a way that has an impact, as we'll see later on.

The sense of superiority that the liberal arrogant elitists have is derived from a self-generated image and, indeed, the image most of us accept—that they are primarily motivated by compassion. Yet, their arrogance is dangerous because it may lead to the advocacy of solutions to social problems that have bad, or even catastrophic, consequences which are not easily corrected. They tend to dismiss criticism from those who are not considered members of their elite. This is a companion to the familiar exhortation "Don't preach to the converted." The admonition here is "Don't listen to those who aren't converted."

In making black or white judgments in the political arena, as the arrogant elitists often force us to do, we rarely get the opportunity to judge how effective an alternate course might have been. And, once these solutions are enacted into law, they are almost impossible to get rid of, no matter how bad they turn out to be.

Since compassion is the underlying emotion which jus-
tifies the arrogant elitism of the social reformers, it is useful
to examine its sources. Thomas Sowell has written extensively on this subject.

> At the center of many [political] controversies is the
> role of compassion. Guilt is often confused with com-
> passion—to the detriment of the whole society, and to
> the special detriment of the least fortunate members
> of society.

I remember reading Sowell's description of the liberal
world view as "unconstrained vision." The word that came
to my mind at the time was *arrogance*. Their vision was that
man's behavior and political institutions should be guided
by those wise ones that I classify as the arrogant elite. They
reject the constrained vision of Adam Smith, Burke, Hayek,
and Friedman that no individual or group of individuals
could possibly understand the immeasurable forces and
emotions of a whole society.

How can this contempt for—or less passionately stated,
distrust of—the common man be reconciled with the doctrinaire liberals' self-image of compassion? They are not nearly
as contradictory as it would appear. Since we have explored
the impurity of compassion and how easily it can degrade to
pity, it is easy to see how these feelings could degrade further to contempt. How else could they maintain the emotional rush that comes with feeling compassion? After all,
it's difficult to feel compassion for someone or something
you regard as your equal. So, the drive to join the nobility of
the compassionate tends to create a class of "weak" constituency. Thus, a corollary to the drive to be compassionate is
the necessity of selecting or creating a lesser or a deprived
class. This necessary ingredient that compassion must assume an inequality between the compassionate and the objects of that compassion, is the inherent flaw in the purity of
that emotion. We conservatives do not deny that inequality
exists, but we are not inclined to supply it to create objects
for our compassion.

There is clearly such a thing as moral greed, which, like all greed, sometimes accepts counterfeit coin.

Arrogant Elitism in Business

In the marketplace, the arrogant elitism of General Motors, IBM, and other industrial enterprises can have equally bad consequences, but the marketplace reacts quickly. The unemployment, the erosion of our industrial strength, the decline in our global competitiveness are a quickly visible result. Free market forces—the public "voting with its feet"— results in a quantitative evaluation of the actions of the arrogant elitists of business. Pain results from the arrogance, but it is of relatively short duration compared to the pain resulting from political, or philosophic arrogance. The most admirable aspect of the free market system is that the arrogant elitists are the ones who feel the pain, but the people ultimately are beneficiaries. In contrast, the arrogant elitists of social movements, bureaucratically enforced, may lose stature, but the people are the victims!

The publicized examples of GM, IBM, and Sears dramatically illustrate the consequences of arrogant elitism in the business world. Here are three great enterprises of American business that gained power based upon the founders' clear insight and intuition about that for which the public yearned. But, having been hugely successful, they became arrogant.

GM's contribution was not just the organizational and management skills of Alfred Sloan or the inventiveness of Charles Kettering, but also a sense of the American consumer's need for aesthetic pleasure from his automobile. The automobile was primarily a symbol of American prosperity and manufacturing genius, exemplified by Henry Ford's development of the assembly line. It was for only a short time, however, that it was cherished as a means of transportation better than a horse. It ultimately also became the symbol of a better life, a status symbol, a differentiator between neighbors. GM exploited the marketing weakness of Henry Ford's assembly line. "You can have any model you want as long as it's a Model T and any color you want as long as it's black!" GM introduced color, power, style, and variety to satisfy a greater psychological need than just for transportation.

Fossilized by the success of this "style" approach to capturing the market, GM, in its arrogance, was not able to detect a shift in the priorities of its customers fifteen years ago.

As gasoline prices soared, GM's customers were apparently looking for smaller, energy-efficient cars when the market research experts of GM were saying they were wanting bigger, flashier, tail-finned gas-guzzlers.

IBM's experience was similar. Thomas Watson was one of the world's great salesmen, who anticipated and benefited from the information explosion. The sales force of "Big Blue" was a powerhouse that ran roughshod over the competition, but ultimately, it became a one-way channel, arrogantly selling what the brilliant technicians in Armonk, New York, decided that their customers wanted. They were not sensing that people were dissatisfied with being tied to a mainframe, no matter how powerful. Their customers wanted "personal" computers. Enter Steve Jobs and the revolutionaries of Silicon Valley.

Like IBM, Sears arrogantly ignored the evolving needs of its customers. For years, its ability to cater to the enormous buying power of rural America through that glorious thousand-acre shopping center contained within the covers of its catalogue was a great triumph of American sales ingenuity. Then the GMs of the world (and the Toyotas) made transportation more accessible. Enter J. C. Penney, then K Mart and Sam Walton, offering neighborliness alongside highly computerized inventory control and volume discount prices, and the whole Sears empire, now grown large, arrogant, and inefficient, was brought to its knees.

Now, my friend Art Martinez, an alumnus of my college, has taken on the daunting job of reorganizing and restructuring Sears. By all accounts, he is doing all the tough things needed—restructuring! Take note, Sam Walton. Ten or twenty years from now the organization you left behind is liable to be doing the same old thing that's been so successful in this decade. Some upstart will discover a new need or convenience that will make your thousand stores obsolete—and in need of restructuring to survive. Will it be interactive TV? The shopping channel? I wonder.

Arrogant Elitism in Government

Has anyone noticed the exquisite irony in the fall from grace of Sears, IBM, GM? Like these fallen corporate giants, the liberal elitists who speak for the government bureaucracy are self-appointed guardians of the consumers, whom they deem not bright enough to know that they are being exploited. But, this popular anti-business attitude within our government is out of touch with today's reality. Even the name of a division of the Justice Department reveals how archaic the principals are—the antitrust division. When was the last time we used the term *trust* to describe a malevolent restrictive business conspiring to prey on the consumers? Not, as far as I am aware, since Ida Tarbell wrote her muckraking exposé of the Standard Oil Trust. Along with Upton Sinclair and other social critics of the early twentieth century, she created the wave of "trust busting" that was such a strong social force in the twenties.

There are those who contend that the amount of control exerted by the so-called robber barons was grossly exaggerated by both Tarbell and Sinclair (not uncommon with muckrakers). But, the image maker's view prevailed, and Tarbell's and Sinclair's characterizations became the reality.

Times have changed drastically. The good guy-bad guy perception of business, though, has remained frozen in the government bureaucracy—and so the appellation antitrust remains. But, what have been the criteria for determining when to bring the awesome force of antitrust into action? Almost invariably, if a business was large and successful, its power was to be viewed suspiciously. The fact that a business became large and successful simply because it met its customers' needs better and at lower prices was rarely acknowledged.

Conservatives recognize that, once a business becomes large and successful, the danger of it becoming arrogant is ever present. But, the added view that, becoming arrogant, businesses inevitably abuse their power is where we differ from those who view all big business as evil. The primary advocate of this malevolent view is the noted political economist, John Kenneth Galbraith. But, unlike businessmen, he does not understand that the marketplace is a better disciplinarian to punish arrogance than a bunch of bureaucrats can ever be.

Helmut Schoeck's seminal work, *Envy*, has this to say about the psychological motivation of antitrust:

> The antitrust actions brought by the U.S. Attorney-General's office against certain firms—which are carefully selected as targets on psychological grounds—are, it is generally admitted, scarcely ever able to show purely economic grounds for the choice of a particular firm. The decisive question is usually as follows: Which firm do its commercial rivals and the general public regard with such animosity that it becomes politically worthwhile to pay the enormous costs of an antitrust action?

Doesn't the antitrust attack on Bill Gates' company, Microsoft, fit this scenario perfectly?

The prime example in the recent past was the relentless, costly attempt to prosecute (some say persecute) IBM. Starting in 1969, the Justice Department initiated its investigation of "Big Blue." IBM, spending enormous sums on research and development, kept offering new models of mainframes of increasing capacity and of decreasing size, culminating in the brilliantly designed series 360 computers. IBM clearly dominated the mainframe market during this period, and businesses were investing enormous sums in more and more powerful mainframes. IBM's control of this market was deemed impregnable.

In 1975 the government brought suit against IBM, resulting in the longest, most expensive lawsuit in history. The final result—the case was considered to be "without merit."

How much taxpayer money was spent prosecuting this case? How much money was spent by IBM?

What irony that the government's long, vindictive attack on IBM was for their domination of the mainframe computer market. Today, IBM is in disarray, restructuring, laying off tens of thousands of people, and losing billions of dollars. Why? Because they misjudged the marketplace in placing all their bets on mainframes—the very thing the bureaucrats decided would be the weapon by which IBM would dominate the marketplace.

Steve Jobs and his maverick entrepreneurs came along and recognized the need in the marketplace for personal computers (PC's). In a relatively short time, large mainframe computers became the dinosaurs of the information age. If anybody in the IBM management had any inkling of the potential for PC's (and there is evidence that there were such people), those multimillions spent upon this lawsuit "without merit" might have advanced the introduction of PC's and provided a worthy competitor to Apple Computer, Compaq, Hewlett-Packard, and others. These upstarts and their allies—the consumers—used the free market system to unseat and dismember the domination by IBM more completely than the gigantic weight of the misguided government bureaucracy.

A similar irony will not be lost on those who remember the lengthy antitrust investigation of GM. I wonder if, under the Freedom of Information Act, someone could estimate the cost to the taxpayers of these and other failed efforts of antitrust actions. Though no case was every brought against GM, the cost of investigating it must have been great—and for what? Would it have been for not producing small, energy-efficient cars? I doubt it. The probable indictment would be for "dominating the market and restricting competition." Ultimately, Toyota and the Japanese found GM's real Achilles heel—its failure to read its customers' wants. The rest is plain to see: The great, invincible GM brought to its knees by the competitive marketplace.

The liberal view of GM is fascinating. It might have been most concisely stated by Harvard's John Kenneth Galbraith in the epitome of liberal arrogant elitism, *The New Industrial State* (1967):

> Size allows General Motors as a seller to set prices for automobiles, diesels, trucks, refrigerators and the rest of its offering and be secure in the knowledge that no individual buyer, by withdrawing his custom, can force a change. Competitors of General Motors are especially unlikely to initiate price reductions that might provoke further and retributive price-cutting.

Galbraith maintained that big companies can set prices:

> Apart from the world of General Motors, Exxon, Ford, General Electric, U.S. Steel, Chrysler, Texaco, Gulf, Western Electric and DuPont is that of the independent retailer, the farmer, the shoe repairman, the book-maker, narcotics peddler, pizza merchant and that of the car and dog laundries. Here prices are not controlled. Here the consumer is sovereign. Here pecuniary motivation is unimpaired. Here technology is simple and there is no research or development to make it otherwise.

Professor Galbraith, just take a sampling of that list of supposedly impregnable companies above and determine what the marketplace has done to many of them in just twenty-five short years!

In my long entrepreneurial career, one of my favorite statements has been "There is no monopoly on brains!" I have seen literally thousands of examples of a single person or small research groups coming up with sudden inventive ideas that the massive research departments of DuPont, GE, or IBM completely missed. Look at the field of biotechnology today. Despite the enormous resources and research skills of Merck, Roche, and Lilly, among others, most biotechnological innovations have come from small groups of scientific entrepreneurs backed by venture capital.

Government agencies are often out of touch with the real business world. It's not just GM, or IBM, or Sears. All of American business is going through a massive restructuring.

Why? To survive in world markets they must be competitive. The liberal elitists didn't understand, but the arrogant elitists of American business learned it quickly, as their survival depended on it. It became clear that, contrary to Galbraith's or Samuelson's views, the world market is uncontrollable by any industrial enterprise, no matter how large. (I do not exclude Japan Incorporated.) The businesses saw their markets go away and woke up, but the liberal elitists and their allies in the government bureaucracy are still in the dream world of yesteryear. Many of them fail to understand that there is a revolution going on in American business—restructuring, downsizing, reengineering companies (all euphemisms for firing a lot of unnecessary people).

I am personally familiar with the process of restructuring. Our company went through a most painful one in 1984, when we lost a lot of money and our continued existence was threatened. We reduced overhead by 40 percent, we reduced permanent staff by almost half, and we retired or otherwise eliminated a whole layer of management consisting of fourteen vice presidents. Today, our company is more than four times the size we were in 1984 (and six times the size of our pared-down company of 1985). In 1995, we were able to make more than three times our previous peak earnings, and we are employing more than three times the number of people we had at peak employment before that traumatic year. And guess what? We have not restored the layer of management we eliminated in 1984! That demonstrates dramatically what the free market system and the fear of failure (discussed in chapter 4) is doing for American industry. That's the success side of the story. But, there is a dark side, too.

Behind those impersonal figures was enormous pain, a not infrequent consequence of arrogant elitism. The emotional toll on those of us who had to do this restructuring was debilitating. We spent many sleepless nights as our compassion for those people who were being fired (I refuse to use softer words) was constantly being challenged by our compassion for the rest of the people who would lose their jobs if the company were allowed to fail. This is one more illustration that compassion is not an unalloyed virtue. Even with that noble virtue one needs to make choices—tough choices. For whom should our compassion be? This constant challenge to make gut-wrenching choices is the reality that many theorists with limited experience often miss. Wouldn't it have been easy to delay making those tough decisions, thereby avoiding the pain of those we had to let go, as well as the pain of those of us who were castigated as unfeeling? What an abandonment of our responsibility to the rest of the people in the company! Should compassion for those whose jobs would be saved be abandoned to compassion for those whose jobs had to be lost?

These are issues that Samuelson, Galbraith, and other liberal academics don't seem to understand. Interestingly enough, the fourth edition of Galbraith's book (1985) contains the same attacks against GM, even though in 1981, GM recorded its first losses since 1921. Galbraith, you missed!

I had my own brush with the arrogance of the antitrust mentality in government. Somewhere around 1965, when our company was considerably smaller and I had achieved a modest reputation as a consultant, there appeared at the door of our small offices two young men from the Justice Department. Asking to see me, they came to my office and explained their mission.

A few years before, the Philips Petroleum Company had acquired the West Coast facilities of the Tidewater Oil Company (the company owned and imperiously run by J. Paul Getty). The two young men (not more than twenty-five years old, I judged) explained that they were lawyers in the antitrust division of the Department of Justice, which was preparing an antitrust suit to break up the recent acquisition of Tidewater by Philips. To my query as to why they were visiting me, they said that they had heard that I was a consultant with significant knowledge of the West Coast energy industry. They wanted to hire me to help prepare their case against Philips.

I was absolutely astonished. "What possible case could you have against this acquisition?" I asked. They explained that with Philips' marketing strength, the company would "restrict" competition on the West Coast. "Are you out of your minds?" I exploded.

> Tidewater is a lousy marketer. Stanocal (now Chevron), Shell, Union Oil, and Richfield command this market. Philips has a reputation in the Midwest for being an aggressive and innovative marketer. It's my opinion that they would increase the competition on the West Coast by turning Tidewater into a better marketer and would provide more competition in the marketplace—not less. You've got it exactly backwards! I am certain the consumers will actually benefit from this merger. Where did you ever get such a silly idea?

I got so wound up arguing with these youngsters that I canceled my lunch date to take them out for a sandwich to try to convince them that their case had no real merit. The climax to this conversation was their final statement. "Dr. Jacobs, we have heard your position, but we would still like to hire you as consultant anyway." To my astonishment, they said, "We would like to hear your full arguments against this action so that we can prepare our legal case to overcome those arguments should someone raise them." "In other words," I said, "you have already made up your mind and are only looking to strengthen a case to which you are already committed. You do not seem to be interested in reexamining your original supposition to see if it has any real merit. I am insulted by your offer to hire me. I am not a prostitute! Please leave."

The sad anticlimax to that story is that the Justice Department did win its case. At great cost, Philips and Tidewater had to unravel their merger. The arrogant elitists of the bureaucracy had their triumph and a few young lawyers advanced their careers on the back of illogical opportunism.

The ironic denouement to this story is that the original Tidewater refinery, now unhooked from Philips, had trouble surviving, was sold, went through several owners, and is now operated to produce gasoline. Today, it has no marketing at all. Its gasoline is sold in bulk to those other oil companies that still dominate the market. In effect, the antitrust "victory" succeeded in reducing competition in the marketplace, as I had predicted it would. I wonder if those young lawyers who visited me know that. Have they ever faced the fact that there were human and business repercussions from their reckless actions?

Arrogant Elitism in Political Systems

It's easy for me to describe the comeuppance of the arrogant elitists in the marketplace when their fall from grace can be measured in quantitative terms. The failures of the ideas of the arrogant elitists of the liberal establishment are much more difficult to quantify—but they are there.

Indeed, all political structures which have been devised or postulated have this Achilles heel. Since government's function is to provide order in a society to avoid anarchy, there is an inherent assumption that an elite will arise to guide that order. If there is an elite, the temptation for it to become arrogant is ever-present. This is not just true in dictatorships, where an arrogant elite is obvious. The danger exists also in all the shades of socialist theory, where the ultimate power is deemed to be in the state.

Think of the human suffering during those long years it took for the failure of the Russian Socialist dream and the arrogance of its leaders to be exposed. And, collectivist/socialist theory is not dead yet because, after all, the motives are so pure, the objectives so sacred, and the compassion so admirable, that the theory remains unassailable. Good friend Sidney Hook—you were so right! The theory is so beguiling that the reality is easily dismissed.

Some contend that progress along the righteous path was diverted by an unrecognized impurity—not in the thought, but in the execution. That is the whole point and the defining moment which separates the compassion of the conservative from the compassion of the liberal. Persistent advocacy of Socialist or "Command Economy" theories, in spite of repeated demonstrated failures, is but another sign of an intellectual arrogance that persists because of the allure and manipulation of nonreferent words.

The paradox is that the conservative who believes that in the long run, the wisdom of the people as a whole is better than any single component in it, also is aware of individual frailty. The inherent weakness in the theoretical construct of compassion is in the imperfection of the men who are chosen to implement the ideas.

Indeed, I make the claim that the compassionate conservative will inflict less harm on mankind just because he is aware that the reduction to practice of his compassion can have harmful consequences. In short, he is simply less arrogant in his claim to compassion. His approach may fairly be indicted as too slow, or too cautious, but the rate at which social change should take place is a separate debate to be argued on its merits.

This question of rate is a subject that is almost always overlooked when discussing social change. Yet, it can profoundly influence the success of the implementation of that change. Social planners or thinkers concentrate upon defining desirable end results and the mechanisms for achieving them, but rarely try to assess the optimum rate for implementation—a factor too important to be overlooked.

Consider this. There is only one route to instantaneous social or political change, and that is revolution. It should be avoided if at all possible because it is always accompanied by hideous human cost.

As a scientist, I have an inclination to apply physical laws to social actions. One I'm particularly intrigued with is Newton's third law, popularly stated as "Every action has an equal and opposite reaction." A corollary to that law is that when a force is applied to a system at a given rate, the resistance to that force is in proportion to that rate. The more intensely a force is applied, the greater the intensity of the resistance to that force.

To give a simple illustration, when a block of steel is slid over another, unlubricated, plate of steel, friction is the opposing force. The more rapidly the block is moved, the higher the friction, which generates heat. If the block is moved so fast that the frictional heat cannot be dissipated, the system will burn up. That's the equivalent of a revolution in solving social problems. Short of burning up, the friction is equivalent to the pain or social costs of that action.

Integration of black and white Americans and totally eliminating sexual discrimination are clearly desirable goals. Accepting that complete attainment will take infinite time, the pragmatic question is, how long should it take to attain a reasonable attainment? Even here, the question of what is reasonable is debatable, but that ought to be the focus. The dream of complete attainment is just that—a dream. The silliness of President Clinton promising universal health coverage was, likewise, quickly exposed.

Even though there are no definitive answers possible, the question of rate of change should become a part of the agenda. There must be room for the conservatives to say, "We agree with your objectives, but you are going too fast! You may induce a backlash or stubborn resistance that will thwart your admirable aims. People find it difficult to change their views or their cultural prejudices overnight." Too often, if we say that, the liberal snorts, "It's obvious you do not really want it to happen, so you're slowing it down to express your disagreement." On the contrary, we would say, "Keep the pressure on at the maximum rate that society can dissipate the friction." How many worthy social causes have we seen undermined by angry rebellion when they were put into action too quickly? Too often, a conservative's caution to slow the rate of social change is misinterpreted by the liberals as being against that change.

Since conservatives are generally more aware of the perils of arrogant elitism in the marketplace, they tend to be more aware of arrogant elitism in the realm of ideas. In the marketplace, arrogance is punished quickly and unequivocally. Indeed, the constant awareness of the possibility of failure is an ever-present specter in businessmen's lives. That is why conservatism is so much more prevalent among businessmen than it is among academics or theorists. Businesses are constantly vying for the goodwill of the consumer. But, government is less affected by errors in judgment. How often do government bureaucracies fail? And failing, what is their punishment? Do the self-appointed arrogant elitists listen when conservatives point out that bureaucracies are not delivering the product that their "customers" want—or that the liberal activists blithely promised that they would deliver? We conservatives are too timid in withholding our approval. We know how uncompromising the marketplace is in bringing retribution to arrogant elitism and should insist that liberal social programs be judged as stringently.

The founders of our democracy attempted to dilute the distribution of power, not just in a bicameral legislature, but in the separation of powers. The Tenth Amendment, which reserved for the states and the people all powers not specifically given to the central government, was a reinforcement of the Founders' fear of the emergence of an arrogant elite in even a democratic form of government.

It is a central core of conservative belief that the combination of our form of democratic government *along with* a free market system has a better chance of being self-correcting than any other system which has been devised. What has corrupted the brilliantly conceived structure of our Constitution has been the emergence of an invisible arrogant elite—the bureaucracy. In my experience, the arrogant elitism in this bureaucracy is very refractory and difficult to overcome. Term limits for Congress will not solve that problem entirely. Only a concerted effort by the people will do it.

Arrogant Elitism in Academia

In the 1960s, left-wing intellectuals were taking over and debauching academia across the country. Our daughters were in college at the time, and I was alarmed by the Gestapo tactics of the revolutionary Left, and by the faculties who encouraged takeovers by radicalized students.

Our middle daughter was at Cornell when black students, carrying rifles, took over President Perkins' office. He capitulated to all of their demands. I wrote a scathing letter to the poor fellow, accusing him of moral cowardice, and he resigned shortly thereafter. I'm sure my letter was but one of thousands by parents who were outraged by left-wing take-over of our universities.

As I learned from experience, academia is the primary sanctuary for liberal arrogant elitists. Insulated from the real world and protected by that two-edged sword of tenure, they tend to give unjustified credence to their theoretically developed social prescriptions. Not that the theoretically derived concepts are automatically invalid, but academia is a place that tends to breed arrogance in its teaching staff and, therefore, these ideas are often presented as basic, unquestioned truths. This would be of little moment except for the temptation to recruit advocates for their ideas.

Universities receive into their care young minds that are just awakening. In the gradual evolution from the complete dependency of babyhood to the prized mantle of adulthood, the most rapid intellectual change for a youth occurs in college. That is when young people are most likely to want to express intellectual independence. The temptation to reject family values and the behavioral mores they grew up with is very strong. This is often expressed in flirtation with radical ideas and concepts. These are especially appealing when cloaked in the mantle of compassion. For the youth, this is his time to make his intellectual declaration of independence.

When the teachers face these thirsty minds, they cannot help but feel a surge of power, and the temptation to mold those minds to their own prejudices is difficult to resist. Unfortunately, it is too easy for teachers to slip over from the examination of ideas into advocacy.

I think it is fair to say that much of the intellectual impetus in liberal thought comes from academia, and this explains the disconnection between the theoretical concepts they formulate and the "reduction to practice" that is the crucible which validates or invalidates those theories. The arrogant elitism in academia is not just hard to combat because of the nature of the system. It is perhaps the most dangerous manifestation of the academic structure, but it can produce a dangerous infection in young minds.

3. The Politics of Envy

What has been the effect of coercion? To make one half the world free and the other half suffocate.

—Thomas Jefferson

Conservatives are troubled because the methods for implementing compassion seem to be flawed and, in case after case, actually result in various degrees of harm to the objects of that compassion. That's why we ask for recognition of our compassion, for we believe we can help prevent some of that harm.

The interesting question to ask is why compassion is such a prized virtue that both liberals and conservatives seek to be associated with it with equal passion. I have alluded to the emotional satisfaction of perceiving oneself in a positive way. But, I also suspect that we demonstrate compassion in order to deny the dark part of our nature. We need to validate our goodness to compensate for all of those sins of man delineated in great detail in the Bible and in most religious dogma—the venal, the covetous, the hatred, the envy, the defying of the Ten Commandments, and a long catalogue of other evils.

One of the most malignant expressions of the dark side that we seek to deny, cover up, and disguise, is envy. For those of us who would like to believe in the "perfectibility of man," it is not pleasing to contemplate that envy may be an intrinsic trait of human nature. In acknowledging this, we may be questioning Rousseau's concept that man is essentially good—or at least almost always. He and Thoreau were, in fact, impractical dreamers whose idealization of nature and man defied any rational evaluation.

The constrained vision that characterizes the conservative is an acceptance, albeit a reluctant one, of envy as part of the dark side of our nature. Conservatives are not willing to give up wishing or striving for the perfectibility of man, but our willingness to recognize envy and its restraining role makes us understand that it works against our ability to attain our wishes.

In a profound book on that subject called *Envy: A Theory of Social Behavior*, the Austrian sociologist Helmut Schoeck argues persuasively that envy is an intrinsic trait of human nature and that no political system can exist which does not recognize the existence of envy in the body politic. For a political system to survive, envy must be curbed and yet catered to in some controlled way.

What is envy? In the purest sense it is almost a direct antonym of compassion. Envy is not the same as jealousy. The jealous person says about his fellow citizen, "I wish I had what he has!" But, the envious person adds a harsher and more reprehensible postscript. He not only says, "I wish I had what he has"; he then adds, "And if I can't have it, I don't want him to have it!" With typical Germanic thoroughness, Schoeck cites example after example in tribal cultures and in modern political systems of rules that are set up to take into account the needs of the envious by appearing to take away unequally from those who have more.

Surprisingly, Schoeck lists a number of social advantages to this most unadmired aspect of man's imperfection. Those who have more of whatever it is that is desirable, go through elaborate rituals to assuage the envy in the political body and, in doing so, produce public good. In modern society, public affirmation of compassion, charity, and other acts of generosity are one result. Schoeck makes no claim that such acts are consciously motivated to deflect envy. Yet, these acts do, in fact, deflect envy and thus serve a useful social purpose.

Schoeck cites recurring examples in sociology, anthropology, and literature dating back to ancient times. Civilization has advanced, he claims, despite the destructive forces of envy. No system has overcome envy completely; at best it can accommodate it by various means.

Communist economic theory, for example, is an attempt to avoid envy, for one cannot covet what is equally owned and distributed. But, supporters of communism often forget that envy is not just expressed over material things. Such differentiators as power, political control, privilege, public acclaim, talent, or anything that expresses a person's differences can arouse envy in people. The simple fact that people do not have equal abilities arouses envy, and that envy is expressed in many ways.

A recent case in point is that of the champion figure skater who is alleged to have conspired to have her archrival physically maimed in order to prevent that rival from attaining the championship. That is blatant envy.

There is often a destructive element in envy that differentiates it from jealousy. Typically, the jealous person places value on the property he covets, whereas the envious often places no value and wants to destroy it. A thief is motivated by jealousy, but an arsonist or vandal is motivated by envy. This was demonstrated during the recent riots in south central Los Angeles. The jealous broke into stores to steal TV sets; the envious set fire to the stores. I consider this to be a significant difference, for the valuation of property is an essential underpinning of the free market system, even though it is expressed as jealousy. In that sense, jealousy, as unsavory sounding as it is, supports the conservative agenda. We do not make that claim proudly. Although one would hope that more admirable motives, such as ambition, ego drive, or the desire to excel, would move people to strive, jealousy must be accepted as a motive that can also ultimately result in public good.

Envy is the ultimate nihilist credo seeking to devalue not only things, but inequality of any kind. The egalitarian drive seems to express a desirable ideal but, in fact, it may have its roots in envy, for envy in action seeks to deny inequality. Is egalitarianism, therefore, a polite and disguised expression of an evil trait? I suppose envy can be described as seeking the least common denominator, whereas the search for utopia is a reaching for the highest common denominator.

Just recently, the *Wall Street Journal* reprinted the chilling chapter "Harrison Bergeron" from Kurt Vonnegut's *Welcome to the Monkey House*. This fictional parody illustrated the horror of corrosive compassion from the opposite side of risk avoidance and toward the "ideal" of equality—especially legislated equality. Vonnegut pictured a fictional society in which equality was pursued at all costs. The skilled dancer had to wear weights so she could not be more graceful than the other dancers. The husband, more intellectual than his wife, had a buzzer go off in his head when he tried to formulate a logical thought. All these devices were conceived and ordered installed by the "U.S. Handicapper General," whose mission was to insure that no person was better than another. This was a society where there was absolute equality—the Handicapper General saw to that. What a hideous picture. It is ironic that Vonnegut, a political liberal, portrays the evils possible when the liberal dream is put into practice.

Unrestrained envy can paralyze human development unless it is contained. But, it is so prevalent that most social structures build into their political systems countless laws, rules, and cultural taboos catering to the envious.

Thus, even though the communist economic model is a paradigm of envy-driven egalitarianism, in actual practice the Marxist society was not reduced to the least common denominator. Not only was political power and control over the citizens unequal but material benefits were unequal as well—despite the high-sounding rhetoric. Because people are—and always will be—unequal, there will always be the potential for envy. We tend to picture envy in situations of unequal wealth, but it exists just as strongly in the art world, in academia, in science, and in all other forms of human endeavor where there is disparate ability.

In certain circumstances, envy has its good side, while compassion, when reduced to practice, sometimes is not the pure unadulterated virtue it is imagined to be. Reprehensible envy can result in good and virtuous compassion can result in bad—what a paradox!

In thousands of ways, our American political system caters to the flow of envy running through our cultural veins. One example cited by Schoeck is the graduated income tax. There it is, for all the world to see. The rich (there is one of those nonreferent words again) should pay a disproportionate share of their income. The demagogue does not call it disproportionate though, because that labels it correctly. Label it instead as fair—that takes the sting out! The tyranny of words surfaces again—the same action with two different labels. Instead of admitting the truth, we make a value judgment by pronouncing disproportionate taxes "fair." But, are *disproportionate* and *fair* equivalent?

In the recent tax debates arguing increased income taxes for higher incomes, George Mitchell, then the Majority Leader of the Senate, said, "The rich must pay their fair share" of the increased income taxes as part of the Clinton administration's feeble attempt to reduce the deficit.

I should make it clear that I admire and respect George Mitchell. I consider him a friend (he kindly wrote the foreword to my autobiography). I have contributed to his campaign, as I have to the campaigns of other Democrats, even though my primary affiliation is with the Republican party. (I believe so much in our two party system that I consider it a patriotic obligation to support honest men of goodwill who serve their country in politics, though I may disagree with many of their views.)

So it is with George Mitchell, who first gained my attention in an exchange with Oliver North during the televised Iran-Contra hearings. "Remember, Colonel North," he said, "that you do not have a monopoly upon patriotism!" I consider George Mitchell to be intelligent, patriotic, and a thoughtful man of integrity. He has always respected my right to disagree with him (as I often do privately and publicly). Perhaps I am partly addressing this book to him and saying, "Remember, good friend Senator Mitchell, that you do not have a monopoly upon compassion!"

I am sure that unconsciously and without intended malice, Mitchell made the statement that the rich must pay their fair share as an expression of his compassion for the poor. But, in fact, this statement is clearly demagogic in its appeal to the human trait of envy.

Take the first obviously nonreferent word *rich*. Who is rich? Is there any universal criterion or even an approximation of who is rich and who is poor? In contrast, who is poor? The so-called poverty level defined by the government is deeply flawed in its assumptions. The words *rich* and *poor* are clearly buzz words of great emotional drive without any real meaning. They are used shamelessly to arouse powerful emotions. When they are used to describe the need for disparate tax rates, their purpose is clearly to cater to the envious.

The U.S. government has an official poverty level. That's how we know who's poor and who's not. But, it's a moving target—manipulated to meet political needs. In constant dollars, the poverty level has moved upward as the standard of living has increased. Since 1970, however, the poor have been at a constant percentage of the population—about 13 percent. I don't know if it's done intentionally, but the numbers seem to be changed so that the percentage of poor in this country is constant. The social purpose behind this is obscure. Can it be that it serves a political agenda to have a constant percentage of the population classified as poor? Perhaps there is a need for the liberal compassion to have a constituency. If there were no poor (an admitted impossibility), there would be no validation of compassion. If the criteria for determining the percentage of people who are poor have indeed been manipulated, the compassionate liberals have shot themselves in the foot, so to speak, for then the hundreds of billions of dollars spent on programs since 1970 to help the poor has had no measurable effect in reducing the percentage of poor! The Great Society has not been achieved, despite enormous cost. How do the compassionate liberals answer that charge?

The validation of the virtue of compassion requires the creation or maintenance of a constituency that needs compassion. "Moral greed" is certainly compelling! Unfortunately, it creates a double dependency. The poor become dependent upon the succor of the compassionate ones and the compassionate ones become dependent upon having a constituency to validate their goodness (or to deflect envy).

Using the word *rich* to justify imposing unequal burdens upon a particular group is calculated, consciously or unconsciously, to cater to the guilt associated with envy. Because envy is such a morally depraved emotion, it is to be covered up wherever possible. Yet, in using the word rich to define a particular group of people, a target is set up that has no other purpose than as a focus for envy. It is certainly not used as a term of admiration or as a measure of accomplishment. Clearly, the term is being used by demagogues to foster envy.

The rich are an easy target, because it is much easier to envy a class, no matter how ill defined, than a single person. As a matter of fact, the fuzzier the term, the more the emotion of envy is diffused and the less guilt one feels in taking away what "they" have. This is an important distinction, for in the tyrannical word manipulation of political demagoguery, envy is thus assuaged without excessive guilt. And, in the same way, the opposite emotion of compassion is satisfied much more if the object of that compassion is a broad, diffuse class such as "the poor."

Take the next most important words in Mitchell's statement: fair share. What do you suppose that means? Notice how carefully the word *disproportionate* is avoided, for that has a much more precise meaning. *Fair share* means whatever the speaker wants it to mean, from 91 percent of one's income (the highest marginal rate during the Eisenhower administration) to any other figure one can get away with. The preposterous ambiguity of the expression *fair share* is thoroughly exposed if we substitute the word *equitable*. That's a pretty nice word, isn't it? Everybody would agree that they are being fair and proper if they deal with a situation "equitably." But, be careful. Substituting *equitable* for *fair* exposes the inequality of the graduated tax idea. The word *equitable* derives from *equal*, and by common derivation to the word *proportional*, that denies a graduated tax, which is disproportionate, unequal, and therefore, not equitable. By definition, an equitable or equal tax would be a single percentage tax. A person earning ten times as much as another pays ten times as much tax. That's equitable, isn't it? "It's not fair," the compassionate liberal says. "It has more impact upon the poor man who is at subsistence level!"

That's a hard argument for the compassionate conservative to counter except for one primary and often overlooked factor: What is the purpose of the income tax? To raise money to pay the government's expenses? Wrong! The primary purpose of modern tax policy in the U.S. is to support social engineering. If the poor need help to subsist, or medical costs need to be made less burdensome, the tax code has been the preferred mechanism to provide help in a politically disguised form. That same political shuffling also introduces a number of features favorable to business or the "rich." Each segment of society—liberal, conservative, business, and labor—shamelessly uses the tax code to achieve narrow political ends that have little to do with just raising revenues. The temptation to use the tax code to achieve social goals is universal. Each constituent argues convincingly for the social benefits of these special wrinkles in the tax code. The primary purpose of the income tax, to raise money, has been lost in the mists of time. Indeed, there is continuous debate, given the graduated tax construction, as to the parameters for the optimum tax return, i.e., what tax structure will produce the maximum income for governmental use over a sustained period?

Arthur Laffer attempted to quantify the idea that taxes can be increased to the point that people have little incentive to earn more or to work harder. I believe it is now universally accepted, not just from American experience but also in

Britain and other countries, that raising income tax rates does not insure that total tax income to the government will rise. Yet, this simplistic assumption still prevails in today's tax debate. The bell-shaped curve Laffer produced showed that there is a point beyond which the disincentives caused a diminishment of taxes collected. No one argues that the concept is wrong; they only disagree as to exactly where the optimum tax rate is. It's just too difficult to measure the exact conditions under which average people will lose their incentive to work. This is often the weakness of economic theory. People are so incredibly complex that predicting quantitatively how they will behave in the future, based upon their behavior in the past, is fraught with danger.

If one were to use equitable instead of fair, then that would argue for the absolute flat tax—every taxpayer would pay the same percentage of his or her income. This has been proposed many times, mostly by conservatives but more recently even by left of center former Gov. Jerry Brown of California. Arthur Laffer has his own carefully thought out flat tax. The estimates vary from 13 percent to 18 percent as to which flat tax would produce the same income as our now enormously complicated tax code. The percentage would tend toward the lower end if there were absolutely no deductions for any reason—for medical costs, unemployment insurance, interest on house payments, charitable gifts, and on and on. How would these and other services, such as feeding the poor, become available without the tax breaks? The answer is simple. The people would buy their own medical plans, retirement income, and other now mandated social benefits to the extent they wished; they could probably get equal benefits for less from private sources anyway. If the government took less away from the taxpayer, he could use his own judgment as to how much of his increased net income he wants to spend. Would that be better than Hillary Clinton or her massive team of so-called experts trying to define what medical benefits the broad population should get? Unless you have a very low opinion of the American people's ability to make choices in their own self-interest, the answer has to be, yes! If she and her advisors say no to that question, they are exposing an arrogant elitism of their own. There is an implied assumption by the elite that denigrates the recipient's ability to take care of himself.

What about the poor, however ill defined that term is? I have not forgotten them. They clearly are an obligation of society, but we'd have to face it squarely by providing a single direct subsidy (not one hidden in the crevices of the tax code). The subsidy would be out in the open, means tested, and constructed with incentives to work rather than to be on the dole. We should have the courage to face up to the compassionate acts society needs, define the costs, and subject them to public scrutiny. Hidden in the tax code as they are now, they are more difficult to find and, more importantly, difficult to quantify. But, how many politicians are courageous enough to cut away all the disguised methods of helping the poor and thus to face up to our obligations directly?

The single tax is an equitable tax plan. Will we ever have one? Not likely, because the envious emotions are not taken into account with a single tax rate. After all, the man earning $1 million per year would have $800,000 left, whereas one who earns $50,000 per year will have only $40,000 left and the man who earns $20,000 per year would have only $16,000 left. Why should the wealthy man have that much more? It lets him buy a better car; he can buy a better medical or retirement plan. Those who wish to cater to envy say, "How can we manipulate the laws to take it away from him?" Envy dictates that a disguised methodology be devised— such as our present graduated tax system.

So far, we have been discussing how to raise income to run the government and the impact envy has upon the methodology. Even our most liberal politicians are at last becoming alarmed by our annual deficit and the mounting national debt. We are simply spending more than we are taking in. As individuals, we know this is wrong. The myth of infinite resources (see chapter 5) has yet to be challenged by politicians in a serious way.

While compassion dominates the spending side of our economy, envy dominates the income side. Curiously, these most contrary moral values achieve an identical undesirable result—a debilitating budget imbalance which many consider a threat to our society.

In a penetrating analysis of the new Clinton tax bill, Alvin Rabushka of the Hoover Institution describes "The Ten Myths About Higher Taxes" in one of a series of "Essays in Public Policy." He punctures all of the prevailing simplistic assumptions that raising tax rates will increase income and lowering tax rates will decrease income.

If his conclusions are correct, and I believe they are, then that lends additional credence to the theory that the graduated income tax and the increased tax on the "rich" are politically motivated by the need to assuage the feelings of envy that are deep in the human psyche and not for the stated hope that tax income will increase. Any honest analysis of fiscal policy will show that the deficit will mount no matter what the total income is if spending is unrestrained. Not just here but all over the world the disincentives built into a graduated tax have been demonstrated to reduce total tax revenues, rather than raise them.

Dr. Rabushka refutes the assumption that raising marginal income tax rates will raise actual tax income. He points out that since the 1950s, receipts have stayed between 17 percent and 19 percent of GDP, even though marginal rates have ranged from 28 percent to as high as 91 percent. On the other hand, the spending rate as a percentage of GDP has risen from 18 percent in the 1950s to 23.9 percent in 1991-1993. Rabushka, thus, clearly demonstrates that the current deficit is without doubt a result of overspending and not of insufficient income. Who is responsible for the overspending? That will have to be argued by the Democratic and Republican parties, or the Congress and the administration. But, it is absolutely clear that it is not possible to reduce the deficit by squeezing more taxes out of the people.

It's certainly true that during the Reagan years, when the marginal rate was at its lowest—28 percent—federal tax revenue was higher than at any time before. But, the deficit also increased because spending exceeded the extra income. Was the excessive spending due to Congress' increased appropriations for entitlements, welfare, environmental, and other socially desirable causes, or was it due to the substantially increased defense budget urged by Reagan? Both statements have validity. Apparently, the myth of infinite resources is not confined to any one branch of government.

Most economists agree that taxing consumption is much more desirable than taxing production, as an income tax does. Most countries in Europe have a Value Added Tax (VAT), which taxes consumption. In England, it is a staggering 17.5 percent. At the retail level, it is quite visible (Milton Friedman says "hidden" taxes, such as corporate income taxes, are the worst kind—taxes ought to be plainly and painfully evident to the taxpayer.)

Unfortunately, the VAT is regressive because the poor are affected adversely by it, and it requires a bureaucracy to administer, especially when there are specific exceptions made to reduce the regressivity. Almost every VAT has a large list of exceptions. To me, the easiest consumption tax to enact is a variant of a motor fuels tax on only gasoline and diesel fuel with a refund to the lowest 50 percent of families. The collection system is in place. I've argued for such a plan with many congressmen, only to have them label it as "politically impossible."

Other Forms of Envy

Envy is evident not just in the tax structure. All of the social engineering methodology of the so-called entitlement programs contain elements of envy, as well as jealousy.

What about uncontrolled envy? The ultimate expression of rampant envy is often a destructive revolution. Even in this extreme expression of envy, the duality of results is illustrated. Despite the enormous human costs and social dislocation, there have been revolutions whose ultimate outcomes have been good. The American Revolution is a good example. The French Revolution, on the other hand, resulted in a wave of oppression, arbitrary sentencing and hanging—all in the name of "the people." As a side comment, Thomas Sowell, in his book *A Conflict of Vision*, uses the American Revolution to illustrate his view of the "constrained vision" and the French Revolution to illustrate "unconstrained vision." And, that is not a new idea. The British statesman Edmund Burke, who supported and admired the American Revolution, denied the pretensions of rationality of the French Revolution. In expressing his admiration of Burke, Lord Acton said, "Against the revolutionist who would reform all of society in accord with a preconceived logical plan, they (Burke, et al) urge the Conservative wisdom of history and tradition, which have evolved institutions that stand the test of time if not of logic."

There are probably many more examples in which envy made a people's status worse. Of note are the many revolutions in Africa, very few of which resulted in any more freedom for people than existed under their colonial masters or even within their own tribal systems.

In describing the struggle to contain the destructive force of envy, Schoeck says:

> Most of the achievements which distinguish members
> of modern, highly developed and diversified societies
> from members of primitive societies—the development
> of civilization, in short—are the result of innumerable
> defeats inflicted on envy, i.e., on man as an envious
> being.

Envy of the rich not only results in the inequitable, graduated income tax, but has beneficial effects on the use of the power of money, not legislated, but there nevertheless. Though a charitable person would deny it as a primary motive, philanthropy nevertheless does deflect envy and, in that respect, it results in social good. The instinctive awareness of envy tends to moderate arrogance, to mute ostentatious lifestyles, and to promote politeness in social intercourse.

Although liberals often implement their compassion by catering to the envious among us, they are not alone. Conservatives, too, have their own envious feelings. Many of them, for instance, envy the political power of government.

I have repeatedly criticized bureaucracy in this book. Though I acknowledge that the people making up these bureaucracies are overwhelmingly hard-working, loyal people, the institutions have, collectively, a power over our lives that I resent, and yes, I envy that power. I do not want power for myself, but I don't want the bureaucracies to have that power, either.

There are today a number of strong movements to curb the power of government and political power in general. Term limits, school choice, balanced budget amendments, and property tax limitations are all supported and favored by conservatives. These can properly be viewed as an envy-driven desire to curb political power. While we conservatives claim equal access to the high ground of compassion, we do not deny our equal responsibility for the dark impulses of the low ground of envy.

Rather than envy the wealthy, we envy those who have political power over us. Most of us would not want to have a political role, but we resent and envy political power in a way that is scarcely different than envying the rich.

In a larger sense, envy also enters into the relations between nations. The widespread America-bashing in Third World countries is no doubt motivated to a great extent by envy. Indeed, one could argue that the seventy-five-year struggle between the East and West was as much motivated by pure envy as by any ideological differences And, one could argue further that the idealistic, unconstrained vision of the socialist dream was doomed to fall upon the naked sword of envy. Schoeck certainly argues that, when he says that no egalitarian or communist system can eliminate envy. His ideas are supported by observations in both ancient tribal cultures and contemporary kibbutzim.

There are many ways of deflecting envy within a social system that actually serve the public good. One of them is the certain virtue of modesty. Publicly displayed modesty may be a true expression of one's persona, but, at the same time, it does deflect envy.

Another is charity. Obviously, philanthropy has many emotional wellsprings, such as a sense of responsibility, gratitude for the system which provided the wealth and, of course, compassion. But, there is also the guilt-driven philanthropy, often observed in the descendants of accomplished and wealthy forebears. I suspect that there is in those descendants a sense of unworthiness and an oversensitivity to feelings of envy in others.

Still another social antidote for envy is the concept of luck. If someone acquires some worthy prizes purely by luck (so the potentially envious might reason), then "he has not demonstrated any superiority over me." Luck is often used as the excuse of last resort in the workplace. When a colleague is advanced to a position that another person covets, how many people can honestly accept the fact that the colleague has worked harder or is smarter? It is easier to attribute his colleague's good fortune to luck—being at the right place at the right time, or making a bunch of "lucky" decisions.

Is there envy in the workplace? It is there, I can assure you. Since business is the arena in which I have spent most of my time for the past fifty years, I have had many chances to observe its presence. Not infrequently, it surfaces in subtle acts designed to destroy the performance of a colleague who has received a promotion.

There is a chapter in my autobiography entitled "Babe Ruth Struck Out 1330 Times," inspired by a cartoon I keep in my office to remind me, metaphorically, that you can't swing for the fences without striking out! In that chapter (a pretty long one), I list many of the mistakes I've made during the history of our business. One of the most serious of these illustrates the existence of envy in a working environment.

During a period in which we were growing rapidly, I had a "brilliant" idea. I decided to follow the conventional wisdom of the business schools (and presumably Adam Smith) and turned various areas of our business into "profit centers." My thought was that rewarding people with bonuses based upon the profits in their particular division would be a powerful incentive. We tried it for a number of years, and it was a disaster!

The self-centered profit motive was infected by envy. Whenever a project manager from a successful division asked for people to be transferred out of another division, all sorts of excuses were made for their unavailability. Soon, we noticed that the percentage of unbilled hours began creeping up. The heads of the divisions were keeping unbillable people because "they might need them" for a project they thought might be "imminent." Many of these anticipated projects never developed and, as a result, our overhead from the rise in unbilled time began to climb. The real cause for not making those key people available, however, may have been envy. Envy and covetous behavior fractionated our company, affecting the overall profits adversely.

One of the requirements for successful entrepreneurship is the willingness to recognize when you've "screwed up." We canceled that system and instituted a profit sharing plan based only on total company profits, and the whole outlook changed.

Noel Watson, who has succeeded me so capably as CEO of our company, has instituted an imaginative management effort to make ours a "seamless" corporation in order to eliminate those destructive factors, including envy, that debase the effectiveness of the whole organization. Recognizing this as a counterintuitive thrust that needs constant repetition, he has used "Jacobs College" to articulate "lessons learned." The company code of ethics, professionalism, honesty, cooperation, and empowerment are taught, and their ultimate appeal to the self-interest of the individuals is underscored.

Empowerment. That's the new buzz word in American management style. It used to be said that "you can't run a business as a democracy." Empowerment introduces much more democracy into the workplace, and the benefits in lower cost and better operations have already been demonstrated. Besides that, there is a little recognized by-product. By giving all employees a sense of ownership in the company, empowerment has the salutary effect of deflecting envy of the bosses. In the most profound sense, we have found that more freedom and less order pays in the marketplace.

Being convinced that envy is a pervasive and powerful force, I am struck by the surprising relationship between envy and compassion. On the surface, they are at the opposite poles of the moral spectrum, but how much of the compassionate drive results from a need to deny or deflect the envy within us? I said before that being compassionate is often an attempt to validate our goodness and to deny the dark side of our nature. Is that envious streak the darkest part of that which we want to repudiate? It seems to me it may be. Recognizing or even sensing its existence leads us, it seems, to try to do good things.

If, however, the striving to be compassionate is reduced to practice and results in undesirable, destructive ends, is that possibly a result of envy coming through after all? All life is bipolar: "Yin and yang," positive and negative poles, force and resistance, movement and friction. Are envy and compassion the "equal and opposite reaction" of social action?

The bipolar nature of morality may be perceived as going from compassion to envy. That is why so many compassionate drives unconsciously contain within them an element of catering to envy, as exemplified in the graduated income tax. How many of the social expressions of compassion in Socialist theory or extreme environmentalism or welfare or universal health plans—all the "do good" formulas—have bad side effects? Is that because of the inherent need to cater to the envy?

I suppose the conclusion is obvious: Man is imperfect and one of the imperfections is that the striving for perfection unfortunately produces imperfect results. The unconstrained vision based upon the perfectibility of man may be one of those theoretical ideas that can never be reduced to practice. The most we can hope for is that we approach it, knowing that we shall never reach it completely.

I must, however, conclude this discussion of the dark side of envy with the optimistic note that the net result is an imbalance in favor of compassion. Even Schoeck says that the advancement of civilization has been a result of learning to contain envy by catering to it just enough to prevent it from dominating the good or compassionate side of our nature. With that observation, I agree.

Finally, a paradox emerges: Compassion, the most noble of virtues, can, in reduction to practice, produce much harm. And envy, a most reprehensible evil, can, by inducing the deflection of its evil-doings, produce much good!

4. The Myth of a Risk-Free Society

Still one thing fellow citizens—a wise and frugal government; which shall sustain men from injuring one another; which shall leave them otherwise free to regulate their own pursuits of industry and improvement; and shall not take from the mouth of labor the bread it has earned.

—Thomas Jefferson

There is another unnoticed and frightening debasement of compassion that strikes at the very foundation of our society, and that is to regard risk as an enemy.

The thought process goes something like this: Failure is painful and traumatic. If you have a heart (or compassion), you want to shield people from failure. Then the logic gets more elliptical: The more you can prevent failure, the less pain will be caused, and therefore, the person who has been shielded from failure will be happier! The arrogant elitist who devises programs to severely limit the risk of failure may, in reality, be enslaving us in a most insidious way. Those shielded from failure become addicted (that's the right word) to this protection, which in turn confers power on their agents, the bureaucrats, who can continue or withdraw their protection.

Between the foolhardy, death-defying, risky adventure, and the paralysis induced by abject fear of failure, lies the whole perilous universe. It is self-evident that there can be no progress without risk, because for a human being, the only absolutely risk-free condition is death.

Ask any American to list the freedoms we enjoy in our country, and he will enumerate a long list with great pride—

properly so. But, I dare say he will omit one that I consider among our most precious—and that is the freedom to fail! To use the dismal word *failure* in conjunction with the lofty word *freedom* may appear to be a paradox, but it is not.

Think about it. Without freedom to fail, there can be no freedom to succeed or even any reason to try. Not only is it impossible to have success unless you can measure it against the potential of failure; the prospect of failure is, itself, an important ingredient in the drive for success. The possibility of failure makes the rewards of success all the more satisfying and desirable. Only by experiencing the pain of failure can one fully appreciate the joy of success.

It is a special quality of the American free market system that the freedom to fail is so pervasive and widespread, which is another way of saying that the opportunities to succeed are therefore also widespread and pervasive—which is good for us! We are indebted to all of those who exercised their freedom to fail, risked the consequences, and subsequently succeeded.

Americans are used to success. Our amazing progress over two centuries has resulted not only from a willingness to take risks, but from our being allowed, and even encouraged, to do so. That is still one of our great national assets. I do not want to see it eroded. No successful business person or scientist is arrogant enough to claim he knows the exact prescription for success, but he will claim he found it by successively exploring many roads, most of which led to failure. Failure is not the end of the world—it is a necessary part of the learning process that ultimately leads to success.

Why is it necessary for us to illuminate and stress this great freedom of ours? Unfortunately, some want to eradicate failure out of a false sense of compassion. While we accept failure in the marketplace, we keep pretending we can avoid it in our political actions.

Today, we are inundated by a flood of social welfare and social engineering actions which are eroding this essential component of our culture. The effort to protect and cushion every person from every possibility of failure is misguided and dangerous, even if the intent is compassionate.

We all know of the child who is sheltered by his parents from every risk, insulated from every possible hurt and from every chance of failure. We watch as that child grows into a miserable, unhappy, fearful, dependent adult—living proof that compassion can indeed become corrosive.

Although not protecting a child against failure can at times seem cruel, a wise parent allows a child to experience some measure of failure. Because failure is painful, the child learns what is necessary to avoid or overcome it—what it takes to succeed—thereby growing into a self-respecting, competent adult who knows and appreciates the joy of success and is eager to work for it. Indeed, the most rewarding aspects of parenthood are those times when a child is comforted after some small failure and counseled as to how to avoid it in the future. The wise parent discriminates.

So it is in our society. By eliminating the fear of failure, the social engineers eliminate the joy of success, thus assuring mediocrity. Those who would protect our citizens from failure of any kind rarely consider the stultifying effects of their well-meaning designs. They pride themselves on being compassionate, but they are actually destroying people's incentive and self-esteem, making dependency a way of life. A government that carries compassion to corrosive limits produces a gray, lifeless citizenry that can accomplish little and eventually will atrophy. Marxism's great emotional appeal was to the compassionate. The adage "to each according to his needs and from each according to his ability," was the ultimate compassionate credo. That's why it became almost a theology—a theology that has now been thoroughly discredited.

What's happening in Russia is a dramatic example of a nation reared in dependency suddenly being set free. The sad part is that now that they are partially free of the shackles that made them so dependent, they may not be able to take advantage of it. If they haven't learned how to handle failure, there is little likelihood that they can cope with, or take advantage of, their newfound political freedom. The chances for success are, therefore, slim. Indeed, having never been exposed to failure, how will they know if they have succeeded? They are absolutely bewildered and fearful, and they may, I fear, turn to a dictator who will declare that he will take care of them; i.e., shield them from failure.

A significant advantage of the free market system over a command-and-control economy is the constant exposure of participants to the possibility of failure. The ever-present threat of failure in the marketplace creates the dynamism which characterizes the system. Reducing the freedom to fail—whether through monopolistic business practices, government regulation, price supports, price fixing, union monopoly, or some other means—reduces the vigor and strength of a nation.

Businessmen face failure in one form or another every day. To remind me of this fact, as I have mentioned before, I have my Babe Ruth cartoon. The mighty Babe courted failure every time he was at bat—and *failed* 1,330 times! That is the game. Let's not hobble those who want to swing for the fences and deprive them of one of their most precious freedoms.

Conservatives who argue that people should be allowed to fail are accused of insensitivity, but that is a stereotype we deny. We should not be deterred, because we know that compassion, when it leads to the destruction of moral strength and self-respect, does indeed become corrosive. The courage to face the possibility of failure is one of the most precious assets a person can have. It takes guts to know that one may fail—but isn't it the gutsy who advance in the world? You cannot confer self-esteem; it must be earned by succeeding against the possibility of failure. The liberals should not forget how many failures they have overcome themselves. Certainly, they courted failure in their leadership of the civil rights struggle.

Social Engineering

The pervasive growth of this cancer in our society has unfolded until it is choking us in the viscous glue of an all-enveloping corrosive compassion called social engineering. It has happened during my lifetime.

The term *Social Engineering* is an oxymoron, for it implies that the precision of the term *engineering* can be applied to the independent and unpredictable humanity of the social animal. Human beings—with whom we associate all those passionate words like love, hate, envy, honesty, family values, beauty, anger, lust—are the antonyms of the engineering construct.

Those of us who experienced the Great Depression of 1929 were grateful for the courageous mobilizing of the force of government to save us from the consequences of the excesses of laissez-faire and irresponsible capitalism. Those ringing words from FDR—"We have nothing to fear but fear itself," the "New Deal," and all the other stumbling efforts to try to do for the people what they were unable to do for themselves, are well remembered. Today, that "fear" is promoted endlessly in the press and in all the social legislation that is prompted by an increase in this fear—the fear of failure! Liberals should recall FDR's ringing words.

At the time, the efforts of the FDR administration were viewed as pure compassion in action—for the first time implemented by the government rather than by business or the charitable works of the very rich. It was a breathtaking adventure. It was risk-taking at the edge of desperation. Little did we realize that we had unleashed an unbridled, omnivorous mechanism for the implementation of the virtuous dreams of the theoreticians. Those who wanted to feel good about themselves could now put their compassionate theories into action by using the seemingly limitless resources of central government. Until that time, only the very rich could afford to translate the emotion of compassion into action in the form of philanthropy. When central government was discovered as the source of funding, it was possible for those without personal resources to indulge their dreams to be compassionate—with money confiscated from ordinary citizens.

Until the Great Depression, those who were not affluent had little opportunity to put philanthropy into action except in the Church. Now, there was an enormous source of funds available to every secular intellectual who could theorize about exercising his drive and inner need to validate his goodness. Thus, the New Deal was born. We have learned, of course, there is a very different spin given to compassion when the funds come not from having achieved some measure of personal financial success, but from money earned by someone else (the people who pay taxes). There are entirely different emotional dynamics attached to using money for compassionate purposes when the sources of the funds are anonymous, or labeled as "public." The dispenser assumes all the emotional power conferred by the control of funds. There is no connection to the sweating coal miner, the auto worker, the secretary, the salesman, or the businessman, who have all worked long hard hours or taken risks to produce the money confiscated by "government." Nor is there any sense of responsibility. The functionary or bureaucrat's responsibility is only to those they help—the objects of their compassion—their "customers." They have little sense of responsibility to their stockholders—us. Their actions are primarily guided by what makes them (the dispensers of the funds) feel good, or to appear good in the eyes of the constituency they bribe with the confiscated funds. Or, even worse, there is no emotional connection at all, i.e., it's "just a job." The disconnection between the supplier of these funds (us) and the dispenser (the bureaucrat) creates a different dynamic to the compassion. The same phenomenon has been observed in many privately endowed foundations.

We must acknowledge that compassion is, after all, at its root, selfish. How many of us can deny the singing in our hearts as we perform a compassionate act? Does it not give us that inner validation that we are good? Does it not improve our self-image? Does it not also assure our external image, whether we seek that approval or not? That's no reason to reject or downgrade compassion, for in the world of action and reaction, of point and counterpoint, that is a small price to pay for the ultimate good of society. However, the final test is that an act is ultimately good for society—not just good for the self-esteem of the compassionate one. This is an extremely important point that bears repetition: The test of the worthiness of compassion is not in how good it makes the compassionate one feel, but rather, in its net beneficial effect to society—and its positive effect upon the objects of compassion.

Those who choose the apparatus of government to implement their compassion have found out by now, I hope, that you cannot legislate compassion. The mechanisms by which we try to express that emotion are imperfect at best and destructive at worst. Legislation is probably the most imperfect mechanism, because it puts the execution into the hands of the state—one important step removed from those who have an emotional stake in the compassionate program—and two steps from the object of the compassion.

Massive entitlements are in danger of devouring our people. From the extremists of the environmental cult, to the massive welfare system, to all the "braces and belt" regulations designed to insulate the people from failure, we are perpetuating the myth that we can provide a society free of risk. And, if we could, is that a desirable goal?

In my autobiography, as I recounted each of my failures, large or small, physical, emotional, I recalled the hurt. I hated every one of those failures, no matter how slight. I do not in any way diminish the agony of failure, and I can wish all I want that I hadn't experienced it, but it happened. Am I a better man for having had those failures? Not necessarily in the accepted sense, for I was not immune to repeating many of these errors. I had the usual angry reaction: "You should have known better!" But, when I made the same mistake a third time—then I became a better man, because I not only lost any arrogance but, more fundamentally, I learned to confront and accept my own humanity, my weaknesses, and my imperfections along with any assets that defined who I am. The real me was that residual core—that combination of good and bad, virtue and impurity, that we all are. This is a lesson I would not have learned in a "risk-free" society.

On this modern phobia to deflect risk and failure, I am surprised that there hasn't been more notice taken of this absolutely stunning reversal of roles between liberals and conservatives. Conservatives are supposed to be the cautious ones, the naysayers, the doomsayers, those who resist the impetuous movements of the liberals. It's very hard for conservatives to argue that the liberal establishment is too cautious; that's not a natural reflexive action for us, but it is becoming a reality. Add up the FDA, EPA, Bureau of Land Management, Fish and Wildlife Service, and all those other agencies whose sole function is to protect us dumb, ineffectual citizens from risks that many of us never knew existed.

This attempt to eliminate risk in our society has occupied the largest segment of liberal activism for the last twenty years. If the major thrust of liberal activists during that time has been to support political actions which are designed to shield people from risk, then they must be judged for these actions. They have become reactionaries! It is on this central and fundamental philosophic thrust that the traditional labels of conservative and liberal have really been turned on their heads. When they say, "I can't prove it will happen, but it might, and so you must avoid the risk," isn't that pure conservatism? Ralph Nader, the high priest of the cult of fear, would shudder at my accusation. But, I say it, "You are an arch conservative!" I wonder how many liberals understand how their cause has been perverted. Instead of being the champions of freedom, they now opt for imposed order. The fact that they justify the need for order based upon a mostly false compassion does not make that order less restrictive.

I have expressed admiration for the courage of those who marched at Selma, who defied Wallace, who refused to sit in the back of the bus, who marched in Little Rock. It pains me to see all of the youthful energy today being spent so fearfully. What has happened? Why have the liberals embraced all of these movements which decry the dangers facing us, whether real or manufactured by extremists? Why are they using their enormous moral force (remember that compassion is their special preserve) and their command of tyrannous words to scare us out of our wits? Why are they forcing us to spend enormous sums of money on more and more bizarre, fanciful, and scientifically dubious quests to shield us from shadowy risks and to force us into a protective cocoon? For the protection of whom? Certainly not the poor, the downtrodden, the disadvantaged, the homeless, the hungry, and the other traditional constituency of liberal compassion.

When I was a youngster, I was puzzled when I heard my parents and friends talking in secretive whispers about someone in our neighborhood who was ill. In those days, cancer was such a fearful killer, it was spoken of only in furtive whispers, and almost shamefully. Today, it's out of the closet, but it's no less fearsome. The word has the ring of doomsday. Despite the great advances we've made and the enormous amounts of money spent on cancer research, the word galvanizes an eerie, fearful feeling of helplessness and certain doom. So many of our resources are spent in reacting to fear of it, that we neglect other, more significant dangers. It's not just the money spent upon cancer research (though that's enormous), but rather the billions spent in mostly fruitless attempts to regulate or to shield us from those things that "cause" cancer.

I put the word *cause* in quotes because it is such an amorphous, indefinable term. There are literally thousands of causes of cancer, and that's why almost any chemical or natural substance can be implicated. As Bruce Ames (an authority I will quote frequently) points out, more than half the natural chemicals we eat, or handle, or contact in daily life will cause cancer. It is the very multiplicity of the causes of cancer that defies the search for a cure. There is no magic bullet, no single cure. Indeed, many specific cancers respond differently to alternate treatments.

In a September 1993 article that Ames coauthored, he cited three studies which estimate that one-third of the world's cancer results from chronic infections. Fortunately, fruits and vegetables contain antioxidants—chemical substances which, when ingested, protect against disease. Citrus fruits don't just prevent scurvy; they also prevent cancer. In a 1992 review of 172 epidemiological studies, 129 of them showed that eating fruits and vegetables protected against cancer. Yet, according to the review, "only 9% of Americans eat five servings of fruits and vegetables per day, the intake recommended by the National Cancer Institute and the National Research Council."

The ultimate expression of the misguided effort to identify substances which cause cancer is the Delaney Clause. In 1958, Congress was considering a new Food Additives Amendment for the FDA. At the request of Congressman James J. Delaney of New York, the following clause was added:

> No additive shall be deemed to be safe if it is found to induce cancer when ingested by man or animal, or if it is found, after tests which are appropriate for the evaluation of the safety of food additives, to induce cancer in man or animal.

This innocent looking statement has raised such havoc and cost the American people so much over the past years that the impact upon us is incalculable.

Take the Delaney criteria in order. "No additives" implies that only additives are harmful. It infers that natural foods are less harmful, and that, indeed, is what most people think. But, the facts are otherwise. Ames argues again as follows:

> Poorer people spend a higher percentage of their income on food, eat less fruits and vegetables, and have shorter life expectancy than wealthier people ... A major contributor to health in this century was synthetic pesticides, which markedly decreased the cost of food production and ensured that most of the crops planted would be eaten by humans rather than insects. Synthetic pesticide residues do not appear in the general population to be a significant cause of cancer.

Ironically, the cancer scare headlines about pesticides impact the poor adversely by increasing the cost of fresh fruits and vegetables. Could it be that the enormous sums spent on the regulatory process and its impact upon fruit growers might be better spent buying more fruit for the poor—or making fruit cheaper?

Ames published a comparative chart of cancer risk associated with a number of common foods, as well as chemicals that have been labeled carcinogens. Here it is:

Relative Carcinogenic Risks	
Alar (average daily intake)	Less than 1.0
1 liter tap water (chlorine)	1.0
3.5 oz. cooked bacon	30.0
1 oz. peanut butter	30.0
12 oz. diet cola	60.0
3.5 oz. shrimp	100.0
1 raw mushroom	100.0
12 oz. natural root beer	200.0
2 slices of bread	400.0
12 oz. of beer	2,800.0
(100 = 0.1% HERP - human exposure/rodent potency)	
Source: Warren Brookes, *Washington Times*, 30 March 1989	

Isn't that an eye-opener? What is important to note is that even these data are extrapolated from tests on rodents— no double-blind tests on humans were done. But, under the Delaney Clause, cancer production in rodents is enough to infer it would happen in humans and, therefore, to ban the additives.

Not only is the Delaney Clause deficient by reason of judging additives only, but it makes a much more grievous error of omission. It says nothing about quantity. If any amount of a chemical can cause cancer, it is to be banned. As the table above shows, if one ate ten pounds of bread a day (if one could eat that much), the potential for getting cancer would be substantial! There are literally thousands of chemicals banned based upon data where rats were fed hundreds of times the amount (per unit of body weight) ordinarily used by people, despite the fact that in normal, or even excessive, use, no causal effect can be shown.

Alar provides a classic case of "cancer hysteria," trumpeted in the press but ill-founded scientifically. The promoter of this scare scenario was Linda Greer, senior scientist, Natural Resources Defense Council. Alar has many beneficial effects, including preventing apples from prematurely dropping. Not only would a ban on Alar raise the cost of apples, but premature fruit drop will encourage fungus growth, which will introduce more toxicity than Alar. It is generally agreed that the Alar hysteria was a media hype of the most egregious kind. And, who was the so-called expert who testified before Congress about the evils of Alar? Actress Meryl Streep, that well-known toxicologist!

There is another problem: Do rats and humans have the same reaction to drugs? The FDA says yes when applying the Delaney Clause, but when testing new drugs it says no! No new drug, no matter its life saving potential, can be declared safe based upon rat tests or by tests on any animals. If drugs are shown to be safe in animal tests, they must still go through Phase 1 trials in which human volunteers receive the proposed new drug while being monitored for any adverse effects.

Although chemical additives and pesticides may be of enormous economic benefit (to the poor, please do not forget), tests on rats are sufficient to ban them. The fact is that, with very few exceptions, no tests on humans would be likely to show cancer unless the tests were continued for years and years. Since there are so many causes of cancer, if a person developed cancer after ten years of exposure to a given additive, is there any reliable way to show that the additive caused it? It gets almost silly to pursue these absurdities. The contradiction seems to have eluded the FDA, as it reacted like a typical bureaucracy to the ambiguity in the Delaney Clause.

According to Bruce Ames,

> The animal testing uses a procedure known as the maximum tolerated dose (MTD). I think we're drawing the wrong conclusions from high-dose rat tests. They are testing enormously high doses—the maxi-

mum tolerated dose in mice or rats, which means you find the level that causes overt toxic effects and back off just a little bit and feed the animal that amount every day for a lifetime. Originally, MTD testing was only designed for those chemicals which people were exposed to in high doses. However, these days every synthetic chemical or food additive is tested using MTD. A high percentage of all chemicals might be expected to be carcinogenic at chronic, near fatal doses and this is exactly what they found. However, people do not ingest most of these additives at chronic near-fatal doses. In other words, humans rarely ever ingest anywhere close to the proportional dose of the substance which is being fed to the rats.

The proof that toxicity in laboratory animals does not correlate with toxicity in humans is supported by the FDA when it tests the toxicity of drugs. Yet, a positive cancer test in rats or mice is immediately trumpeted in headlines as "Chemical 'X' Causes Cancer!"

The classic example of the irrelevance of MTD testing is saccharin. This chemical has been in use for over one hundred years. When it is tested by this high dosage method in rats, it is definitely carcinogenic. Therefore, if it were to come up for approval today, it would be rejected. Thankfully, no one in the bureaucracy has the temerity to ignore one hundred years of history in which no case of cancer has ever been traced to the use of saccharin. Why not? The answer is that human use is so far below the presumed carcinogenic levels that the inferences of the rat test are worthless.

This is part of the compulsion to advance the myth of a risk-free society. So, excessive regulation, senseless testing procedures, and doomsday scenarios using that still frightening word, *cancer*, result. Conservatives believe in protecting people from risks— but from real ones. Even for the real ones, let's spend our energies in some relationship to the probability of the risk. We should ask, "What is the shortening of the average person's life span by the expected effect of those risks?"—or use some other comparative table. By the former measure, the carcinogenic effects of most addi-

tives are insignificant. Yet, cancer is such an emotional bogeyman that it is constantly being used as the prime criterion for safety of almost everything we use.

There is another important factor here that must not be
overlooked, and that is the almost intractable legal system.
Lawmakers unfortunately enact thousands of laws almost
too casually. Talk to any congressman or senator and they'll
admit that even with their swollen staffs, they are so inundated that they rarely can study new legislation adequately.

The Delaney Clause is a perfect illustration; casually
passed, it has been a burden to our regulatory system even
though practically no one supports it (except the bureaucrats
who owe their jobs to it). There have been complaints about
the Delaney Clause for thirty-five years from all quarters, yet
there is no way—or any imperative—to change it.

The Food and Drug Administration is a good example of
the exponential growth of regulatory agencies. Its original
purpose was solely to limit risk—legitimate risk, I might
add, for I hope it's abundantly clear that risk avoidance is a
proper arena in which government can help people. What I
object to is extending that help to such extremes as to strangle
the possibility of substantial benefit.

The original FDA was started in 1906 as a labeling watch-
dog by the Food, Drug & Cosmetics Act. It was based upon
the simple assumption that, if people know the ingredients
in a food or medicine, they will be smart enough to decide
whether or not to use it. Later, it became apparent that,
particularly with drugs, the average person could not judge
the toxicity of products with complicated chemical names.
So, doctors were given a monopoly on that decision making.
The "prescription" system was the mechanism. It was a rational decision at the time, as doctors were free to use their
own clinical experience to judge the worthiness of different
drugs. They did not have to depend upon an agency to tell
them what was good for their patients and what was not.

Until 1957, the FDA mission was essentially to prevent
the use of drugs which had serious toxic reactions. It left the
judgment of the efficacy of the drugs up to the doctors. Then
came the famous Thalidomide case. This chemical was dis-

covered in Germany and was becoming widely used as a tranquilizer overseas. At the time, the FDA's oversight of toxicity took into account the experience of overseas use.

When it came before the FDA for approval in 1960, Dr. Frances Kelsey resisted approval while she investigated reports that the drug caused peripheral nerve damage. Then in 1961, reports began coming in of hideously malformed babies born to mothers who took Thalidomide as a tranquilizer during pregnancy. Dr. Kelsey became a pop heroine of the media.

Then a curious thing happened. In the hysteria of the moment, there was a flurry of legislation that not only tried to prevent the problem of the side effects of Thalidomide, but added totally new edicts. The Kefauver committee had been investigating the pharmaceutical industry because it was so "powerful" (it hasn't changed much, has it?). In 1962, the Kefauver-Harris amendment was added to the Food, Drug and Cosmetic Act. The FDA was suddenly charged with testing not only the safety, but also the efficacy of new drugs. Thalidomide could not be blamed, because there was no question of efficacy of that drug as a tranquilizer. It should have been banned or at least limited in use purely on the basis of bad side effects.

With few exceptions, doctors were careful in prescribing new drugs and, of course, they were guided by the FDA's studies of toxicity. Evaluating the efficacy of a drug takes considerable judgment and experience, especially in balancing benefits with possible side effects, where there is room for wide difference of opinion. Doctors believed they were best qualified to make that judgment for their patients, but the FDA took that out of their hands.

The 1962 law fundamentally changed both the agency and the drug development process. Judgment of efficacy was turned over to a bureaucracy as the rigid rules of the IND (Investigational New Drug) were formulated. The broad clinical evaluation of the medical world was no longer admissible. Rather, a rigidly performed, staged process, known as Phases 1, 2, and 3 trials, became the only FDA criteria for efficacy and for safety. It was not realized at the time that new drug introduction would be seriously hampered by giving the responsibility for judging efficacy to a government bureau. The FDA went beyond being regulators into being "partners" in every sense of the word, as their judgment was imposed upon the researchers and developers. The FDA got the common bureaucratic disease: "We have the authority to approve. Therefore, you must obey our rules!"

The staff of the FDA was 1,678 in 1960. Today, it is over 9,000! And, under its aggressive bureaucratic leader, David Kessler, it is constantly looking for new areas to regulate.

What has resulted from all this bureaucratic control of new drugs? There is much literature on the subject and substantial data available to support the following conclusions:

1. The average time to approve a new drug application (NDA) went from seven months in 1962 to thirty months in 1967. Despite many attempts at streamlining the process, the average now is still over thirty-two months—just to get permission to initiate a study of the drug.

2. The time between application for approval to study a drug and final release of the drug for sale has gone from about four years in 1962 to over ten years now. If one adds in the several years that drug companies spend in animal testing prior to the NDA, then the elapsed time is even greater.

3. The result has been fewer new drugs. From 1975 to 1979, the number of new domestically developed drugs dropped to 50 percent of those approved in the previous decade.

4. Many pharmaceutical companies find it easier to let foreign companies develop new drugs since they can be tested in half the time. With their marketing power, the domestic companies simply make licensing agreements. We are thus losing the commanding lead we have had in this important area of science—new drug development.

I've alluded several times to the "invisible" costs imposed or mandated by bureaucracies created to support the unreasonable pursuit of a risk-free society. Of course, we count on government to protect its citizens, in some measure, against risks. But, the "in some measure" has been expanded so much in modern political thought that it threatens to destroy us, instead of saving us from harm.

It's difficult to calculate the real cost of these regulatory or mandated rules, but I am convinced that it is enormous. There is little doubt that medical costs have been rising at an astronomic rate. Is it that doctors overprescribe tests? Is it because hospitals are inefficiently run? Is it because the lawyers bring so many malpractice suits? All are true to some extent, but why? They are all clearly a reaction to onerous bureaucratic mandates.

The FDA is both friend and foe. It supplies valuable oversight of toxicity. It attempts to prevent medical charlatans from taking advantage of the unwitting. But, on balance, its grip upon us is too firm, too oppressive, and too bureaucratically hidebound. The protection it gives us is obtained at an unacceptable price: Life-saving drugs and beneficial additives are being kept out of reasonable reach.

In their book *Risk & Culture*, Mary Douglas and Aaron Wildavsky put forward the thesis that the risks which society is willing to accept or, conversely, those which it considers worthy of Herculean effort to avoid, are not decided on a rational basis. The authors maintain that, rather, the acceptable risks are dictated by a cultural bias, which explains the book's title.

To show the cultural bias, the authors quote a Harris survey of three cultural entities: The general public, corporate executives, and federal regulators. The differences in perception in each category were startling. For example, the poll revealed that "twice as many people in the general public, as compared to the executives, think there is more risk today than 20 years ago." Here is the tyranny of words in action. The general public has been exposed to so much inflammatory language, pointing out the risks they face, that they accept this myth without question.

Abraham Maslow, the non-Freudian psychologist, makes the point that the fervent risk avoidance posture is a result of our unprecedented prosperity. He contends that our extraordinary high standard of living has given us the time and opportunity to worry about risks that affected people very little when they were struggling to survive. Though

Douglas and Wildavsky tend to minimize this, it has the ring of truth to me. I don't think it's incompatible with the theory of cultural bias.

I agree with Maslow that our very successes give us time to worry about risks that heretofore were relatively unimportant, but the risks we consider most necessary to avoid are selected, not by rational analysis, but rather by cultural bias. This is how the single-issue activists ply their trade in tyrannizing us with the frightening pictures they conjure up.

At the root of the selection process is the lack of any relationship between the probability of risk and the cost to avoid it. There are quantitative methods of risk assessment. In the large amount of environmental work our company does, we use risk assessment routinely. It is a very touchy subject because the logical end point of such calculations makes us terribly uneasy. How much is a life worth, for instance? The absolute numbers should never be taken literally, but the appearance of a "godlike" judgment makes everyone uncomfortable. However, the point of the cultural bias is that the risks which society chooses to avoid (usually at great cost) have little relationship to probability or cost.

The culprit here is that pervasive need to validate our goodness and our worthiness by viewing ourselves, or having the public view us, as compassionate. Certain risks have more compassionate content than others! In the case of radiation deaths, the imagery of nuclear holocaust—slow, lingering death—certifies the compassionate value of preventing those deaths.

Nobody personifies these scare tactics that raise the compassionate juices better than that inveterate publicity seeker and self-characterized ascetic, Ralph Nader. He was propelled into the public eye with his criticism of the safety of the GM small car, Corvair. This early GM attempt to match the Japanese onslaught of energy-efficient small cars did appear to have design flaws, though I have heard unconfirmed claims that the crash data on the Corvair were severely flawed. Whether true or not, Nader's proclamation that the Corvair was "unsafe at any speed" legitimized his role as a consumer advocate. In its arrogant attempts to deny those design flaws and discredit Nader, GM simply validated him. Have you ever heard Ralph Nader praise anything or anyone other than the trial lawyers? He knows that his only credibility and access to publicity come from scaring us to death over dangers in a device or in a social system which does not protect people from failure—invariably, a failure for which he claims the user bears little responsibility. How he degrades his audience!

There is another compassionate theme that is invariably coupled with these attempts to shield people from failure. All of the malevolent, awful things that will befall the common man are invariably caused by outside forces—forces of villainy such as business, or evil people who smoke, or sightsee, or drive cars, or use too much energy, or whatever. It is rarely acknowledged that many of these victims may, in fact, bear much of the responsibility themselves. What bothers me most is the inherent, but false assumption, that those who have been victimized do not have the intellect, or the knowledge, or the will, or the judgment to have any effect on what happens to them. Doesn't absolving man of any responsibility for what happens to him, in the end, demean him?

The environmental movement is an easy target. I know that criticizing Rachel Carson is almost like attacking Mother Cabrini or Mother Teresa. *Silent Spring*, the progenitor of the environmental movement is, in fact, highly flawed, unbalanced, and scientifically suspect in many areas. Like all yellow journalism—and like many of Ralph Nader's causes—there are elements of truth in it, but not the whole truth by any means. Sensationalism is the venue and book sales the objective. To read Rachel Carson, one concludes that there is absolutely no virtue to any chemical insecticide.

I happen to have a deep personal interest in, and some knowledge about, the main focus of her attack in that book, the now infamous DDT.

During World War II, as a recent graduate Ph.D. in chemical engineering, I went to work for Merck and Company, the chemical and pharmaceutical giant. Among a number of projects I was assigned to, one was to develop a commercial process to manufacture a then-secret but sensational micro-biologically produced germ killer (antibiotic as it was later called) developed by Fleming, Florey, and Chain in England. It was called penicillin.

I also was assigned to a highly secret product that had originally been made by a Swiss chemist in the mid-1860s. It had a long chemical name, which I shortened to DDT for convenience.

I was not told what its use was, but was given the reference to the original laboratory procedures and asked to duplicate the process in my laboratory and to find a way to produce it in large quantities in a very short time. Working around the clock, I successfully produced the first five hundred pounds of DDT ever made anywhere, as far as I know.

The next day the drums of this product I had so laboriously produced were picked up by U.S. Army trucks. During that final push to make the five hundred pounds, a valve on one of the vessels broke. I was covered head to foot in a two-inch coating of pure DDT, and I'm sure I swallowed a lot of it. But, I took off my work clothes, showered, and finished making the product.

Two weeks later, Merck received a message from the surgeon general of the army thanking them for producing that five hundred pounds of DDT. It had been shipped by air to Italy, where there was a typhus epidemic raging among our soldiers. Typhus is a deadly disease spread by body lice which lodges in soldiers' uniforms. DDT, it turns out, is absolutely lethal to body lice, so they dusted it in the soldiers' uniforms and the epidemic was stopped in its tracks. In his message, the surgeon general estimated that the lives of five thousand soldiers were saved. When Rachel Carson made her claims, did anyone try to track those thousands of soldiers who dusted their clothes with DDT and lived in daily contact with it for many months to see if any developed cancer? And, if they did, would it have been prudent or humane to refuse to use the DDT and not save those five thousand lives?

Add to that the fact that DDT is absolutely deadly to the anopheles mosquito, the carrier of malaria. With DDT, this deadly disease was finally manageable. Millions of people avoided malaria because of DDT.

Now, against those heroic things that DDT did which no one remembers, and Rachel Carson gives little notice to, it is a fact that repeated exposure to DDT will collect in the liver, potentially leading to cancer. If sprayed on grass, cows will collect it in their milk and possibly pass it along to people. However, I am not aware of any fatalities that have ever been proven to have resulted from this method of transmission. Despite the millions of tons of DDT that have been used, I am not aware of any deaths having a proven causal relationship to its use. As Anthony Woodlief noted in a recent article,

> This campaign to eliminate man-made pesticides began long before Alar, and has proven deadly. Sparked by Rachel Carson's *Silent Spring*, in which she asserted that chemicals were destroying the earth, environmentalists went on a rampage in the 1960's to ban the pesticide DDT. Before the advent of DDT, Sri Lanka suffered about 2.5 million malaria cases from mosquitoes a year, of which about 25,000 were fatal. Using DDT, Sri Lanka lowered the malaria rate to 110 in 1961.
>
> Then came the environmentalists. Armed with questionable research showing that DDT was harmful to humans and the environment, several groups, including the Environmental Defense Fund, the National Audubon Society, and the Sierra Club persuaded the Sri Lankan government to abandon the use of DDT. Within a few years, the incidences of malaria rose to pre-spraying levels, and thousands of people died. But, as far as Laurie Mott of the Environmental Defense Fund is concerned, there is "no room" for consideration of the benefits of pesticides.

The World Health Organization, however, assessed these benefits at over five million lives saved by DDT within the first eight years of its use. Furthermore, a study by Dr. Edward Laws of John Hopkins University revealed that workers exposed to high levels of DDT for ten to twenty years developed no cancer. Dr. Walter Ebeling, an entomologist at UCLA, noted that single doses of five grams of DDT had been given to people to treat barbiturate poisoning without adverse effects. Five grams of DDT was about four times as much DDT as the average American would take into his system in a seventy-year lifetime. When speaking of DDT, Dr. Ebeling asserted that "probably no other compound, not even penicillin, has saved as many lives."

Finally, after thirty years, rational voices have finally been heard. In a retrospective review of Rachel Carson's *Silent Spring* in *Reason Magazine*, Drs. Bruce Ames and Thomas Jukes (professors of biochemistry and biophysics, respectively, at the University of California, Berkeley), mount a devastating attack on this "bible" and progenitor of the environmental movement. It is more strongly worded than I would have written it, but I quote it primarily as an antidote to the enshrinement of Rachel Carson as a saint.

> Rachel Carson's *Silent Spring* (1962) became the inspiration for the environmental movement. Its elegant prose expressed passionate outrage at the ravaging of beautiful, unspoiled nature by man. Its frightening message was that we are all being injured by deadly poisons (DDT and other pesticides) put out by a callous chemical industry. This message was snapped up by intellectuals, and the book sold over a million copies. Many organizations have sprung up to spread Carson's message.

> Rachel Carson set the style for environmentalism. Exaggeration and omission of pertinent contradictory evidence are acceptable for the holy cause.

The article convincingly refutes the distorted condemnation of DDT and decries the senseless criticism of this most worthy and beneficial product. Because of my intimate involvement with the development of DDT, I applaud this analysis.

Without debunking any of the negative effects of these and all of the thousands of other chemicals that were given the *Silent Spring* treatment, no one, least of all the liberal establishment that preaches the avoidance of risk, has ever proposed a comparison of the advantages of these products against these projected detrimental effects. If one were to ask the more rational question, "How can we take advantage of the benefits of DDT and avoid or minimize the presumed bad side effects?" There are many obvious answers. The hysterical answer was an outright ban. Such was the power of Rachel Carson's inflammatory rhetoric that no rational method of avoiding or minimizing the risks she pointed out was ever proposed. The negative impact upon society was ignored as Rachel Carson's virtuous validation was enshrined. Instead, almost everybody in this country stands in abject fear of what is really a relatively benign chemical that could be of enormous benefit to people.

On the other hand, penicillin, the other great life-saving chemical that I am proud to have helped bring to market, somehow avoided this treatment—despite the fact that it has caused quite a few deaths and DDT has not been proven to have caused any. It was later discovered that penicillin could cause allergic fatalities. No one has ever bemoaned the discovery of penicillin or caused it to be banned. In fact, Fleming and Florey received the Nobel prize for discovering a new class of antibiotics that turned out to have lethal side effects. If this had been given the Rachel Carson treatment, think of all of the lives which would not have been saved—including mine! I am also certain that if penicillin were submitted to the FDA today, it would have a very tough time being approved.

I recount the story in my autobiography of how a courageous Dr. D. W. Richards (later to win the Nobel Prize) defied U.S. Army regulations and injected me with penicillin in early 1943 when I was dying from a particularly virulent septicemia. I may have been one of the first civilians penicillin was used on. If I were one of those people who are severely allergic to penicillin, Dr. Richards may have killed me. But, he took a risk that saved my life. He risked failure. So did I, and I have survived!

People know that there is risk in life. They face it every day. But, the arrogant elitists of the liberal establishment do not choose to let the people make their own choices. They are constantly warning us of dangers we never knew existed, invariably exaggerating both the extent and the seriousness of these dangers. Rarely, if ever, do they balance those against the positive values. I am depressed by their dark view of our culture.

Unfortunately, this has resulted in enormous costs to our society—costs that come from somewhere and, ironically, are often diverted from other compassionate agendas.

Go down the list. The tortuous processes of drug approval in the FDA. The infamous Delaney Clause, that hysterical reaction to the scariest word in the American lexicon, cancer. The endangered species list, forest preservation, atomic energy, global warming, ozone depletion, asbestos, and on and on down the line.

Why should conservatives object to all of this caution, this avoidance of risk, especially when we are generally viewed as the cautious ones? We object simply because there is no discrimination. (Remember that degraded and denatured word?) And, why is discrimination, in the good sense, needed? Because there is an enormous cost to all of these endeavors. While I am willing to argue with Rachel Carson or Ralph Nader on the merits of any particular fear they promulgate, it's against the mass of all of these fears that I feel so helpless because, as I argue in the next chapter, we do not have infinite resources. So, the promotion of the idea of a risk-free society is not just wrong on moral grounds; it is, I insist, not a desirable social goal. It suffers in the real world where we are all forced to make choices every day—choices of which risks we are willing to accept and which are unacceptable ones. The indiscriminate fear projected for each risk the activists discover threatens to turn us into an unadventurous, immobile, catatonic society.

5. The Myth of Infinite Resources

To preserve their independence we must not let our rulers load us with perpetual debt. We must make our election between economy and liberty, or profusion and servitude.

—Thomas Jefferson

Obviously, we do not have infinite resources available. Why does it need constant reiteration? Great harm is done by ignoring this simple fact. Society's resources are too precious to squander on trivial and low-impact ventures while major problems in our society are starved for support. Though we would wish otherwise, not all compassionate programs can be implemented. Limited resources force us to choose. When the choice is difficult or painful, it's too easy to ignore the limitations.

In pursuing compassionate objectives indiscriminately, we may starve the more worthwhile projects of their funding. If the science behind the risk assessment is faulty or suspect, it is not permissible to say, "It could possibly happen." The familiar question, "What are the chances of being run over by a truck?" is of the genre in which such debates belong. With many of the predictions of catastrophe, one is reminded of Chicken Little, who ran around shouting that "the sky is falling!"

The mirage of infinite resources is reinforced when we deem them to come from Washington. Even worse, through the use of regulations we unobtrusively spend people's resources that are then unavailable for other compassionate ends. This leads to the every-man-for-himself approach to

solving social problems. Each advocate commits the ultimate sin—he refuses to measure the relative value of his
particular cause against all others. Has any social activist
ever admitted his program did not work—or that it was less
important to society than some other cause?

The temptation to apply the quantitative techniques of
engineering are very strong, but I fear that we are captives
of the very indeterminacy that always plagues the advocates
of social action. After all, how can you measure pain, dependency, self-esteem, independence, pride, and those hundreds
of other factors, beyond being fed and clothed, that influence the quality of life? But, even if we can't reduce these
variables to numbers, we must raise the consciousness of
people to recognize that each social action must be evaluated
and compared against all others and then, finally, judged.
The single-issue advocates rarely have the courage to face
the fact that the people may not choose to pay to avoid a
given risk if they knew that another risk was being ignored
or starved for funds. It is not permissible to disguise the
need to choose.

Thoughtful social activists should be prepared to defend
their ideas against those of their compassionate competitors.
Who should make these decisions of choice in a democracy?
A well-informed people should! No omnipotent commission, no computer program, no super "brain," no engineer
devising new quasi-quantitative criteria—just the people.
Once the people know they must make choices, I have sublime confidence in their judgment. But, the key here is that
the people be well informed. This places a moral responsibility upon the activists to state the problem accurately and
to evaluate the cost of the solutions honestly. Based upon
my observations, most social activists fail this basic test of
morality. The press with its much vaunted "objectivity" often fails this test, too. The bad science, the distorted statistics, the exaggeration of what might happen, and sometimes
outright lying are all considered acceptable behavior by those
who desperately seek the validation of their compassion—
their moral greed. The complicity of the media, "60 Min-

utes," and press reports sensationalizing Meryl Streep's "testimony" in the Alar scam was a disservice to the American people.

With every new cause there should not only be a justification of the need, there should also be an attempt to make a relative comparison to other needs. Where are the investigative reporters when we need them? They, too, are gullible when the notice of a scare or hazard arouses feelings of compassion.

This does not say that the emotional content of compassion for each program is any less, but rather, that the social benefit to the community may be. This is a distinction which needs constant repetition. Discrimination should be based upon benefit to society with no judgment implied about the strength of the compassion impelling it. Activists often judge merit based upon the emotions they can arouse rather than based upon real impact upon society.

As one of "constrained vision," I hold that the people are the best judges; but they must be made aware of how things are—that resources are limited.

Where is the selfless politician, the academic, the philosopher, or the journalist, who can rise above advocacy, who can be trusted by the people because he has no ax to grind, to preach that there are not infinite resources? Who would present the alternatives fairly and say to the people, "You must make choices! And, your choices shall be our command!" There are a few of them, but their voice of reason is rarely heard. Since they tend to be rational, reasonable people who present facts rather than passions, they tend to be overlooked. It is sad that it takes an entertainer like Rush Limbaugh to put these serious evaluations in the confrontational and emotional terms that are the standard weapons of the arrogant elite activists.

My late friend Aaron Wildavsky, a professor at U.C. Berkeley, was the bete noire of many of the activists. He created a whole literature skewering them and their pretensions of virtue. In addition to questioning the scientific claims, he also questioned them on philosophic and moral grounds.

One of his repeated complaints about some of the activists was that they did not even understand the notion of trade-offs. To them, everything they proposed must be examined in absolute isolation, instead of being subjected to measurement upon any comparative scale of desirability.

The dilemma is a simple and historic one. Sidney Hook would attack the simplistic notion of a choice between "good and evil." He said to me one time, "It's only in fairy tales or in the manufactured discourse of religion that such choices exist. In life, most decisions are between different degrees of good or, more familiarly, with 'the lesser of two evils.' One rarely, if ever, has the luxury of making a simple choice between 'good and evil.' " How true! In these cases, the choice, to give the advocates full credit, is between good and good, i.e., which is the better one of the good choices?

The activists, with their smug and incorrect assumption that only they are motivated by compassion, drive ahead in pursuit of their narrow sphere of interest. A particular mission of conservatives ought to be to convince the activists that they have competition, even from their own like-minded brethren. Just as products rarely have monopolies, so ideas for implementing compassion rarely are the only good ones around. I guess competition is another one of those tyrannical words that gets the compassionate juices of most liberals boiling. Competition implies winning or losing, and losing is painful. Therefore, competition is undesirable, because one party (the loser) will suffer. This distrust of the natural order of things is more common in liberal thinking than even they recognize.

My experience as a businessman colors my selection of words. Competition has existed from the dawn of time. Shall we ignore Darwin and all the competition between opposing forces and species that has resulted in the world as we know it? Most people understand the triumph of good over evil, but is it so hard to understand the need to recognize that one good is more beneficial to mankind than another good?

What I am proposing is to apply the inevitable test of competition to the selection of a worthy social agenda just as Darwin articulated the natural selection of animal species.

Of course, the idea of using such a conservative methodology as free market selection of ideas will be repellent to some. In order to accept the need for competition, the fact that resources are finite must be acknowledged.

Some think there is more flexibility in resources than really exists. The instinctive reaction is "How can we tax the public to raise more money, and not have to face painful choices?" There are two hurdles. One is that there is a finite limit on tax revenue (the Laffer curve), and the other is that the activist or his handservants, the bureaucrats—not the public—keep expanding the choices. The myth of infinite resources has unfortunately infected our whole political process. There isn't a politician of any note who doesn't deplore our unbalanced budget, but few of them seem to have the discipline to make hard choices.

The state of Oregon faced this problem in trying to contain medical costs. A system of rationing or of grading the importance of medical conditions was proposed recently in that state, where health insurance costs were becoming unmanageable. Choices had to be made. Should cosmetic surgery be funded equally with removing a brain tumor? This, of course, is a facetiously chosen example. The point is that thousands of such choices needed to be made and a panel of experts pondered for many months before coming up with a long list of prioritized medical conditions. It was immediately attacked in the press and by many citizens.

As expected, an arbitrary allocation by a committee, no matter how expert, is just more government rather than free choice. It's the old syndrome, "We (the elite) know what's best for you." Should the individual be allowed to make the choice of a face lift and forfeit the funding for a brain tumor? That's the dilemma. We must be careful about being arrogant in our effort to protect our people from risk—especially freely chosen risk. We should ponder whether the freedom attained is worth the cost of allowing the foolhardy to make bad choices.

Broad health coverage has a widely accepted compassionate purpose, but the cost implications are so massive that the issue of limited resources cannot be avoided. Let us put the problem of choice under the harshest light. Suppose that the people in Oregon were given a budget for major surgery. There are certainly people who would spend it for a face lift and not have any left for a brain tumor if it should come. Which is better, to allow that free choice or to legislate the choice? To choose the latter is a blatantly elitist position. There is little doubt which choice of medical procedure most rational people would make. But, that's because I've given an obviously easy example. I think that only very broad limits should be put on choice to prevent obvious self-destructive choices, but other than that, let the citizen decide what he wants. Not always, but in most cases, the choice will probably be a wise one. And, that's the most anyone can hope for. The bureaucratically established choices, even from a panel of experts, will have just as many aberrational judgments as a freely derived one. That I believe.

The imposition of order can only be bought at the price of freedom—precious freedom. In everyday experience, the free market system, with all of its discipline, would not exist if there were infinite resources. The need to make choices is the heart and soul of the Adam Smith model. Another way to put it is in the classical definition of the study of economics: "The study of the factors which govern the allocation of scarce resources."

It may be worthwhile at this point to examine this central core of conservative thought. Starting with Adam Smith, there have been thousands of learned treatises written on this subject. What is the free market system in its simplest terms? Why is it so important to conservatives? And, is it really that good? I bring this into the discussion because the whole foundation of *The Wealth of Nations* is that there are not infinite resources. Adam Smith's tenets would be absolutely groundless if there was an infinite supply of anything people wanted.

To the conservative, the free market represents democracy in its purest form, as Adam Smith enunciated it a long time ago. In making any decision of choice, each individual casts a vote and the final summation measures the success or failure of the product or service. John Kenneth Galbraith maintained that people have only restricted choices when big companies dominate the market so much that they determine the menu from which the public can choose. Although at any moment in time this may have some validity, John Kenneth Galbraith, in the long run, has been proven dead wrong, time after time, and especially recently. The examples of General Motors, IBM, and Sears Roebuck, already cited, are only three of hundreds of examples denying Galbraith's thesis. What he would have the government break up because it's big and, therefore, evil, the marketplace and intelligent competition has accomplished much more efficiently. The very examples he cited have since then been vanquished in the marketplace. GM, IBM, and Sears—those supposedly impregnable behemoths—were toppled by Adam Smith! Ironically, Galbraith does not attack the absolute power that has now been bestowed upon the massive bureaucracies that dominate our daily lives. Where is the challenge to the restriction of choice imposed by big government? Does it not also offer a limited menu and stifle competition?

When there is an intermediary of enormous size and inertia marketing an activist's ideas, the consumer's free choice is also severely blunted. Galbraith's "demons" today are not big business but big government. There is, unfortunately, a vast difference in power between big government and big business. Because government is perceived to be a creation of the people, it is much less responsible to market forces. Its power is, therefore, more invasive and difficult to defeat. This is what Fredrick Hayek studied in *The Road to Servitude*. Nevertheless, the market forces are there. Thus, term limits for elected officials are becoming increasingly appealing. The public, for whom so many elitists have little regard, are finding a way around the unresponsiveness of the politicians to what their constituents are really feeling. Self-interest, Adam Smith's energizer, is hopefully beginning to work even in the area of big government.

I am sure none would intellectually gainsay that resources are finite, but what is the emotional need to ignore that fact? Compassion, combined with a dominant unconstrained vision, has a self-validation that is hard to resist. In the liberal view, compassion tends to prove that the perfectibility of man is attainable and, more importantly, to prove that those who prescribe the formulae to attain that end have a special virtue. Thus, the fact of finite resources is a bothersome intrusion into an exquisitely constructed and highly moral vision.

Not unlike an addictive drug, the spell of compassion can lead one to ignore the real world, with its harmful side effects and realities, such as imperfect people or finite resources. Another by-product of this emotional narcotic is a feeling of superior moral strength, as some drugs make one feel physically strong. Perhaps the comparison that is more apt is to the psychotropic drugs. Compassion is an "upper" of seductive power.

If it were purely a question of how to allocate governmental resources, the problem would be somewhat easier to evaluate, although it still would be very difficult to make the government responsive to the market. The problem is that most of the newer liberal activist agenda also involves enormous mandated costs to the private sector and to local governments. Though hidden, these costs are nevertheless still subtracted from the total national resources available. But, because they are not a direct budgetary item, they escape public scrutiny. The limit of our resources is not just defined by the imbalance of the congressional budget, but is exacerbated by an enormous expenditure of our nation's resources that are mandated to be spent in the private sector.

It's easy to be deluded into thinking the resources of government are somehow different and have dissimilar limitations than those of ordinary people. One need only be reminded that all government funds are simply confiscated (a harsh word, purposely used) from the consumer, removed from his discretionary allocation and shifted to the discretionary allocation of the bureaucracy—often to be simply squandered.

Dixy Lee Ray, former head of the Atomic Energy Commission and former governor of the state of Washington, estimated that government expenditures just to support the first Clean Air Act of 1990 have amounted to $1.4 trillion to reduce air pollution by 90 percent.

Incidentally, Dr. Ray's book, *Environmental Overkill: Whatever Happened to Common Sense*, is a dispassionate, scientifically accurate analysis of the emotional environmentalist's sometimes outrageous excesses. We won't debate whether the expenditure of $1.4 trillion was a fair price for that substantial improvement, though that question does deserve study. It would be interesting, however, to ask the constituents of the underclass, the hungry, or the homeless, how much of that enormous sum they would like to have diverted to their needs in exchange for perhaps only an 80 percent improvement in air quality.

Dr. Ray illustrates the principle of asymptomatic cost extrapolation by stating that increasing the air quality improvement by only 5 percent, i.e., from 90 percent to 95 percent, would cost another $1.6 trillion—more than doubling the cost to get only an additional 5 percent improvement! This principle applies almost universally to cost versus improvement phenomena. The asymptomatic curve will generally look like this:

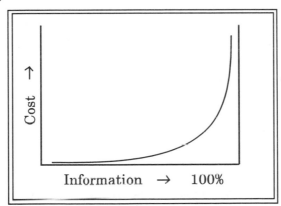

Though I use this asymptomatic curve to illustrate Dr. Ray's attack upon environmental excesses, this phenomenon applies to a myriad of social questions. How "universal" can health care be? How much money should be spent to save one life from asbestos exposure? How much money should be spent eliminating all chance of side effects from a new drug before introducing it? These are questions rarely asked because they force us into the uncomfortable position of deciding how much a life is worth—a decision forced by limited resources.

Most excessive environmental regulations are regressive, benefiting the middle class most and taking funding away from the poor unevenly. Regressivity is the major objection of liberals to most consumption taxes, but the regressivity of mandated regulation and of costly alternative fuels is rarely acknowledged. They are, in fact, a consumption tax. Why have the doctrinaire liberals adopted the extremes of environmentalism without recognizing that they are draining resources from the traditional constituency of their compassion?

For those who declare universal health coverage to be a desirable social goal, especially for the poor, I ask this question: Is the amount of money being spent upon further improving air quality a better expenditure of a trillion dollars than spending it on universal health care? Is that a painful choice? Of course it is, but it can't be ducked.

The Clean Air Act of 1990 finessed the problem of making the public aware of the extra cost by transferring much of the cost to the private sector, which in turn passes it on to the consumer. The refining industry is currently spending billions to retrofit their refineries to meet requirements set by Congress almost too casually. The cost for getting the incremental improvement was simply hidden, and a publicly exposed comparison with other government spending was avoided. But, the cost was not avoided by transferring it to the private sector.

How much of our resources will this absorb? The lowest estimates that I've seen say that the price of gasoline will increase by 16 cents per gallon in the most polluted areas, such as in Southern California. California, in its zeal, went one better than the U.S. Congress by passing an even stricter Clean Air Act (CARB). As a result, there will be an added annual burden upon the consumers of over $12 billion per year. Nationwide, the added cost will average 10.8 cents per gallon.

Compare this added cost to the anemic 4.25 cents per gallon direct tax included in the Clinton tax bill to help balance the budget. Gasoline taxes are regressive and are resisted, especially by liberals, on the basis that the poor are impacted disproportionately. Is the 10.8 cents a gallon any less regressive because it's for environmental reasons?

While reviewing a PBS documentary about the lobbyists who try to shape health care policy, Walter Goodman of the *New York Times* mentions "the activities of groups that want a national health plan paid for by Washington, more or less on the model of the Canadian system." "Paid for by Washington." What an enticing idea! What disingenuous fakery! Who wouldn't want a health care system paid for by somebody else? It's been said so many times: Washington is the place where all the money collected in the form of taxes is funneled to meet our goodness credo. "Paid for by Washington," indeed!

There's no such thing as a free lunch. Washington can't pay for anything. Government has no money of its own. Every dollar Washington gets comes from the pocket of a taxpayer—from you and from me. Goodman would have been accurate had he said these groups "want a national health plan managed and operated from Washington," using our money—much of it consumed by the bureaucracy.

One area in which the myth of infinite resources plays havoc is the discussion of alternate energy sources. This is a subject which sometimes reaches bizarre extremes. However, the term *alternate energy* has taken on a virtuous sheen— another demonstration of words taking on special meaning. Because an energy source is alternate, is it automatically good, as this term has now come to imply?

Many of the proposed alternate energy sources are based upon dubious science and often have their own undesirable environmental effects. I suppose I could be classified as an expert in this field since our company has at one time or another studied most of the alternative energy schemes. Sometimes there are serious technical questions, but more often, there are serious economic limitations. One should not be put off by the term *economic*. That is simply a shorthand recognition of the limitation of resources. Comparing the economics of alternate energy sources simply tells you which route uses more or less of our resources.

Take our foray into solar energy. Our company backed the development of a system of reflectors based upon the ideas of some bright engineers from the Jet Propulsion Laboratory of Caltech in Pasadena, California. The device was an assemblage of long parabolic mirrors with metal tubes at the focal point, or center of the mirrors through which a fluid circulated. Assembled in a frame, these mirrors were slowly turned to keep facing the sun. With significant subsidies from the Department of Energy, we convinced a local laundry to let us build such a unit to provide them with the large quantities of hot water they needed. ("Think of all the savings," we said, "in not having to buy all that gas.")

It was a clever, ingenious design, but we kept bruising our knuckles on reality. First, because the mirrors had to be prevented from twisting, the structural steel frame turned out to be very heavy, requiring a much larger motor to rotate the mirrors (an energy consumer!) than we had anticipated. We had to mount the mirrors on the roof of the laundry (people tend to forget the very large areas that are necessary to gather any significant energy from the sun). Because of the weight, we found that we had to reinforce the roof. Since the sun only shines during the day (and not every day at that), we had to increase the sizes of the hot water storage tanks as another added cost. The final result? The system was so costly, even with the government subsidy, that the owner not only refused to pay for his share, but forced us to dismantle and remove all of the machinery. We lost a pile of money trying to make that scheme work.

The point of this story is to underscore how so many brilliantly conceived schemes for alternative energy do not live up to their advance billing. Many, if not most, alternative energy schemes turn out to be uneconomic. The advocates then say, "Isn't it worthwhile to use such clean energy even though it costs more?" We must ask, compared to what?

If the cost is higher, then that represents an expenditure of those resources that we agree are not limitless. The next question must be "How much more?" You need to know the answer to that in order to answer the inevitable next question, which is "Should I support the spending of that amount, as compared to burning natural gas in a power plant with scrubbers? Would those extra resources be better spent for other uses that may contribute more to the quality of life or to relieve the burden of the disadvantaged?" The answer to that may be yes, but it will depend on the compassionate justification for that alternate use of those resources. Again, which compassionate cause deserves which share of our limited resources?

Clearly, choosing a more expensive process because it is environmentally better is making a unilateral vote that the particular environmental improvement at issue is more important than any other compassionate cause upon which that money could be spent.

It is admittedly simplistic, but every family faces such choices almost daily. If you buy a Cadillac instead of a Toyota, you don't have the money to buy that new refrigerator. If families had infinite resources, they would not be forced to make choices, and the free market system would not function. It is exactly the same in public spending. The total resources of the country are the sum of the total resources of the people of the country. Since no individual or family has limitless resources, then the country does not have limitless resources either! Doesn't the appalling debt we are accruing tell us exactly the same thing? The liberals have finally recognized the deficit in the budget and are now climbing on the political bandwagon, but at present they are only deploring it—not much else. Liberals have yet to realize that the majority of Americans are fiscally conservative because that's the way most of us run our own lives.

I must insert a caution here. I am not implying in any way that our limited resources are static. It is an admirable quality of the human mind and of freedom that we have an infinite capacity to create wealth. But here again, rate is critical. We must not and cannot spend our resources faster than we can create them. We must not mortgage our future beyond our capacity to create new wealth. At any one time, our resources are finite, and we get into deep trouble when we forget that.

The single-issue activists, with their passionate, narrow focus, seem to set the ground rules for us. How little are vital questions asked, such as "Compared to what?" or "In place of what?"

On a much broader scale, it's interesting to look at competing environmental demands. Environmentalists these days are carried away by their smashing P.R. conquests. With this nation's unquestioning support and adulation, they get in the press that they have spread their wings of zeal to the whole world. Witness the absolute travesty when the United States was asked to support a worldwide attack on global warming in Rio de Janeiro at unknown, but surely astronomic, cost. The "science" of this highly publicized demon is so dubious and so uncertain that massive financial support of it is an incredible misuse of scarce resources.

Why not take a single global environmental issue about which there is no scientific question and to which the solutions are not only known but have been applied with great effect in the United States? According to a comprehensive United Nations study, there are 3.2 million children who die every year from drinking unpurified water. This is in every sense a worldwide environmental crisis. It is a real problem that's here now. The unnecessary deaths of all those children ought to break everyone's heart. The solutions are tried and tested. Unfortunately, it's not as apocalyptic as global warming or species loss or ozone layers (another quite dubious "scientifically" predicted disaster). All of these latter are of the "chicken little" category: they *might* happen. But 3.2 million children *are* dying—every year. Where is the sense of values? I have not calculated the cost of the plants needed to purify the water for those children, but I dare say it's insignificant compared to the monumental and, as yet unknown, cost of taking care of projected catastrophes that may, or may not, take place sometime in the future.

Will an activist get headlines if he goes before the U.N. to point out the serious problem of 3.2 million lives lost and to ask for "X" billion dollars to prevent those deaths? Probably not. The prediction of apocalypse and destruction of the world by us heartless people is so much more newsworthy. Moral greed needs constant reinforcement.

The activists seize upon emotionally compelling injustices as if there were no others in the world—and each has his pet which he promotes blindly to the exclusion of all others.

But, liberals should be of good cheer. There will always be injustices, inequalities, sadness, tragedy, and other causes deserving of their admirable compassion. In fact, we conservatives will provide a few more. How about the reduced standard of living of the poor because of the profligate spending of our limited resources (used, I might add, upon the comfort and environmental purity for the elite of the middle and upper class)? And, how about the rapidly approaching insolvency of our country? There are more than enough worthy targets for compassion in our society, without having to manufacture new or spurious ones.

I must conclude this chapter by saying that my engineer's heart has been infinitely gladdened by at least some in the media. I refer to a TV news special by Emmy Award-winning reporter John Stossel that aired on ABC on 24 April 1994, entitled "Are We Scaring Ourselves to Death?"

Stossel took on the task of rating risk quantitatively. He spent much time during the program punching holes in many popular myths about risk. He especially attacked the statistics often used as a basis for the scare stories. The best illustration of this is his deflation of a common statement we all believe: "Violent crime is increasing." Many famous people were shown making that statement. Stossel shot holes in the data from the FBI and the Department of Justice (who disagree with each other) and showed, to my satisfaction at least, that violent crime is actually decreasing. I have independent confirmation of that from James Q. Wilson—the country's foremost criminologist. He says, "That's the good news. The bad news is that teenage crime is increasing at an alarming rate."

In discussing crime, as well as other "scary risks," Stossel said that the most common mistake is in applying the absolute numbers to show an increase of whatever risk is being trumpeted. Scaremongers simply forget that our population has grown over that same period of time. Thus, the risk per unit of population may not have increased at all.

Stossel adopted the techniques of risk assessment specialists by asking the simple question, "How much will the average life span of the people be reduced if they are exposed to each of those risks?" The numbers he came up with are eye-opening, to say the least. To insure that he hadn't slighted any risk, Stossel made sure to use the "worst case scenarios." He used a graphic chart in the video show, but here are his data in a table:

Risk Assessment from John Stossel's Program
"Are we Scaring Ourselves to Death?"

Risk	Life Expectancy Reduced
Flying	1 day
Toxic Waste	4 days
Fires	18 days
Pesticides	27 days
Air Pollution	61 days
Murder	113 days
Driving	182 days
Smoking (from lung cancer)	5 1/2 years
Poverty	7 to 10 years

Look at that last item. Doesn't it validate the misallocation of our finite resources? Toxic waste—that scary subject—reduces life expectancy by four days. Poverty reduces it by seven to ten years!

In that list, Stossel estimated the reduction in life expectancy for smokers at five and a half years, but quickly amended that statement by saying that the figure is not for the whole population. Using that figure he asked, "Isn't it a little silly for a smoker to worry about flying or using his cellular phone?"

I suppose the point Stossel was making is that people make a choice in smoking, so those people are choosing a risk three hundred times that from air pollution, over which they do not have much control.

The discussion that took place after this program is most illuminating. An observer who was there said that the environmentalists were thunderstruck and tried to dismiss the numbers, but Stossel stuck by them. The most important and revealing exchange took place on the question of having to make choices because of finite resources.

> JOHN STOSSEL: [voice-over] The danger [of] excessive regulation, say economists, is that it can backfire. By slowing the economy, the regulations may shorten lives by making people poorer, and as the chart shows, being poor shortens lives much more than other risks.
>
> [on camera] Now, Linda Greer, you're the head scientist of one of the country's leading environmental groups. You've been furious at my saying this. Here's your chance to respond.
>
> LINDA GREER, SENIOR SCIENTIST, NATURAL RESOURCES DEFENSE COUNCIL: Well, I think that you'll find that there are a number of people in the audience that are furious with what you're saying, because in a lot of ways it doesn't make sense. Your numbers are screwed up, but I'm not going to get into that. What I'm going to get into—
>
> JOHN STOSSEL: We'll get into that.

(My note: If the numbers were wrong, wouldn't Ms. Greer have taken the challenge and thereby destroyed the whole premise of the program?)

> LINDA GREER: No, I want to get into something else. I think the major point is this. What you're saying is something like this: "Well community, you have a choice. You can have a burn unit, you can have an emergency room, or you can have a terminal cancer ward. Which one would you like to have?"

(My note: How's that for dissembling?)

LINDA GREER: What we say is that this country is a wealthy country. This country can afford to have all three of those problems taken care of with no problem.

JOHN STOSSEL: And there is enough money to do it all?

LINDA GREER: There is undoubtedly enough money to address the major risks, and many of the risks you've addressed tonight are major risks.

Let me interrupt here and ask the reader to look at the list and classify those they consider "major." Would pesticides be included?

JOHN STOSSEL: Peter Huber, you wrote a book on junk science. Is this junk science?

PETER HUBER, SENIOR FELLOW, MANHATTAN INSTITUTE FOR POLICY RESEARCH: No. Your numbers are essentially right. One does have to make choices. People who have more money do live longer. Living is something that money can buy, and basically, if you look in your wallet, there are $200 missing there. They were spent on toxic waste in the last 10 years on your behalf. You didn't get much for that $200. It's about $200 per household. If you had spent it yourself on other things, you'd probably be better off.

AUDIENCE MEMBER: Regulation is costing our economy $600 billion a year. Linda Greer mentioned we as a nation can afford all this. But, you know, it's individuals who produce this money we're talking about, who earn this money, and these people are acting like it's a common pool, that we'll just all lump it together, and then they'll get to sit down in Washington and decide how to divide it up. And I think we ought to be able to make decisions about how we spend our own money.

JOHN STOSSEL: Ms. Greer?

LINDA GREER: Well, I disagree. I think that the government should provide a certain baseline of protection to the public. And look at a country like the former

Soviet Union, which didn't spend a dime on environmental regulation, and they're not exactly rolling in
wealth.

(My note: The nonsequitur is used here in a classic way.)

This is an eye-opening exchange, especially since Greer
supposedly has credentials as a scientist. If one were to take
her literally, then what are "the major risks . . . addressed
tonight"? They certainly wouldn't include flying. How about
toxic wastes or pesticides? They are pretty low on the list,
but can you imagine Linda Greer, the generator of the Alar
scare, admitting that pesticide risk is unimportant? Of course
not, and she'd be right—except for missing the point entirely.

No one is suggesting that none of our resources should
be spent avoiding those risks on this list. All a pragmatic
conservative maintains is that the amount we spend upon
each of them should have some relationship to the risk as-
sessments shown by John Stossel. Throughout these discussions, the same theme keeps repeating. Are we spending our
limited resources for the maximum benefit to our society, or
are we spending them to reinforce a special group's right to
call themselves compassionate? If you deny that our resources
are limited then, of course, none of these arguments has
merit. But, the dream world of unlimited resources is just
that—a dream world.

With all the objects of compassion that we have now and
will discover in the future, we will never be able to avoid the
responsibility of making choices. If, like children, we avoid
making those choices because they are difficult or unpleasant, I'm afraid the real world—the uncompromising physical world, the laws of nature, and all those natural restraints
that we conservatives are perhaps, too conscious of—will
force the issue of responsibility upon us, for the choices must
be made. This is when the tyranny of words and the irresponsible rhetoric and the wanton corruption of nonreferent
language will finally be overwhelmed by the immortal and
unrepealable physical laws that we scientists insist will be
the final judge of the worthiness of our compassion.

Part Two

The Consequences

6. The Quality of Life and the Environmental Religion

The earth belongs to the living, not to the dead.
—Thomas Jefferson

Quality of life is a nonreferent term. The claim that the elimination of environmental effects will automatically improve the quality of life is open to serious question. Improvement in quality of life derives from many other sources as well. Over the past seventy-five years, our quality of life has improved dramatically because of the positive contributions of science and technology. Why do so many people search desperately for catastrophic retribution? Is it a secret fear that we are undeserving of our good fortune? Yet, to turn this into a public guilt is a destructive political agenda.

One would think that those who believe in the perfectibility of man would rejoice at the incremental steps we've taken toward the good life. The ingredients of the quality of life that we take for granted are far different today than fifty years ago. Man's drive to rise above the muck and to live the civilized life was once considered a celebration of his ingenuity; today, for too many, it signifies man's affront to nature.

I believe passionately that an important ingredient in the quality of life is the environment. I deplore the impairment and danger of impure water, air, and waste. Indeed, our company is on the front lines in environmental engineering and remediation in this country. I am proud of what we are doing to clean up the environment. My concern is solely with those environmentalists who do not exercise discrimination. Too many activists force us to waste enormous energy upon unworthy targets and low-impact problems.

Interestingly, the almost $1.2 billion backlog of environmental work our company has is primarily for government agencies, mostly the Department of Energy and the Department of Defense. In the urgency of meeting past military needs, there was little time to consider the environment.

To their credit, the Department of Defense and the Department of Energy are now moving aggressively to remediate environmental problems at their installations. But, funds that could be allocated to clearing hazardous waste sites are often spent on questionable environmental matters. Intelligent choices need to be made concerning the legitimacy of projects being labeled a threat to the environment.

Our company will continue to pursue environmental projects that make real sense, and there are plenty of those. We solve the problems that activists only talk about. We pioneered the study of waste minimization and indeed wrote the "bible" on this subject under a grant from the Environmental Protection Agency. This is the pure free market in operation. "Don't spend money to treat what comes out of the plant as effluent," we say, "but go back into the process and learn how to prevent those horrible things from forming." Despite this advice, the cry continues for regulation, regulation, and more regulation, punishment, fines, and now, to our horror, even prison sentences.

Shall we spend our brainpower to avoid risk, succumbing to the myth of a risk-free society? Shall we hold back medical treatments that will save thousands of lives because we might lose a few from some undiscovered side effect? Shall we make the cost of energy so high that the poor are deprived of it? Or, should we free our brainpower to realize its maximum potential to add to our standard of living? I argue only for a reasonable balance between creating wealth and improving the standard of living and minimizing the undesirable side effects. Let us not idolize the doomsayers. Instead, we must rediscover our obligation to spend our resources positively, with courage, with risk-taking, and with the pioneering spirit that has made this country great.

I recently discovered that my faith in the ultimate good sense of the American people, although sorely tried at times, may finally be justified. In an article in *Fortune* magazine entitled "Environmentalists on the Run," the stupidity of the environmental juggernaut of the last thirty years was detailed. With their $400 million per year budget, the members of the Carson crusade have abused their power, and ordinary people are fighting back. This article simply reinforces all the criticisms I've made—obsession with cancer, wide-ranging clean air, water and other bills expanded to a tangling restrictive, and costly network by bureaucrats.

I will point out only two of many interesting observations. The government of Peru is suing the U.S. government because, following the U.S. classifying chlorine as a possible carcinogen, Peru stopped treating their drinking water with chlorine. The result: A cholera epidemic that killed thousands. This is compassion?

Finally, it was reported that three former EPA administrators—Russell Train, William Ruckelshaus, and William Reilly—believe that what's ultimately needed is a new federal agency of scientists and economists that would assess risks, weigh costs, and benefits, and help policy-makers set government-wide regulatory priorities. Is it possible that the activists will listen to this whisper of common sense from three of their former acolytes? There is some sign that this thinking is now being taken seriously. Unfortunately, there are so many existing problems now integrated into law and the bureaucracy that reversing the momentum will be difficult.

My most vivid memory from the days of Carson hysteria is of the governor of Oregon pleading for a release from the total ban on DDT. The Douglas Fir forests of the Northwest had been infected with the Tussock Moth, against which DDT was especially effective. His request was refused. The activists could prove no entry of DDT into the food chain by the contemplated spraying of these precious forests. Instead, they concentrated upon the claim that DDT would cause the eggs of certain birds to have thin shells, thus perhaps reducing the population of those birds. As a result, millions of board feet of Douglas Fir lumber were destroyed. The irony is that those in the movement to protect endangered species are now supplicating the flock to preserve those same trees (those that haven't been destroyed by the Tussock Moths). This is an example of the kind of irrationality that has swept the nation—an irrationality that I compare to excessive religious fervor. The witch trials of Salem come to mind.

When I decided to pursue an engineering career, I had no idealistic dream that my objective would improve the quality of life. I simply took it as a matter of course that I would learn how to design or make things that people would use to make their lives less burdensome. But, as I began to learn how to design these things, I was confronted with the reality that people would not use them just because I made them; they had to want them. And, the primary reason for wanting what we made was to improve the quality of life.

In the years since then, I have lived to see the quality of life of ordinary people go from a subsistence level to the comfort that we take for granted today. The past sixty years have seen the development of plentiful energy, improved sanitation, a transportation and energy infrastructure, dramatic drugs, a revolution in farming, computers, information systems, a vast welfare system, an unbelievable rise in the level of real income, and an equally dramatic rise in the living standards of those we still define as poor. Also, let us not forget those much-demeaned pesticides that improved our food supply so dramatically. The list is much larger, of course, but I'm proud of my small contributions to this enormous leap in the standard of living that has taken place. Beyond these material benefits, technology has also given us a dramatic increase in leisure time to indulge our aesthetic needs. I wish it were possible to put on a scale all of these elements which have, over the past seventy-five years, made our lives so much easier, then to place all of the negative by-products on the other side of the balance pan. The positive products of our technological society would so outweigh the negatives that there would be no contest. What I'm trying to argue is that the quality of life can be improved by the adoption of reasonable measures to help reduce unwanted by-products. At the same time, it should be realized that even Draconian regulatory measures can only improve the quality of life incrementally—and then at perhaps a prohibitive cost.

It's not just that improving the air quality, for instance, from 90 percent to 95 percent will cost twice as much as improving it from zero to 90 percent, but whether not having that additional 5 percent will diminish our enjoyment of the life that's already been made so easy for us. Add to that the enormous resources involved in getting the extra improvement (which then become unavailable for perhaps more important improvements in our quality of life), and the price of limited improvement becomes prohibitive.

There is a dramatic, almost ludicrous, way to illustrate how our improved standard of living has also had enormous environmental benefits. I think everyone will agree that the dramatic centerpiece of improved quality of life in the first seventy-five years of this century is the often reviled automobile. There are approximately 144 million automobiles on the road in the U.S. Suppose the automobile had never been invented and produced by the genius of Ford, Kettering, Durant, Chrysler, etc., and that we had to depend upon the horse for our transportation needs. Or suppose, even more plausibly, that the zealots can scare our people enough to ban automobiles. To supply the equivalent "horsepower" available now, there would have to be sixty-six horses for each man, woman, and child in the United States—a total of sixteen billion horses. It's almost impossible to visualize that many horses roaming the countryside.

And, what about the environmental impact of those horses? In addition to the tons and tons of what I will politely call waste, don't forget the amount of methane gas emitted by all these animals. I suspect it could be enough to suffocate us; if someone lit a match it might incinerate us! Furthermore, it would take some thirty billion acres of arable land to grow the hay to feed those horses, more than thirty times the total arable land in the United States. Are those who brought us the automobile not to be honored for freeing us of the enormous environmental damage they avoided by their invention? Are they to be castigated because the automobile also brought smog?

I frankly reject the criticism we scientists have taken because, in fact, the ratio of good to bad that we have produced for the American people is so heavily weighted toward the good. Our critics should not forget also that we engineers and scientists are the ones they have to call upon to correct environmental damage. How many of the activists who specialize in pointing out each new problem they discover (or invent) are capable of devising workable remedies? Very few, I would venture. Their technical skills are so minimal that they rarely conceive of any alternative but a ban. Their so-called solutions are regulations and bureaucracy.

Another frequent target of environmentalists is the use of pesticides and fertilizers in raising our food crops. Despite the popularity of "organically grown" foods, the cost of such foods exceeds those now produced commercially. What exactly are organically grown foods? The term is absolutely meaningless in any etymological sense. I suppose it means that animal manure is used to fertilize the crops. What are the actual ingredients in these natural fertilizers that cause the crops to grow? Simply nitrogen, phosphates, and potash—the same ingredients used in chemical fertilizers. There are indeed other micronutrients that are important too, but we can add those to fertilizers easily. How do you suppose we arrived at the components of chemical fertilizers? By analyzing those elements in natural fertilizers which did the job.

All the nitrogen, phosphates, and potash needed by the crops we grow has to come from somewhere, or we will deplete the native soil of its natural nutrients. Ascribing special mysterious virtues to organically grown foods is voodoo science. Between the use of chemical fertilizers and the enormous increased efficiency of motor-driven soil preparation, food production has far outstripped Malthusian predictions. Science overcame what appeared to be an irrefutable law when it was made. Shall we deprive the poor of the cheap food made possible by these unjustly reviled insecticides and fertilizers? The question I raise is whether the very affluence we have attained allows us the luxury of indiscriminately deploring environmental damage.

There is a subtle transition taking place which is scary. The extreme measures of some environmentalists elevate matters of preference to matters of morality. Thus, the similarity to religious dogma is exposed. In a recent article, Steven Landsburg, an economist at the University of Rochester, made the point with a simple illustration:

> A proposal to pave a wilderness and put up a parking lot is an occasion for conflict between those who prefer wilderness and those who prefer convenient parking. In the ensuing struggle, each side attempts to impose its preferences by manipulating the political and economic systems. Because one side must win and one side must lose, the battle is hard fought and sometimes bitter. All of this is to be expected. . . . [But], to vest one of these preferences as morally "right" and the other as morally "wrong" is a concept of a religious origin.

It's interesting to note that the methodology employed by the Marxists in the thirties is being employed in promoting this new religion of environmentalism. For example, the use of front organizations, each with a certifiably worthy and emotionally supportable mission, is common. My view that these extreme activists are members of a religious cult is not shared by all conservatives. Edward C. Krug of the Committee for a Constructive Tomorrow takes an opposite view and declares the environmental movement as anti-religious—if one believes that "Man was made in God's image." He, in fact, calls it a new but undeclared political party. It is an intriguing concept that deserves consideration.

There is substantial support for Krug's claim about the enormous war chest that these groups amass. Here is a list prepared by the Pacific Research Institute clearly indicating that their budgets exceed the sum of the Democratic and Republican parties:

Annual Revenue for Selected Environmental
Organizations in the United States

Organization	Annual Revenue
The Nature Conservancy	$109,604,000
National Wildlife Federation	78,753,000
Ducks Unlimited	70,594,099
Sierra Club and subsidiaries	39,282,479
Greenpeace, U.S.A.	33,930,747
National Audubon Society	33,601,514
Natural Resources Defense Council	13,475,075
Environmental Defense Fund	12,902,741
The Wilderness Society	10,928,494
Defenders of Wildlife	4,082,459
National Parks & Conservation Assoc.	3,361,200
Izaak Walton League	1,554,000
Trout Unlimited	2,538,176
Total:	$414,607,984*

To Krug's view that the environmental movement is an undeclared political party, I add: Environmental groups enjoy a significant advantage over the two major political parties. Most of their funding is tax deductible, in contrast to political contributions. Even more pertinent, there is no limitation on the amounts they can receive, as there is on political contributions. Indeed, many of these environmental groups get direct government funding—emphasizing the alliance between the bureaucrats and those who create the need for the bureaucracy.

If the organizations above are classified as 501(c)3 (an IRS code), they are prohibited from overt lobbying. But, they are allowed to "educate," which gives them wide latitude in

---

*Source: Pacific Research Institute, 1994. Not all of these are activists. The Nature Conservancy, for instance, buys land, presumably at market price, to preserve for future generations. That's commendable as long as they don't use the government as their enforcer.

visiting congressmen, preparing papers for their staffs, etc. They are not allowed to contribute to campaigns, but they have so many members who can contribute to those congressmen who pass environmental scrutiny that their clout is powerful.

For those who are not familiar with how the political process works, it is often a surprise to find how dependent congressmen are on their staff members. There are so many bills to be considered that the staffs of congressmen wield great power. Skilled lobbyists help these staffers by preparing position papers with closely reasoned, but one-sided, arguments. Blessed with the mantle of compassion and carefully cultivated media support, the conclusions of these reports are hard to resist. There is no anti-environmental lobby. The most that can be mustered is a tired Republican Congress complaining that "it costs too much!"

How did extreme environmentalism and all of its cousins take such a powerful hold on our society? How did it become virtually deified as a religion? The influence of the media cannot be disregarded—although I recognize that the media is an all too convenient whipping boy for conservatives. There is, however, some merit to the argument.

In a devastating op-ed piece in the *Wall Street Journal*, George Melloan asks the question, "Why do so many reporters and editors suspend their normal skepticism when that major word 'environment' is involved?" He cites an Associated Press report criticizing President Bush for not strongly supporting efforts to fight global warming at the infamous Earth Summit at Rio de Janeiro in June 1992. What he decries is the implicit assumption by the press that global warming is a proven fact, that it is caused by environmental emissions, and that it is harmful. Each of these theories has been challenged repeatedly by knowledgeable scientists. Indeed, as Melloan points out, one prestigious scientific institute used the historical data of temperature records for the past one hundred years in the computer program which is the basis for predicting future global warming. It found that "the greenhouse effect has not had any significant impact on global warming over the past hundred years." And, this was tested by using the very computer program that is the basis for predicting future global warming. Yet, Melloan says, "the A.P. dispatch only talks about Bush's grading of 'D' for his efforts to fight global warming." The A.P. assumes global warming as fact and "the only issue is doing enough to fight it."

Melloan is right. The press prides itself on its "world weary" skepticism, yet it's been taken in by environmental tales. I can only speculate that it has been hooked by the repeated claim of compassion. It has not recognized that compassion put into practice is not automatically virtuous.

It is interesting to trace the growth of the environmental movement to its place today as a secular religion. The underlying psychological force was the same in the progression from Marxism and socialism as the centerpiece of compassionate activism, to the civil rights movement, the upheavals in the universities, the rejection of military action in Vietnam, and the "great society" and its aim to eliminate poverty and hunger. The need to feel compassion, to feel good about oneself, to fight against the forces of evil can become addictive.

Indignation, compassion, the revealed truth, concern for evil perpetrated upon unsuspecting people: These were the parameters set by Rachel Carson for the new breed of environmentalists. These were the ingredients for a new cause to supplant the ones which came before. It was a new movement to substitute for the civil rights movement—by then won, at least in principal; the dissatisfaction with Vietnam; and "the great society," which by then seemed to be easily attainable, simply by spreading enough money around. Now there was a new passionate movement to fill the void.

The irresistible lure of compassion, the central core of most great religions, has driven the secular world to develop this passionate new cause. Unfortunately, the extremists of environmentalism have lost their rationality. By continuing their steadfast intolerance and denying their fallibility, they may actually be promoting a decrease in the quality of life that we have so bravely obtained.

7. Who Is More Important?

If we can prevent the government from wasting the labors of the people under the pretense of caring for them, they will be happy.

—Thomas Jefferson

I have a confession to make. When contemplating writing this chapter, I was troubled. I was afraid I might come across as too argumentative or perhaps too angry. I had a concern that I may be giving credence and recognition to movements that will become victims of their own excesses. Nevertheless, I felt compelled to recognize that there is a dangerous ideology proliferating. Unchecked, it will seriously limit the already scarce resources we have available to implement our compassion for those who are in desperate need of it. We must stimulate the immune system of the body politic to resist this virulent infection.

As may be obvious, I tend to have an argumentative style and I know the origins. In college, I faced the rigors and terror of the Socratic method. Professor Emeritus John C. Olsen was cherubic, white-haired, and portly, with a walrus mustache. He established chemical engineering as a separate discipline from industrial chemistry (then a subdivision of the chemistry department). When I met him, he had retired as head of the Chemical Engineering Department at Poly, but he continued to teach.

I'll never forget my first encounter with the Socratic method in his class. He asked me to answer a question about some fundamental chemical engineering theory that we were studying. I answered confidently. Without comment he then asked another, related, question. I answered that confidently, too. Then another, and another, and still another, each following from the previous answer. The jolly looking Santa Claus at the front of the class turned into an ogre in front of me as he drilled the questions in, never once rendering an opinion about any of my answers along the way. Finally, he asked one last question, and to my chagrin I gave an answer that directly contradicted my first answer! I was suffused with embarrassment and anger. "Professor Olsen," I asked, "which answer was right?" He responded, "You decide! Next student please!" Despite my anger and frustration, I determined to learn to cope with this method, and as I learned it, I became an admirer of it. Later, when I started teaching, I adopted the Socratic method, lock, stock, and barrel—so much so that I had students complain about the cruelty of my unrelenting style.

Though I learned not to overdo it, I have used variations of the Socratic method throughout my business career. Rarely have I accepted the first answer to a question. I tend to probe and dig to see what's behind opinions expressed by people. I've overheard more than one conversation in which one of our young guys was advised by an older hand, "Don't give Joe any bull. He'll expose your cover-up pretty quickly. You'd better be able to back up your conclusions because he'll grill you!"

The pretension and the self-righteousness of a marginal but extremely powerful group who place themselves under the umbrella of the legitimate environmental movement has stirred up those juices of the Socratic method that I learned from Professor Olsen.

I write this chapter with all of the anger and argumentativeness exposed because that is the way I feel. I feel that way because I am a compassionate man who deeply resents the wasting of the precious resources that mankind has acquired on causes that essentially denigrate and cast doubt upon a human being's right to the place we've earned on this planet.

The environmental movement which occupies so much of our attention these days and consumes so much of our resources has, for the most part, a sound underlying motive in the compassionate goal of improving the quality of life of people by improving the environment around us. My criticisms are only directed to the extremists and those who worship environmentalism as a religion, imbuing it with moral sanction. As a proactive, pragmatic movement to improve our environment, it has a desirable goal and one that I support. The recurring conservative criticism is not in the importance of the issues, but rather, in the defects in the proposed solutions and the lack of discrimination in the use of our resources. Imparting a moral dimension to environmentalism as to a religion is an effective shield against pragmatic evaluation.

In improving the quality of the air we breath and the water we drink, there are definable goals that can be expressed quantitatively. Though we may argue vehemently as to how much improvement we want, the desirability of improving air and water quality for people is disputed by no one. What is often overlooked is the importance of "cost-benefit ratios"—a mechanistic but essential concept. When allocating resources, we must consider the value—and the cost—of each ingredient that contributes to our quality of life: Plentiful energy, transportation, infra-structure, housing, cheap and nutritious foods, improved pharmaceuticals, health care, and in the broad sense, more leisure to enjoy aesthetics.

We get the secondary or derivative benefits of environmental improvement after the fundamentals of our standard of living are adequately provided. You are unlikely to enjoy an opera if you are hungry. Enjoying the beautiful trees or a verdant forest is only a dream if you are homeless. Can one aspire to enjoy the beauty of the forests if the lack of resources for energy makes transportation too costly? Shall we leave the trees in the forest untouched but essentially inaccessible, or shall we cut down some of those trees to build a parking lot to accommodate the cars people drive, in order to give people a chance to enjoy those trees? For whom should those trees be preserved—only those who have the resources to travel to see them or the time to hike to them? That's the practical dilemma we conservatives insist must be faced.

We must make rational decisions about the way our resources are allocated between all the conventional contributions to our quality of life and the environmental factors. Conservatives maintain, indeed we insist, that though the motives are well based, the compassion of many activists has been too narrowly focused. The environmental movement carries with it excesses that, by consuming resources that could be beneficially used elsewhere, may have substantially diminished the net value to our society of that movement. Even within the environmental arena, the allocation of resources has been so badly skewed by fringe activists that they severely denature the improvement of the quality of life we could expect from sensible environmental improvement.

On the one hand, the justification of the environmental movement's concentration upon air and water is clearly that there is a demonstrable improvement of the quality of life for all the people, though often environmental laws are regressively in favor of the middle and upper class. Other fringe movements, all lumped under the carefully crafted, made-up word *ecosystems*, are not by any means in that category. They are, in fact, regressively against all people, rich and poor alike. Because a direct benefit for people cannot be demonstrated, they are deemed "morally right" in order to evoke guilt for "disturbing the ecosystem."

Quite correctly, the environment is influenced by man's interaction with his surroundings. What is not said, is how much influence he has upon that interaction. It is in assessing man's influence that conservatives take issue with the passionate advocates of the endangered species, et al. There are so many effects from natural causes that exceed man's influence that these activists elevate the power of man as an evildoer far above his real place in this cosmos. Man pictured as a destructive being is paradoxically paired up with a denigration of man in relation to other animal species and the aesthetic environment. If it is agreed that man's influence upon the ecosystem is highly exaggerated, then the projection of guilt upon us, which is the major weapon used by eco-terrorists, will lose its impact. How much sulfur is spewed into the air by industry as compared to the eruption of Mt. St. Helen's?

By advocating a stasis, a freeze-it-as-it-is attitude, and indeed to advocate a reversal of advances we've made, we deny benefits to those aspiring to them. How many of the radical "greens" recognize the essential immorality of their position (ironically labeled as compassionate) because they simply cannot freeze one section of our lives without freezing them all. In many ways, they are clearly enemies of the poor.

The poor shall remain poor; the homeless shall remain homeless; the cold shall remain cold. For, as many of the greens admit, the ecosystem is interdependent. More accurately stated, it is a zero sum game. Can we provide homes for the homeless out of thin air? No! We must cut down trees. Can we succor the poor without providing them with more of this planet's bountiful resources? Can we provide transportation without providing the fuel? The advocates of "small is beautiful" or "stop the planet I want to get off" are not kind people; they are not compassionate. They are, indeed, selfish and self-centered, denying for the underclass any hope of getting more of our planet's resources to improve their lives. How they can pretend to wear the virtuous cloak of compassion is beyond me. Look at John Stossel's table (chapter 5), which clearly demonstrates that being poor shortens the life span substantially more than all other causes put together.

One of the great dividends of the enormous improvement in productivity in this century has been to give people the leisure and, in many cases, the resources to enjoy aesthetics—all of those needs within us that we can enjoy as a surcease from our struggle for survival. But, aesthetics cannot be quantified, nor can we have any common agreement of that which is good or bad. Can we agree on which paint-

ing pleases us? Can we decide whether a tree is more important to preserve than a Frank Lloyd Wright building? Can
we decide between *The Pieta* and the stainless steel abstract
in front of an office building? It is the grossest sort of censorship to declare that certain creations of nature or man are
morally superior.

Although there is little trouble in accepting the joy of
these aesthetic dividends, it should never be forgotten that
they are by-products of our high standard of living. Although
art has been with us throughout history, it has always been
secondary to the primary need for survival.

In a world of finite resources, even the quantifiable objectives of clean air and clean water should be examined and
compared with other demands upon those resources. The
alternative agenda of aesthetic needs or of species preservation occupies, in my view, a secondary place which must
withstand even more demanding scrutiny, since the impact
upon the quality of life is so subjective. Therefore, the choice
of which aesthetic values we spend our resources on should
be subjected to more intense scrutiny and evaluation than
other, more direct environmental improvements.

As a result of the efforts of a relatively small group of
activists, these by-products of our affluent society have taken
on a holy stature; they have become an entitlement, if you
will. Codified into law and given official sanction, they consume our resources beyond their relative importance in the
overall environmental movement and especially in the
broader agenda of our quality of life. The coupling of the
narrow activist's zeal, with the natural bureaucratic need to
expand regulations, has created a monster.

What is clear is that these actions (many of them now
laws) were probably motivated originally by compassion for
the people and the aesthetic pleasures of which they might
be deprived. However, that connection has almost lost any
meaning. What has happened is that many of these movements, especially those led by the endangered species activists and certainly the anti-vivisectionists, is a transfer of compassion away from the people to the animals themselves.
This is probably based upon the false assumption that all

compassion is of equal weight and of equal benefit to the world. But, given all of the other compassionate causes, we are obligated to discriminate—to make choices. Causes should be judged by their benefits to mankind, not by the purity or intensity of the motive impelling them.

I pointed out before that resource allocation is not just a matter of choosing not to spend on defense in order to shift resources to environmental purposes. That would make the choice seemingly simplistic. There are many other compassionate causes that compete for those funds, so the choice is, more properly, which compassionate cause shall be supported.

The *Los Angeles Times* recently devoted fifty column inches to an article describing the sad condition of our national parks. They attributed this to many things, including the terrible things people do to these premises. Another is the budgetary restrictions—the Park Service has been handed a burden of scientific and environmental missions by animal and other activists that are costly, time consuming and controversial, thus depriving the Park Service of funds for the conventional policing, guiding, and enhancement of the parks' beauty.

Where is the Sierra Club? Isn't this their primary purview? Unfortunately, they have been diverted to holier causes. What started out as a rather benign club of middle class people who shared a common interest in hiking in the High Sierras in California, has now turned into the one thousand pound gorilla of the environmental movement. The watershed in the transition of this friendly hiking club into the nation's leading activist environmental group probably was reached some twenty-five years ago. At that time, the Walt Disney Company proposed a large resort development in the foothills of the Sierras near Yosemite National Park. Fresh from its spectacular creation of the first theme park, Disneyland, near Anaheim, California, Disney proposed to build the Mineral King Development near Yosemite.

I don't remember the details and certainly am not qualified to defend the concept, but the Sierra Club led the opposition to the Disney scheme. This was not unexpected since, by its very name, the Sierra Club would be the natural opponent to any commercialization in that area. Aside from the question of whether it was justified to oppose such a venture on the basis that there would be too many people (an elitist view if I ever saw one!), the opposition of the Sierra Club was not unexpected.

The confrontation was highly publicized, with almost daily headlines as spokesmen for Disney and the Sierra Club were quoted and public opinion was being courted. Those headlines, I suppose, provided a heady narcotic of media attention, which seduced the sedate members of the Sierra Club. The final rush of the publicity "high" came when Disney canceled their multimillion-dollar project, and the little Sierra Club brought the mighty Disney to its knees. From that point on, the Sierra Club, under the leadership of David Brower, whom Virginia Postrel describes as the "archdruid of the environmental movement," started its ascension (with appropriate media notoriety) to the top of the environmental activist heap. They have become the most powerful environmental political lobby in Washington. David Brower has now gone on to found even more radical environmental organizations. I suppose that the protection and upkeep of our beautiful national park system is now beneath the Sierra Club's concern.

If the value of compassionate acts is measured by its effect upon people, I make no excuse for making mankind the primary focus of my compassion. Against all of the dark forces of nature and the competition of other species, we have earned that position. This does not disallow compassion for animals or other creatures, for it is one of the foundations of our claim of a preferred position on this planet that we are not totally selfish. Though not always, we are considerate of our fellow man and we are considerate of other creatures. In short, we are compassionate, and that is a distinguishing feature of the human species that separates us from others and, indeed, exalts us. I ask: Does it make any sense to validate ourselves as compassionate human beings by denigrating or belittling ourselves?

How much is the quality of life improved by spending

substantial sums for the protection of the desert tortoise or the snail darter or the Stephens kangaroo rat? It's a sad misapplication not only of funds but of compassionate energy. The argument that these measures are necessary to preserve our ecosystem is, as far as I am concerned, just so much "new speak." It is arrogant to think that we mere mortals can manipulate the ecosystem or protect it against natural forces.

The absurdity of some of these laws was highlighted in a recent story in the *Los Angeles Times*. It told of the homeowner in Riverside County who wanted to clear the dry sage brush around his home to avoid the potential fire hazard. He was prevented from removing that brush because it was deemed to be a habitat of the Stephens kangaroo rat, an endangered species. His home was destroyed in the recent fires in that region, when the brush around his home was kindled—just what he wanted to avoid by simply removing a small amount of the brush. He was quoted as saying, "My home was destroyed by a bunch of bureaucrats in suits saving a rat I'd never heard of!" What do you tell this man—go sue the environmentalists?

What has happened is that the compassion which should primarily be for the benefit of human beings has now been turned around, with little apology, to compassion for animals, or vegetation, or swamplands, usually using the so-called ecosystem argument. Are these concerns of ultimate benefit to the human race—as compared to spending the same resources to feed the poor? The absurdity of this compassion gone berserk is exposed by a listing of just a few of the more than eight hundred species currently on the official list of threatened or endangered species, such as: The San Marcos Salamander, the Arkansas Fat Mucket, the Tuna Cave Cockroach, and the Kanab Ambersnail. Shall we go on?

There are literally thousands of examples of the negative impact imposed by the bureaucrats who enforce these laws. Many of these might seem trivial, as in the case of the homeowner who lost his home to preserve the Stephens kangaroo rat; certainly, it was not trivial to the poor homeowner I quoted. But, many of these rulings have much more substantial consequences.

Does anyone remember the infamous snail darter? This was a tiny obscure fish that some "authorities" said could only be found in the path of the Big Tom Canal project, a multibillion-dollar waterway to be built through Tennessee to provide barge access to the Mississippi. The transportation cost savings for products manufactured in the lower mid-East were enormous.

With the unchallenged statement that this was the only spot where this endangered snail darter existed, the activists stopped that project in its tracks for a number of years as the case progressed through the courts. Finally, the project got the go ahead. I don't know if anyone has calculated the cost of the delay, but it must have been enormous.

Less than a year after this had finally been resolved, I happened to notice, buried in the back of my daily paper, one paragraph saying that zoologists had discovered many other colonies of snail darters in small streams hundreds of miles from the officially declared "last habitat." How many millions of dollars were wasted by this delay? There is a point here that is not often noticed by the public. Political institutions and bureaucracies are rarely held accountable for their stupidity and documented errors. Financial responsibility is rarely accepted by a bureaucracy.

I cannot trace the actual players in the infamous case of the snail darter, but certainly, the Department of Fish and Wildlife was the bureaucratic instrument by which this project was delayed so long. They should have been held accountable. The Corps of Engineers should have sued them for costing that arm of the government (read: The taxpayers) many millions of dollars by their purely arbitrary rulings based upon very bad science.

You can bet your bottom dollar that if a private company had been hired to do an environmental impact statement and had provided a written report stating, unequivocally, that this area was the last refuge of the snail darter, thus causing this expensive delay, the Corps of Engineers would have sued the company to a fare-thee-well. Who represents the taxpayer when his money is shamefully wasted by ineptitude and bureaucratic bumbling of another government agency?

But, this is just a side issue. The real problem is a basic one. The government was not justified in depriving the people of this country of the economic benefits of the Big Tom project, even if that was the last habitat of the snail darter. Remember that economic benefits are directly translatable to improvement in the quality of life. The emotional environmentalists do not seem to understand that simple fact. They would have mounted a media campaign portraying the advocates of the project as selfish businessmen who willingly sacrificed poor little fish just to cut transportation costs—forgetting that real people were being affected adversely in order to preserve the snail darter.

Why do we give these movements credibility? How can anyone be deluded into accepting these as "compassionate" issues? An apparently harmless law to save endangered species (not a bad idea in the abstract) has probably been expanded to many times the size originally envisioned by its congressional proponents, as they, too, stand by helplessly as the bureaucrats and activists turn a well-meaning law into a juggernaut of abuse.

An article entitled "All Creatures Great and Small" by Charles Oliver, which appeared in *Reason Magazine* in 1992, illustrates my point. Oliver recounts how, in 1964, the Department of the Interior established the Committee on Rare and Endangered Wildlife to study the state of native plants and animals. Two years later, the committee said eighty-three native species were endangered. (There are nearly eight hundred species on the list now.)

After Earth Day 1970, environmental activists campaigned for a law to protect threatened species. In 1973, Congress passed the Endangered Species Act, which empowers the federal government to devise "means whereby the ecosystems upon which endangered species and threatened species may be conserved." This places the focus on the locations where threatened species live, not on the species themselves. The act also gives the Fish and Wildlife Service "all methods and procedures which are necessary to bring any endangered species or threatened species to the point at which the measures provided pursuant to the Act are no longer necessary." Fish and Wildlife must do whatever it deems necessary to preserve a species, *regardless of cost*. Fish and Wildlife now controls eighty-seven million acres of property, and since the agency believes another three thousand species may merit listing, that acreage will only go up.

The act does not use the biological definition of species— i.e., two individuals are members of the same species if they can produce fertile offspring — but instead considers species to be animals that have nearly identical physical characteristics and geographical locations. As a result, decisions are often made based on subjective criteria. As Aaron Wildavsky pointed out, "Some taxonomists say there are eight species of squirrels, others say there are as many as eighty-seven. The disagreements can be quite large." In 1984, Wildavsky and economist Julian Simon said that the estimates of species loss provided by the worst doomsayers were "pure guesswork."

This was confirmed just recently in an article in the *L.A. Times*. The gnatcatcher, a tiny bird that lives in the dry brush of Orange County in Southern California, was placed on the endangered species list. Consequently, a group of home builders were prevented from building homes on their property in that area by the endangered species bureaucracy. Was denying the owners the right to use their property an involuntary appropriation of land? Was this a violation of the "takings clause" of the Fifth Amendment? No one seems concerned about the home builder being adversely affected. The preservation of the gnatcatcher was also used as an excuse for prohibiting a quasi-government group, the Orange County Transportation Corridor Agencies, from establishing a transportation route through the dry hills where the gnatcatcher lives. Thus, expropriation of the home builder's property led to the usurping of the rights of whole communities.

The home builders and the transportation agency sued

the Department of Interior and, happily, the judge ruled against the department. The point at issue reinforces the contention of Wildavsky and others that these arbitrary decisions are made upon flimsy scientific evidence.

According to the article in the *L.A. Times,* apparently, a Massachusetts ornithologist spent several years studying the gnatcatcher. In 1988, he wrote a scientific paper in which he concluded that the California gnatcatcher was essentially no different from gnatcatchers found in large portions of Mexico and the Western United States. This paper was criticized by other scientists (the newspaper does not report who they were or their credentials). The ornithologist spent two years restudying his data and finally issued a new report in 1990 saying that his conclusions in 1988 were wrong! I understand that the Mexican variety of the gnatcatcher had different coloring on its beak. The issue the judge ruled on was a demand made by the plaintiffs simply to see the original data upon which these two contradictory scientific papers were based. They wanted to see whether the data were any good or if there were good reasons for the ornithologist reversing his view. Urged on by the environmentalists, the Department of the Interior refused to give the plaintiffs the data and that was the basis of the judge's ruling in favor of the home builder and the transportation group. Here are two quotes from the *Los Angeles Times* story, which summarizes both positions:

> Thornton [attorney for the plaintiffs] said the ruling "effectively repudiates" what he called the efforts of environmentalists "to illegitimately twist the Endangered Species Act into a tool for stopping development in general, and specifically halting construction of the San Joaquin Hills Transportation Corridor" in the coastal hills of Orange County.

> Joel Reynolds, senior attorney with the Natural Resources Defense Council, which had petitioned the Interior Department to list the gnatcatcher as threatened, disagreed.

> "This is absolutely a step in the wrong direction, one

that could have a devastating impact on the habitat planning program to protect endangered species," Reynolds said. "The listing of the gnatcatcher is the foundation upon which the conservation efforts in Southern California have been based."

In bemoaning the "devastating" impact upon the habitat planning program, Reynolds made it clear that the program is what is important. Pray tell what ever happened to the dear little gnatcatcher?

I can't resist remarking on the wording of the statement "the gnatcatcher is the foundation." If this small bird is the foundation of the conservation effort, that seems to be a very weak base. Does Mr. Reynolds mean that if, by chance, there are other gnatcatchers found, the whole conservation effort would collapse? Doesn't that trivialize the grandly named conservation effort beyond belief?

There is also the question of property rights. Whatever happened to the Fifth Amendment? The "right of eminent domain" is established in law, but it requires that a property owner be reimbursed fairly when his property is "condemned" for public use. But, what about a property owner whose property has been substantially devalued by an environmental edict issued by a bureaucracy? Is he not entitled to compassion or some fair treatment? How much was the land devalued? I see very little difference between outright seizure and sterilization of private property by edict. Do the landowners and the agency who wanted to build a transportation system have a cause for action under the Fifth Amendment? That's for some lawyer to answer—or perhaps Congress, as has recently been proposed.

Activists who seek to protect subspecies are actually defying evolution. As biologist Norman D. Levine wrote in the journal *BioScience*, "Perhaps 95% of the species that once existed no longer exist. . . . What species preservers are trying to do is stop the clock. It cannot and should not be done. Extinction is an inevitable fact of evolution. New species continually arise, and they are better adapted to their environment than those that have died out." Wasn't natural selection a factor in human development?

I wonder if these activists understand the profound damage inflicted by this campaign to prevent people from using large blocks of land, based upon the rather flimsy excuse of saving the habitat of an obscure bird like the gnatcatcher? In depriving the people, they are especially depriving the poor—for, by taking desirable land out of the available pool, the price of other land goes up. These higher costs impact the poor adversely.

Very few of the environmental activists recognize or acknowledge that their programs are regressive. Since regressivity is a major litmus test used by the liberals for social and tax policy, it's surprising that they haven't tested environmental legislation the same way.

It is pretty clear that if the primacy of the conservation movement as represented by the gnatcatcher is accepted, then the inevitable result is an unfair impact on the poor. The progression is fairly obvious. Land is taken off the market and public transportation for the people is blocked. As a result of withdrawing land and transportation from the supply, the remaining land in the area goes up in value and congestion increases. The landlords in the cities will find the worth of their holdings increasing (remember supply and demand) and the cost of housing will clearly increase, impacting the poor most. That's regressivity. Saving the gnatcatcher habitat increases the slumlord's ability to gouge his renters.

Anyone who has bought real estate recently knows how enormously complicated it has become. Environmental impact statements are required every time you turn around. Who assumes responsibility for environmental problems caused before they were declared illegal? The cost of property has escalated significantly as a result of the activists. Who pays? The people—including the poor.

When trying to understand what motivates activists, I tend to resist conspiracy theories, with their vision of people meeting furtively in back rooms to plan an assault or plot the overthrow of an existing social structure. On the other hand, there is often a commonality of thought or a common philosophic thrust that binds people to actions which appear to be conspiratorial. One of the best analyses of the conjunction of the ideas of the radical "greens" was an article written in *Reason* magazine in 1990 by editor Virginia I. Postrel entitled "The Green Road to Serfdom." She declares:

> But beneath the rhetoric of survival, behind the Sierra Club calendars, beyond the movie-star appeals, lies a full-fledged ideology—an ideology every bit as powerful as Marxism and every bit as dangerous to individual freedom and human happiness. Like Marxism, it appeals to seemingly noble instincts: the longing for beauty, for harmony, for peace. It is the green road to serfdom.
>
> If we are not to turn down its path, we must first recognize it for what it is. Just as socialism seduced many people by masquerading as an elaborate form of charity, so this green-ideology-without-a-name disguises itself as simple concern for a cleaner world. But there is a difference between the ordinary desire for clean air or pretty places to hike and the extraordinary passion to remake the world.

What this means is that there is a morality imputed to this movement that rises above science, and brooks no rational comparison to other worthy compassionate movements. Though presented under the cover of compassion, it rises above it in order to resist the discrimination which would put it in its proper place.

Postrel recognizes that there are hundreds of separate organizations which seemingly fractionate this movement, but are, in fact, held together by a common ideology. She makes a comparison with a similar phenomenon within the Socialist movement, which I saw firsthand in the 1930s.

Yet, these ideas are somehow so appealing and persuasive that a *New York Times* poll showed that 80 percent of the people believed that the environment should be protected "whatever the cost." With my faith in the ultimate wisdom of the people, I am dead certain that this view will be repudiated as these radical ideologues are consumed by their own excesses. The Stephens kangaroo rat, the snail darter and the gnatcatcher—those little "defenseless" creatures—shall destroy their idolaters.

On the other hand, there are those in this movement who are, in fact, crafty political animals. David Brower, the "Archdruid" of the environmental movement, said:

> I founded Friends of the Earth to make the Sierra Club look reasonable. Then I founded the Earth Island Institute to make Friends of the Earth look reasonable. Earth First! now makes us look reasonable. We're still waiting for someone to come along and make Earth First! look reasonable.

Postrel quotes absurdity after absurdity, such as Jeremy Rifkin's justifying an entire system of political economy "based on the ideal of never expending energy." The inevitable result of that idea is its terrible brutalizing of the poor and the disadvantaged, whose way out of the ghetto cannot be postulated without giving them access to energy. Did it ever occur to Rifkin that the only system that doesn't expend energy is simply death—that every time he breathes he produces energy. Life is defined by energy! The cells in Rifkin's body demand energy and the food he eats and the air he breathes produce it!

Finally, Postrel confirms my own observations that these people have "an utter contempt for humanity." She supports that view with a chilling quote from a research biologist for the National Park Service—ending with the sentence "Until such time as Homo Sapiens should decide to rejoin nature, some of us can only hope for the right virus to come along."

What motivates these activists who have such contempt for us? There must be some way of having these warped people accept the real place of man in the cosmos. We are neither all-powerful against the overwhelming forces of nature nor unwanted intruders into an inhospitable universe. Those who say we are less than what we are and those who exalt our status against nature are both wrong. We should be proud of the accomplishments of the human race and humble before the power of nature to destroy us.

At one time, I viewed these animal rights and endangered species people with amused tolerance, but I have been persuaded that their ideology is really threatening to our society and they cannot be ignored. If these fringe activists were merely academic theoreticians, it would be less threatening. But, their activism goes well beyond polite discussion in Ivy League halls, as they inject their ideas into the political vascular system of our country.

There is a clear parallel between this modern activism and that which I observed firsthand during the thirties when Marxism took to the streets. The parallel extends not just to the attempt to reduce theoretical ideas to practice but also to methodology. The proliferation of hundreds of front organizations in the thirties confused the public, and the artful use of *democracy* in many of the names put an acceptable face upon these Marxist-backed organizations. "The Democratic Front for . . ." was a common naming style during those times.

Compare that with all of the front groups pushing the ideology of the fringe activists. The proliferation of organizations containing warm, fuzzy words such as *Friends, Earth,* and *Humane* is a chilling evocation of the Marxist model. Although these modern groups do take to the streets occasionally, they have found another much more receptive venue to put their ideology into practice, and that is in Washington, D.C. The bureaucracies are their target because they help to create them. Bureaucracies are hungry for causes and hungry for laws which they can use as a springboard to spread their regulatory control over us. Did the Congress which voted for the endangered species legislation, a well-intentioned act, ever visualize that their legislation would be used as a basis for declaring eight hundred (growing to three thousand) species as endangered? And, did they know that it would be used as a springboard for one of the most blatant land grabs ever seen? Even worse, it has been used to restrict the fundamental right to own and use property, the basic underpinning of our economic system. There is, unfortunately, a symbiotic relationship between the activists and the bureaucracies who wish to retain and expand their power.

If proof of the hunger for growth is required, how about this? Until very recently, the Fish and Wildlife Services was a sleepy corner of the Department of the Interior. In 1982, the limited Endangered Species Act of 1973 was expanded by eliminating the original act's requirement to consider the "economic impact" of these acts:

> "We add over a hundred species every year," brags Endangered Species Deputy Director Robert Ruesink, speaking of his department's growing power. "Often lawsuits brought by environmental groups force us to add them." He adds: "Then we can go to Congress and ask for more money." And get it. Today, with a full-time equivalent staff of 7,300 and a budget of $1.2 billion, the Fish & Wildlife Service is the third-largest bureau in Interior Secretary Bruce Babbitt's empire, after the Bureau of Indian Affairs ($2.2 billion) and the National Park Service ($1.5 billion). *(Forbes Magazine,* 18 July 1994).

One insidious by-product of these emotionally charged issues is a frightening tendency for these bureaucracies who are the allies and partners of the fringe activists to become militant. I have heard of one case, which I cannot verify, that the Fish and Wildlife Service sent a force of men to a company's offices, unannounced, to seize some files. They wore flak jackets and side arms! Does this government agency have its own army? How many other bureaucracies have their own armed forces? I have an answer to that question. At a seminar including speakers from the American Civil Liberties Union (ACLU) and the National Rifle Association (strange bedfellows), Gene Guerrero, the speaker for the ACLU asserted that there were fifty-three agencies of the U.S. government who had the right to carry firearms and to make arrests. Are we approaching a police state? Scary, isn't it?

Let's take on some of the easier targets: The animal rights activists who decry the testing of drugs upon "poor helpless animals" who suffer such pain in order to help man develop drugs to benefit human beings. The irony is that the activists demand humane treatment of these animals. I think that "humane" means to treat the animals as human beings! Do they see no contradiction here? Whatever affection and love we have for animals does not justify equating them with humans, nor is our love for them decreased one whit by denying that equivalency. Is the humility that these activists parade as a virtue really that, or is that feeling of virtue the same old eternal drive to validate one's goodness?

Animal rights is a favorite cause for entertainers. One of them reportedly said, "I think [biomedical researchers] should experiment on murderers. What the hell are they doing to pay us back?" Does this woman understand the enormity of her immorality? Buchenwald, Dachau, and Nazi doctors' experiments on Jews are to be revived? Does simply substituting murderers for Jews make it O.K.? Is that what she suggests?

It's bad enough that the basic, soundly motivated environmental movement is burdened by excesses in setting goals so high that they place unwarranted burdens upon society. But, carrying the excesses of these fringe activists in support of inconsequential issues weakens the movement even further. The irrationality of driving spikes into trees and carrying out all those bizarre activities serves the legitimate environmental movement badly. Being of "constrained vision," I have faith in the ultimate common sense of the American people, but I struggle to keep that faith in mind each time I see these activists engaging in such destructive practices.

Finally, the attack on the rights of property owners is a fundamental attack upon our society and culture. Will the arbitrary actions of the Fish and Wildlife Service, which has taken more than eighty-seven million acres out of use, stop there? I doubt it. Some have suggested that taking control of property out of the private sector is a hidden agenda of the ideologues of the endangered species activists. Such actions enrich other land owners and impact the poor in a regressive way. They defy the "takings" clause of the Fifth Amendment. Where is the Department of Fish and Wildlife budget for reimbursing the people whose land they render partially worthless by bureaucratic regulation?

If it appears that I am exaggerating this bureaucratic land grab, look at this table:

Agency	Designated Wilderness	Recommended for Wilderness	Under Study for Wilderness	Grand Total
Wilderness Acres Managed by the Federal Government				
Bureau of Land Management	369,000	400,000	22,400,000	23,169,000
Fish & Wildlife Service	80,700,000	19,300,000	3,400,000	58,000,000
Forest Service	32,100,000	2,500,000	9,300,000	43,900,000
National Park Service	74,300,000	36,800,000	8,900,000	28,600,000
Totals:	88,569,000	15,200,000	118,300,000	222,069,000

Source: Pacific Research Institute, 1994

Isn't that terrifying! The ironic part is that the National Park Service and the Fish & Wildlife Service have already gotten Congress to designate much new land as national parks or wildlife reserves. The agencies have not been able to get the funds to close these purchases and to establish the parks and reserves they convinced Congress were so important—yet they are voraciously grabbing for more!

I say, "Enough of this nonsense!" Unfortunately, we cannot easily dismiss it. I, therefore, repeat my plea more emphatically. We must stimulate the immune system of the body politic to resist this virulent infection!

8. Education

Enlighten the people generally and tyranny and oppressions of body and mind will vanish like evil spirits at the dawn of day.
—Thomas Jefferson

There is at least one area of public policy in which few liberals will question the motives of conservatives, and that is in support of education. The desirability of an educated citizenry is undisputed. However, unconstrained and constrained visions result in well-defined differences of implementation. Refreshingly, those arguments can be judged on their merits, without questions of motive.

Teaching is at the core of education, and education is at the core of a democracy. Without an educated citizenry, political actions will inevitably become tools of oppression.

I claim no expertise as an educator, but I do have considerable experience and hands-on knowledge. My love of teaching has been an important part of my adult life. When I try to analyze the contributions I have made in helping to build the enterprise that bears my name, perhaps the most important is that of a teacher. Thus, in my later years, I have comfortably assumed the position of "non-executive" chairman.

My former "students" now run the company and I dare say, more successfully than I could. Not only that, they have, themselves, become teachers.

When Noel Watson, our CEO, first told me about the formation of Jacobs College and the hope that everyone would thus understand what the "Jacobs" culture was, I frowned. "Noel," I said, "I am worried. Have we grown into a rigid organization in which there is only one way to do things, enshrined as the 'Jacobs way'? This is the kind of cultural stasis that did in GM, Sears, and IBM. I hope that we are not being arrogant enough to think that we have discovered *the* way to serve our clients. As our company grew, we were always looking for new and novel ways to do things, and I hope that we still are. We were risk-takers in innovation of methodology but prudent as to financial risk. Are we in danger of institutionalizing what we have learned into something rigidly structured, with a 'how to' manual that must be followed slavishly? Are you telling me that we have become an arteriosclerotic organization that only does things one way, the so-called Jacobs way?"

"Absolutely not," said Noel. "Exactly the opposite! You know me better than that. But as we've grown to more than 15,000 people, we have hired many who have come from companies whose culture is much more hierarchical than ours, including turf building, risk avoidance, selfish ambition, etc. It's quite a change for them to come here and to experience our open culture and rigid honesty with each other. They often feel insecure because we don't have absolute rules other than our 'minimum acceptable standards' (which are, in fact, quite high!). As you know, I am proud of the fact that we are the leanest, lowest overhead, major company in our business. Our flat management structure will not work unless we push decision-making downward. We cannot push decision-making down into the organization structure unless those people know how we make decisions. We, thus, avoid telling them how to handle a particular business problem, but rather the principles which guide us.

"What we are trying to do is to have them understand the process we use to make decisions. We are prudent risk-takers, but only when accompanied by ruthless honesty. 'When you screw up,' we tell them, 'You should be the first to recognize it, ask for help, and fix it quickly!—No hiding it and hoping it will go away. No excuses—'It was the other guy's fault!' Just, 'I screwed up!—Help!' Don't expect your boss to tell you that you've screwed up. He doesn't have time!

"The ultimate purpose of Jacobs College is to have our people understand the entrepreneurial and innovative way of looking for new and less costly ways to do things. If we are going to trust them to make important decisions at the lowest level, they should know how you and I and the rest of the top management approach problems. Then it's more likely that their answers will meet our high standards."

Needless to say, I beamed with pride.

Of all of the community service that I have participated in during my business career, education has been, by far, the major focus. Why? I suppose it goes back to high school.

Because I was shy, introverted, bookish—an omnivorous reader—my social skills were virtually nonexistent. I loved words as I read them, but I could not articulate them. Shyness tied my tongue, so I joined the Public Speaking Society at Brooklyn Technical High School. What a new world for me! What a power I felt. There was a dimly lit passage out of my shyness.

One of the courses in high school was "machine shop." Our shop teacher was a Scotsman with great skill as a machinist. One day, he shyly asked me if I would help teach him geometry and trigonometry. He had never even attended high school. It took courage for him to acknowledge his need to a student. Teaching him, I learned how to simplify, explain, and illustrate—to a man old enough to be my father. Talk about boosting a weak ego!

When I graduated from college and could not get a job during those Depression years, I accepted a graduate fellowship to earn a master's degree. Polytechnic Institute of Brooklyn, my alma mater, had a very large night school attracting people from all over the metropolitan New York area. To earn extra money, I taught undergraduate courses every night, to students often considerably older than I. Polishing my verbal skills, learning to simplify, explain and convince, I continued teaching until getting a doctor's degree in 1942, when I got married.

This was a critical point in my life. I now had my "union card" for academia. Should I remain in teaching, which I loved so much? I knew I could teach and could have made that a career. Was I ready to settle my future to a prescribed and predictable path at age twenty-six? What was out there? Did I have the guts to face the unknown world of business? Could I be successful in it, or would I fail as I secretly feared I might? Compelled to test myself, I thus chose to enter business life.

When I went to work for Merck in 1942, Vi, my wife, and I decided to live in Brooklyn Heights, and I commuted to Rahway, New Jersey, a long, arduous trip. We wanted to be near our families in Brooklyn, but just as importantly, I wanted to continue teaching at Poly in the night school— now at the graduate level. I had about seven years of part-time, but extensive, college teaching experience, every moment of which I cherished. Then we moved West, and I maintained only sporadic contact with Poly.

Teaching, as I have said, is the core of the education that we revere in our democratic society. What about teachers? What are their characteristics, good and bad? What kinds of people are attracted to teaching? What are their rewards? As when discussing liberals and conservatives, we can only talk about averages or middle ground.

First, the psychological rewards are enormous. The emotional satisfaction is not unlike that derived from compassion, and there is, indeed, a large component of compassion in most teachers' makeup.

There is also, of course, the power. I'll never forget the feelings I had when a man thirty years older than I hung on my every word as I explained trigonometry to him. And there were those older students, after a full workday, attending my night classes at Poly, absorbing my "wisdom." Not unlike compassion, the power to shape minds is so satisfying to one's self-esteem that it, too, can be like a powerful narcotic.

Like all power, that of the teacher can be abused. The quantitative limits of science and engineering are restrictive, but in the softer sciences and human affairs, the temptation to move over the line between discussion and exploration of ideas to outright advocacy is sometimes difficult to resist. When the powerful influence of a teacher is combined with the intellectual hunger of students, the result can be explosive. Revolutions often originate with the military, whose power lies in weapons, or in the university, with its power of ideas.

Almost everyone agrees that there is a crisis in education in the U.S.—not just in higher education, but even more insidiously in elementary school education. There clearly is an arrogant elite in much of the educational establishment. This elite is openly contemptuous of the free market approaches to education. This is especially true of professional educators—those trained in the so-called skills of teaching— who are not to be confused with scholars.

In *The Last Intellectuals* Russell Jacoby complains about "a vacancy in culture." There is no core of intellectuals to speak in the vernacular to the educated mind. They are speaking rather "only to each other and only to get tenure—or to get a raise."

There have been two penetrating books published recently that expose the corruption and the erosion of the quality of higher education in America today. One is Martin Anderson's *Impostors in the Temple*, primarily focused upon once-proud Stanford University. While Anderson spends some time exposing the corruption in the administration, including a particularly sad account of a professor's alleged seamy relationship with a young man, he aims much criticism at college boards. As I can attest, most college board members are well-meaning, but often ineffectual, people who dutifully carry out their community service. Anderson contends that university boards, being volunteers, do not exercise proper controls of either their administration or their faculty. The latter, especially, with their role in management of the university, tend to ride roughshod over the mostly passive board members.

According to the Association of Governing Boards of Universities and Colleges, in 1985 there were 48,000 trustees governing some 3,200 institutions, 86 percent of which were private. The typical trustee is an old, white, male business-man, with no or few advanced degrees. By my observation, they are often intimidated in an academic atmosphere, though they may be effective leaders in the business world and not easily intimidated in their normal milieu.

It appears that the aura of academe casts a spell over many usually self-confident businessmen. Remember that both administration and faculty are teachers. As such, their command of language is exceptional—they exploit the tyranny of words very effectively. Also, they are so used to being authoritative in front of their students that, try as they might to be deferential to board members, they come through as experts whose opinions are not to be questioned. Many directors give a reflexive deference to teachers. It is surprising to see powerful captains of industry sitting mute as academics express their opinions.

Anderson directs most of his criticism against the tenure system and the degradation of scholarships into fractionated and wordy studies of minutiae. He stops just short of a position which I believe is necessary to arrest the disastrous slide of American higher education into less than mediocrity—the introduction of the free market into recruitment and retention of faculty.

Thomas Sowell's book, *Inside American Education*, does not disappoint those of us who are his admirers. Sowell states unequivocally that the quality of American college education has declined, and that ideology has supplanted academic skills. He especially indicts campus racial policies, the fractionation and balkanization of colleges enslaved by multiculturalism.

It is tragic to see that the powerful forces of desegregation, unleashed by liberal activism in the sixties, are now being suddenly reversed by a bitterly divisive drive for cultural diversity. After all, what is multiculturalism but another word for segregation? Isn't that irony obvious to those who tyrannize us with that new word? Under the false banner of ethnic pride, we are resegregating America into not just blacks and whites but many more subdivisions—all of them fractionating, not integrating, thus refuting the American dream of the "melting pot." In one of his early books, Michael Novak talked about "The Unmeltable Ethnics." He has told me that many of his observations were made in Johnstown, Pennsylvania, where there was a large colony of Lebanese-Americans. Fiercely and loyally American, they also revered their Lebanese heritage. From his work, I concur that we children of immigrants do not melt, we amalgamate—a subtle but important difference!

Donald Eastman of the University of Georgia noted that young blacks are often pressured to resegregate.

> Once the burden of the Negro, segregation has now become a politically correct comfort zone for African-Americans, to judge by the many black leaders, teachers, students and ministers who preach the rhetoric of separatism and racism. Black high-school and college students are often pressured by other black students to avoid integrating fraternities, sororities and other white-majority organizations. They are encouraged to "stay with their own."

The responsibility for these excesses lies with an arrogant elitist hold on education and an unwillingness of either the private sector or the government to take control away from the educators.

Most schools are run inefficiently by business standards. When taking into account income from endowment, scholarship funding, and capital gifts, the cost of educating a college student is probably three or four times that paid for with tuition. I once had a study made that showed that publicly funded colleges on the average cost about 40 percent more to educate a student in engineering education than do private colleges.

The business people who serve on college boards often do not understand how a university operates. They believe that the board has the same role as it does in industry, representing the stockholders (the public at large and the donors). Jane Jacobs points out quite accurately that most business people fall into the category of "Commercial Moral

Syndrome," whereas most of the university people fall into the category of "Feudal Moral Syndrome." As a result, the two groups approach the governance of a university from quite different perspectives.

By tradition, that governance is shared by the board, the administration, and the faculty. The faculty do not regard themselves as employees. Just recently at a board meeting of the UCLA management school, we were discussing the fact that some of the highly specialized faculty, whose major interests were in research, were not agreeing to teach any of the "core courses," where the students at the beginning of their education would benefit from contact with these "stars" of the faculty.

One of the board members exploded, "What do you mean they won't agree to teach at least one of these courses? Who pays their salary?" Looking toward the dean of the school, he said, "I wouldn't tolerate that in anybody that works for me. Just tell them that they must do it for the benefit of the students!" I calmed him down and explained the concept that, in contrast to the business paradigm, a university was governed traditionally by a "community of scholars" that included the faculty. The faculty could be persuaded, but they could not be ordered. Tradition aside, there were a number of faculty present, and I'm sure my friend's anger did not go unnoticed!

We have mentioned tenure several times. Martin Anderson says that it is archaic and prevents the university from becoming as good as it should be. I agree. Tenure is so institutionalized, however, that I doubt whether it can be abolished very easily. Tenure is simply a euphemism for a lifetime employment contract that, except in extreme cases, only works one way. The professor can resign any time a better job comes along, but the university cannot fire the professor except for cause. For the star members of the faculty, tenure is no problem, since they can negotiate tenure with a new institution if they are unhappy and want to move. For the mediocre, however, giving up tenure to test the marketplace is too daunting. This is why tenure is most stoutly defended by mediocre teachers.

Talk to any teacher about the value of tenure (in many specialties it is almost the major milestone in a teacher's career), and the rallying cry is "academic freedom," as though that were the only guarantee of academic freedom.

In reality, academic freedom is only marginally connected to tenure; it is almost totally a product of the culture in which a scholar works. Did tenure in the great German universities guarantee academic freedom during the Hitler years? Of course, it didn't. Dissident after dissident was shot, harassed, and imprisoned by the political tyrant. I'm sure the equivalent of tenure existed in communist Russia, too. Yet, how many dissident scholars were banished to the Gulag?

In the practical, everyday world of Western culture and especially in America, academic freedom is so ingrained into our culture that no university of any stature would use unorthodox scientific or political views as a basis for dismissal—tenure or not. Presumably, the censure of a faculty member's peers would govern how his or her ideas are accepted. Academic freedom is a straw man of no real consequence in defending tenure.

Often, the most insidious attack upon academic freedom is from tenured faculty who are intolerant of views that are not politically correct. In fact, an attack upon academic freedom is more likely to come from tenured faculty than from a university's administration or board. Teachers reluctantly conform to the politically correct views of their colleagues in order to increase their chances of becoming tenured, knowing that tenure is often denied to those whose views are not politically correct. Even worse, tenure covers up slothfulness, mediocrity, and the study of minutiae, as Martin Anderson observed.

One of the characteristics that has always surprised me about academia is the stark contrast between the teachers' obvious academic brilliance and the often childish, petty, social milieu in the academic world. I often jokingly say that I decided not to pursue an academic career because I couldn't take the faculty teas. Though teachers are bright, intelligent, and intellectually challenging people, there is often an undercurrent of opportunism or, in many cases, sheer politicking in academia.

The weakest link in the tripartite management of the university is the board of directors. If we in industry are dissatisfied with the product of our universities, we must stop passively serving on university boards and start taking a more active role. The graduates help us survive and insure the continuation of our society. To the businessman I say, "How much effort do you spend in insuring the quality of the raw materials you use? You select your suppliers carefully, and you get to know enough about how they produce the raw material you need, to set quality specifications." It is in the self-interest of business people to devote the time to education that it requires.

It isn't just raising money, for that seems to be the primary role to which most boards are relegated. The boards must take their management role much more seriously. If they did, even their fundraising efforts would be much more effective.

I believe also there is a crying need for a training course for university board members. They must learn how a "community of scholars" is managed and the importance of their role in that management. Audit committees must really audit. Management experts must examine the management structure. Are the overheads excessive? Are the services supplied really necessary? Is a restructuring exercise in order? Academic committees must examine the relevancy of courses. Are they salable to the students? Do they turn out the product needed in society? Research committees must examine the research effort—not against industry standards, of course, but against theoretical research standards, for business people can understand the difference between the two.

From my experiences, I would opt for a recently retired CEO from industry to serve as full-time chairman of a college board, and an active board of senior executives in industry (and government) who participate much more fully in committees and helping in management decisions. They should plan succession as carefully as corporations do. The weakest leg of the three-legged stool of university governance is the board, and it must be substantially strengthened if the mediocrity of our higher education system is to be reversed.

Large boards are necessary to raise capital and endowment money by networking for fund-raising, but there should be a carefully selected executive committee who meet often enough to really help govern the school. As Ronald Schmitt, former president of Rensselaer has said,

> Education is losing the innocence of an earlier age when the purity of our motives and our dedication to a high calling provided sanctuary from the harsh world around us. Changes (are needed) to regain the confidence and full support of the larger society and the body politic. (*National Academy of Engineering*, Spring 1994)

As concerned as I am about the sad state of higher education, I am even more alarmed at the status of our primary education (commonly referred to as K through 12). Especially in the state of California where I live, the public school system has become chaotic, and there is a widespread dissatisfaction with it. Comparative statistics support this dim view of our elementary schools. There is little point in reciting a litany of surveys attesting to this. I'll just pick one that was reported in the local papers. In reading comprehension in fourth grade, California ranked forty-ninth among the fifty states.

Perhaps my own public involvement with this issue can be a focus for this discussion. I was a major financial supporter of a recent attempt to enact a charter amendment in California called Proposition 174. It was, I hasten to add, soundly defeated.

Why did I support Proposition 174, the so-called School Choice Amendment, though our three daughters are now in their forties? Just as I think businessmen should pay more attention to collegiate education, there is a similar incentive to worry about our primary schools. After all, they produce the raw materials for our high schools and colleges. If our grade schools are deficient, then the product of the high schools and colleges is likely to be deficient.

I was recruited to support "school choice" by my friend Joe Alibrandi, chairman of the Whittaker Corporation and a member of the board of directors of Jacobs Engineering Group Inc. Joe is one of the most dedicated activists and participants in community affairs that I know. His enthusiasm, incisive thinking, and deep caring about our society and our country make him a much admired citizen.

When Joe was asked to chair the committee on education of the California Business Roundtable, he characteristically jumped in with both feet. First, he commissioned a substantial study of our school system and other school systems throughout the country. Although the unadmired educational system in California was the primary focus, it was found that the same malaise and deficiencies were found nationwide in varying degrees. Why?

Education throughout history has been a product of family and of church, from the ancient myths and parables to cultural or tribal taboos and values. However, in a modern agricultural and industrial society, education became a community function. During the growth of America, the one-room schoolhouse was the symbol of community dedication to education as men worked in the fields. But, in the industrial communities, the schools were more concentrated, though they were still an expression of the community's culture. Teaching under those conditions was dominated by genteel young women who had enough education to be able to supply the information for the children to learn. Teaching quality was ragged in both content and methodology. It was assumed that the maternal instinct would guide these young women in teaching.

In the early twentieth century, under the leadership of John Dewey at Columbia University, there was a recognition that education of our youth was so vital to the growth of our nation that it should not be left to chancy educational experience. Teaching was to be elevated to a profession. There arose the concept of the Teachers College, almost exclusively attended by women at that time. Here they were taught *how* to teach, more than what to teach. This was at a time coincident with the rise of Freudian psychology, which had a profound influence upon teaching techniques. As soon as teaching became recognized as a profession and the methodology of teaching became somewhat stylized, the fundamental values of society, which are a by-product of teaching, also became stylized. Thus, the "teachers of the teachers" were, inevitably, arbiters of cultural values—a force not often recognized. The church and family were slowly undermined as the arbiters of morals.

As the teaching profession studied Freud and recognized the profound impact that early childhood experiences could have upon the adult, a neo-Freudian frenzy overtook the teaching profession, giving rise to a protect-the-child-against psychological-damage syndrome.

Sidney Hook and I argued this many times. An ardent admirer and former student of John Dewey, he insisted that Dewey's ideas had been thoroughly corrupted. Perhaps so, but nevertheless, out of fear of damaging the "psyches" of the youngsters, teachers shied away from being judgmental.

Thomas Sowell illustrates this starkly. An international study of thirteen-year-olds found Koreans ranked first in math, and Americans ranked way down on the list. Yet, surveys showed that thirteen-year-old Americans are three times as likely to think they are as good at math as the Koreans of the same age! Sowell blames the neo-Freudian obsession for making the students feel good about skills they do not possess. Koreans and other Asians emphasize high standards. American children must feel good; Asians must *do* good.

The absurdities that result from this position are many. For example, in some schools the grading system has been eliminated. The myth of a risk-free society is thus foisted upon our children early. If elementary school is an extension of the learning started in the family, then the wisdom of the parent who refuses to protect children from minor failures as part of the learning process is negated. To let children be deluded into thinking that failure is not a part of living is not compassionate; it's cruel. What is even worse, they become willing listeners to the siren song of the welfare society. They accept that government is obligated to protect them from failure in life. They are "entitled."

Life in the real world grades us every day. By avoiding a subjective judgment of a child's ability, is a teacher really being kind?

An insidious by-product of the nonjudgmental teaching methodology was the gross distortion of the separation of church and state guaranteed in our Constitution. One should not teach values, this doctrine said, because values involve moral judgments, and moral judgments are derived from religion. Schools thus dilute and corrupt the moral teachings of family and church.

Another irony is that by concentrating upon teaching methodology, course content has suffered severely. Not only are teachers proscribed from teaching moral values, but they are now also woefully deficient in teaching substantive knowledge.

The centralization of power in the hands of a teaching bureaucracy coincided with gradual usurpation of local school boards. These were originally formed to reflect community values in education. In California, the erosion of the power of the school boards was accelerated by the anti-tax revolt. Proposition 13 severely limited property tax increases, and local property taxes were the primary source of funds for local schools. When communities had to appeal to the state for school funding, they lost their control and were increasingly at the mercy of a massive state and now national educational oligarchy.

At one time, education was the primary bastion of self-governance. It cannot be overemphasized how centralized control of education has co-opted freedom in our society. Milton Friedman makes the acerbic observation that education in the United States is so centrally controlled that it follows a textbook Socialist methodology. Education is the core of democracy. When it is commanded by a central authority, order replaces freedom.

Concurrent with this diminution of local control, public education became a monopoly—the most pervasive, all-encompassing monopoly ever known in this country—hijacked by a union. It goes by the innocent pseudo-professional name of the National Education Association (NEA). There are, of course, many subdivisions, such as the California Teachers Association (CTA), but this so-called national association is, in fact, a union.

In a devastating article in June of 1993, *Forbes* magazine labeled it the "National Extortion Association," pointing out how teachers' salaries and the cost of educating a student (K through 12) have grown exponentially in constant dollars while SAT scores in math and verbal skills plunged dramatically. This puts the lie to professional educators whose pat answer to the complaint about the poor education system is always, "Just give us more money." Extracting dues from teachers involuntarily in a rigid, "closed shop" environment and selling group insurance to enrich the teachers union have given the NEA enormous power. The NEA's monopoly of our most important social product—schools—is much more pervasive and decidedly more arrogant than GM's position in the automobile industry.

Not only does the National Education Association dominate the teaching profession in this country, but it also dominates the management of education as well. Virtually all of the bureaucracy and the permanent executives of education departments are, or were, members of the NEA. So, in any collective bargaining between teachers and the school administration, the NEA members are bargaining with other NEA members or former members who are now management.

One needs to be as careful about examining statistics in education as in any other arena. There is so much dissembling and so much self-serving that irresponsible and contradictory numbers are common. The statistics I use for

California are probably good averages and, if they are not taken too literally, serve to illustrate the problem.

It costs about $5,200 per year to educate a K through 12 student in California. Less than 50 percent of that goes to the actual education of the youngsters in the form of direct costs— teachers' salaries, cost of property, maintenance, heat and light, etc. All the rest is consumed by an overbearing and cumbersome bureaucracy of "professionals" with layers and layers of management. It's no wonder that conservatives have said that the free market system can do better than that. The free market brought GM to heel. Why not the NEA and the CTA?

Proposition 174 called for vouchers for $2,600 to be issued to parents to spend for any school of their choice. Why was the proposition defeated? The easy answer is that the National Education Association and the California Teachers Association mobilized massive financial support to defeat it. They recognized that if Proposition 174 passed in California, it would sweep the nation, for there is nationwide discontent with elementary school education.

It has been estimated that between $15 and $20 million was spent by the CTA and the NEA during this campaign— more than five times that spent by the proposition's supporters. There were other reasons it failed, though. Especially among the white middle class, it was often viewed as a "Catholic school" bailout, even though the church carefully avoided any endorsement. The Catholic school system is, of course, the largest private school system. No one criticizes the quality of its education. In the ghetto, some disadvantaged mothers scrimp and save and hope to get their children into the Catholic schools. There are a large number of excellent grade schools under the control of other religious groups as well.

Many public schools in affluent neighborhoods are reasonably well run because the parents spend so much time with them. Therefore, there was not much support for Proposition 174 in these areas. Unfortunately, the message we were not able to get across, even to the black community, was that the primary beneficiaries of school choice were the children in the disadvantaged neighborhoods who had no alternatives to the abysmal inner-city schools. Polly Williams, a black woman from Milwaukee, was a fervent supporter of school choice in her city, and she convinced me of this.

I have said much about monopolies and the ability of the free market system to overturn them. Institutional monopolies are now beginning to crumble too, and thus the educational bureaucracy is doomed. Choice in education is not dead. There are organizations springing up all over the country and many philanthropists are financing choice in the ghettos. The pressure in the marketplace is mounting, and I am certain that eventually the NEA will suffer the same fate arrogant elitists do everywhere else.

I am not anti-union. They are an absolute necessity when workers are exploited. I am, however, against arrogance in unions, just as I am against arrogance in industrial enterprises, in bureaucracies, and for that matter with any elite.

I am in an industry (construction) that for years was dominated by unions, many of whom became arrogant with their power. In the sixties and seventies, construction unions were in the vanguard of inflationary wage increases. Inevitably, there arose a burgeoning non-union or "open-shop" movement.

Our construction operations at one time were all with union workers. We even had so-called national agreements with the union's headquarters in Washington. When the competition from the open-shop people was hurting us, we went to union headquarters in Washington and pleaded for relief from many of the very onerous work rules. We were met by diffident and rather arrogant union leaders who refused to believe that they were threatened. Today more than 80 percent of our construction work is done by our open-shop—or more euphemistically called "Merit shop"—construction forces. Despite this, our relations with the unions today are outstanding. With their superior training and recruitment procedures, unions are becoming competitive. (Isn't that a wonderful word?) The teachers union as it operates today is doomed!

I have mentioned the multicultural movement in college ranks. I cannot understand liberal endorsement of this movement, which essentially negates the great civil rights victories for which they should have great pride. Even more insidious, however, is the introduction of bilingual teaching in grade schools and its handmaiden, bilingual ballots. As a child of immigrants, who was raised in an ethnic conclave in Brooklyn, I say that is wrong, wrong, *wrong*.

Where did any of the Latino leaders (for Spanish is the "second" language of California) get the idea that they are being compassionate or kind to Latino children by telling them they could avoid the pain of learning the language of the country where they lived? No one ever taught me Arabic in school, but I acquired pride in my ethnic heritage from my parents. I acquired that alongside my parents' obvious pride that they, and especially their children, became Americans. Bilingual education is a shining example of compassion grown corrosive. Is it painful for a child who is raised in a home where only Spanish is spoken to have to learn English? Of course it is, but no more so than learning to spell or do arithmetic or any other skill. To let those children out into an English-speaking society with the idea that English is a second language is not compassionate; it is cruel.

Another manifestation of this trend for balkanizing our society is the hyphenated name. Why must ethnic or racial antecedents define differences in Americans?

What is the sense of African-American? Aren't people from Morocco, for instance, African-American? Though touted as a source of ethnic pride, African-American is a word manipulation to denote an American whose skin is some shade of black, and that's all. Why should the color of skin be used as an identifying characteristic of an American? We have red-headed Americans (perhaps of Irish origin). We have blond, blue-eyed, Americans (perhaps of Scandinavian origin), and we have slant-eyed Americans (of Korean, Japanese, Chinese, or Vietnamese origins). Why don't we stop all this nonsense. Is there anything that would promote commonality and the brotherhood we cherish more than the elimination of all those hyphenated names? Why accent differences? We are simply *Americans*. This does not diminish pride in our ethnic origins, but it does say that our primary identification and loyalty is as Americans. The hyphenation only impels wrong generalizations that should be avoided.

Theodore Roosevelt put it very well when he said, "There is no room in this country for hyphenated Americans—the one certain way of bringing this nation to ruin, of preventing its continuing to be a nation to all, would be to permit it to become a nation of squabbling nationalities."

Introducing multiculturalism into our society via the educational system is misguided at the least and a time bomb at the worst. It will destroy our country as no rival country has been able to do. The extension of this faulty thinking to the printing of bilingual ballots is the typical progression of consequences from a basic faulty assumption. We need not apologize for insisting that those who come here adapt as well as they can to our common culture. I have not diminished my pride in my Lebanese culture by becoming an enthusiastic, loyal American. Just look around the world. Multiculturalism is one of the leading causes of national disintegration.

Lebanon is a country that never really became a country because of the fractionated allegiance to thirteen or more confessional religions or tribes. I know that situation well, and the Lebanese are a caricature of what multiculturalism in extremes can do. Fifteen years of suicidal intertribal fighting laid the people prostrate, to be rescued only by Syrian self-interested intervention. Some of the brightest, best educated and most sophisticated people in the Middle East, they have never understood the obligations of statehood. Despite their westernized culture, they have difficulty in acknowledging that they owe primary allegiance to their country rather than to their "tribes."

The U.S. has benefited immensely from its abundance of natural resources, but its great strength has come because of the enormous energy from successive waves of immigrants who became Americans. Despite the natural tendency to huddle together in ethnic enclaves, the lure of the melting pot made us all Americans first and "whatever" second. We were taught to cherish our heritage at home and in the community, but we were also taught to cherish America in school and in the community. Multiculturalism is a disease to be feared as much as the dependency of the welfare system. It is another example of compassion gone awry.

Our failures in education are mortal ones. Where is the pride in our country? Where is the pride in the values that made us great? Where is the legacy of pride we should leave to our young people? Let the people of this great country take back control of education from "professional educators," from monopolistic and socialistic unions, from tenured mediocrity, from multicultural fractionation, and from "politically correct" teachers who do not value and revere scholarship. Let us teach pride, self-esteem, independence, self-reliance and the recognition that, with all of its faults, this is a country of which the whole world is jealous—and perhaps envious. We must vow to keep it that way and to continue to improve it rather than to denigrate it. We must dare to teach common values of morality, self-help, brotherhood, and caring. Let's take back control from those who march under the banner of political self-serving and corrupting compassion. We must teach our children that a "moral sense" is a celebrated part of them. Those who would deny that are our mortal enemies.

9. Junk Science

Our greatest happiness does not depend on the condition of life in which chance has placed us, but is always the result of a good conscience, good health, occupation, and freedom in all just pursuits.

—Thomas Jefferson

Bad laws based upon bad science cause immeasurable harm to people. The term *junk science* was probably coined by Peter Huber in his book *Galileo's Revenge: Junk Science in the Courtroom*. In it, he explores how bad science presented by prejudiced witnesses with marginal scientific credentials becomes endorsed by the courts. What results is a core of legal rulings that give almost irreversible validity to questionable science. Bad science becomes legitimized in bad law.

The Oliver Wendell Holmes lectures of U.S. Supreme Court Justice Breyer, which were subsequently incorporated into his book *The Vicious Circle*, recognized the significance of this dangerous trend. Although he approaches the problem of societal risk from a legal standpoint, he does accept that real science and economic factors should guide legal decisions. Huber's book, on the other hand, cites case after case where these factors are ignored or minimized.

Justice Breyer is right to worry about this problem since, in our litigious society, legal decisions have a special validity that often overrides scientific judgments. Yet, most judges or juries are ill equipped to discern differences between good science and bad science. Driven by the need to right wrongs, to protect the victim in the courts, the responsibility tends to be placed upon the most convenient or affluent sources. The complexity of scientific analysis is too daunting and complicated; thus, poorly supported science often carries the day—especially when presented in unequivocal black and white terms, as it often is, by those who let their passion override their objectivity.

In fact, real science is most complex. Many alternative explanations must be examined, and the weaknesses in each evaluated. In almost any scientific evaluation, the possibility of something happening is never zero. It takes rational analysis and in-depth technical knowledge to determine the probability of it happening. However, the prospect that something might happen is, unfortunately, the last refuge of junk science.

Breyer takes a course very similar to that taken by John Stossel in his TV program "Are We Scaring Ourselves to Death" (chapter 5). He tries to assess relative risk. For example, he argues as follows: Each year 2.2 million people die in the U.S. On that basis, each of us has about a 1 percent chance of dying in any one year. He then proceeds to measure all other risks against that random 1 percent chance of dying.

About 22 percent of all deaths are the result of cancer. Therefore, the average person's chance of dying of cancer in any one year is 0.22 percent (22 percent of 1 percent). But, what causes these cancer deaths? In their book *The Causes of Cancer*, Doll and Petro attempt to answer this question. Though recognizing some wide variations in the data from various sources, they arrive at a middle ground which appears reasonable. Approximately 35 percent of these cancer deaths are caused by diet. Not from additives or pesticides as Bruce Ames has clearly shown, but from unhealthy diets or natural carcinogens which exist in all foods. Thirty percent come from tobacco. Pollution causes about 2 percent of those cancer deaths and ranks lower than alcohol as a cause of cancer. If these figures are correct, then the average person's chance of dying from cancer caused by pollution is .0044 percent.

Breyer then points out the problems that arise when regulations are considered for public action. The first comes from "tunnel vision," which is Breyer's term for the narrow activism that calls for complete removal of the risk posed by any hazard chosen as the target. Risk analysis becomes an emotional exercise rather than a rational one. For those who have adopted a theistic approach to environmental risk, such rational calculations are not tolerated because they tend to dilute the moral imperatives derived from the compassionate motive. Moral greed fuels this harmful extremism.

Tunnel vision leads to two unacknowledged consequences. One is substituting one risk for another. Breyer says that when a bureaucratic ruling deprives a farmer of a pesticide with small cancer risk, he then grows a new, hardier variety that contains more natural pesticides, which may actually be more carcinogenic (see Bruce Ames). The farmer creates a new risk more dangerous than the one he is told by the bureaucracy to avoid. The myth of a risk-free society dominates the methodology. The fundamental error, repeated over and over again, is that risk avoidance is equated with compassion, and that is very often wrong.

The other factor Judge Breyer recognizes is the one I've also pointed out: The myth of infinite resources. He says, "The resources available to combat health risks are not limitless. The money is not, or will not be there to spend—on more serious or social problems—prenatal care, vaccinations, cancer diagnosis, housing, education, etc." Judge Breyer is simply reinforcing the need for *discrimination* in the expenditure of our limited resources.

The point is that, even with known risks, the principle of limited resources requires hard choices, which those with "tunnel vision" avoid. Much worse than that are the enormous sums spent avoiding hazards that *might* happen based upon spurious or, at best, questionable science. This is called the "precautionary principle." Does that fancy wording validate spending enormous amounts of money because "it might happen"—especially when we are deprived of those funds for catastrophes that are happening? (Remember 3.2 million children die each year from impure drinking water.)

It is comforting that there is a rising recognition of this need to make choices. Judge Breyer is just one more to add to the list of the people who come to their conclusions from different vantage points. Each chooses a different method of assessing relative risk, but the very fact that they prepare tables of relative risk shows a recognition of the principle of finite resources. What is it about the zealots that makes them avoid making choices—or assume that a world without choices is possible at all? Except for those motivated by moral greed, the need to discriminate is quite clear. The refusal to recognize that resources are limited is, in many ways, child-like, wishful thinking.

This is the first time I have referred to the myth of infinite resources in terms of maturity, but the analogy is apt. After all, when young, don't we dream of having everything we want? And, isn't the impossibility of this one of the first realities we learn, unless our families are sadly and foolishly indulgent? Having accepted that, to continue the analogy further, how do we decide which we choose and, therefore, which we reject? How do we learn to discriminate? That's why thoughtful people search for a scale of merit—to help us choose. One of the troublesome, emotional problems arising from the need to choose is the necessity to reject. For a compassionate person, rejection of a constituency is painful, and it dilutes the psychological rewards of compassion. It's tough to say, "You will not get my compassion (or the resources) because I have only a limited amount, and I choose another, more worthy cause that I deem to be more important than yours." There is a profound truth here. The human heart has a limitless capacity for compassion, but our capacity to translate that compassion into action is finite and limited. Constrained vision is a product of constrained resources—not of constrained hopes.

The Harvard School of Public Health's Center for Risk Analysis made its comparison in a different way. They calculated the cost of saving one life by a number of preventative techniques, including reducing exposure to various environmental risks. The results confirm again that our priorities are wrong, our fears are often groundless, and our resource allocation is destructive.

Here are a few conclusions from their report (quoted from a *Wall Street Journal* article by David Stipp):

Findings so far suggest that:

Medical care generally saves lives at less cost than workplace safety or environmental measures.

Extravagantly large sums are spent to alleviate minor cancer risks.

Oregon's ranking of Medicaid services—touted as a possible national model for setting medical priorities—falls far short of maximizing cost-effectiveness.

(An aside here: The most well intentioned and well qualified "commission" cannot judge as well as the people themselves, reacting in the free market.)

Some sixty thousand deaths could be averted annually in the U.S. if the $21.3 billion spent on 185 major life-preserving programs was reallocated, so that more went to the most beneficial measures and less went to the others. Cost-effective spending could cut about $31 billion in health care and other costs without increasing the death rate.

Critics often blast risk-analysis studies as biased guesswork dolled up by spin-control experts to look like hard data. However, outside researchers say that the Harvard study, begun in 1990, appears quite rigorous. Some 90 percent of its data were drawn from government studies or peer-reviewed ones in technical journals. "Nothing comes close to [the study] in breadth and the number of interventions analyzed," says Paul Slovic, a risk expert at Decision Research, a Eugene, Oregon, think tank.

Here is the table:

Lifesaving Costs
Median cost of a year of life saved by various interventions

	Cost
Childhood immunizations	Less than zero
Prenatal care	Less than zero
Flu shots	$600
Water chlorination	$4,000
Pneumonia vaccination	$12,000
Breast cancer screening	$17,000
Construction safety rules	$38,000
Home radon control	$141,000
Asbestos controls	$1.9 million
Radiation controls	$27.4 million

Source: Harvard Lifesaving Study

I was a bit puzzled by the concept of costs being "less than zero," but that was explained by the fact that more money was saved as a result of these interventions than it cost to apply them. For every $1.00 spent for prenatal care, $2.51 is saved.

There is only one item on this list that I question, because it is something with which I have direct experience. That is the cost of construction risk. Our company employs between five thousand and eight thousand craftsmen at any one time. The construction trades tend to have high accident rates, for craftsmen are always dealing with unstable situations—temporary platforms, ladders, awkward angles of work, etc. When you add to that the "macho" image construction workers like to project, this makes safety a serious problem.

A number of years ago, as our field workforce expanded, we decided to make a determined effort to improve our safety record. What impelled us to do that? Compassion, of course! I have seen enough accidents occur so that when a serious injury is reported, it is not just a statistic to me. I can see the body falling and hear the bones breaking; I can see the blood, and the pallor as the poor guy goes into shock. Thoughts like these plague me whenever an accident is reported. But, there is another reason to improve safety: It pays. This is another case where compassion and self-interest intersect.

I wonder if the costs of the safety rules in this table are only for those necessary to make the workplace safe, as exemplified by the OSHA rules. If so, they should have subtracted from them the savings in workers' compensation and liability insurance premiums, which can be significant.

In 1991 and 1992, we received the top award from the Business Roundtable for best safety performance of all the major contractors in the U.S. In five years, our company has reduced the number of injuries in our workforce to 2.4 reported incidents per 200,000 labor work hours. Compare that with the national average for the construction industry of 14.2.

There is another statistic that measures the seriousness of the reported incidences, and that is the time lost as a result of the incidents reported. In that, we've done even better. In 1993, we reported 0.36 lost work days per 200,000 labor manhours, compared to a national average of 6.7. We are proud of this record and guard it zealously.

One time, when I was touring one of our construction sites with the construction superintendent, I noticed his jaw tighten and his eyes turn angry. He looked up into the structure and yelled, "Listen you blankity blank, if you don't tie off immediately, you're outta here; you can go pick up your check and you're blackballed from any job I'm on!" "Tying off" is a procedure in which workers above a certain height must wear a safety harness to clip onto a strong beam as they work. If they slip, they will avoid injury. The blazing anger and profanity of that superintendent exemplified real compassion in action—tough love!

This underscores a fundamental statement that I have made repeatedly—the worthiness of compassion can only be measured by its public good. Will anyone doubt that reducing accidents in the workplace is a compassionate act? Injuries and death are avoided. Self-esteem is enhanced because people are proud to work in a safe environment. Is the discipline imposed cruel, or is it compassionate?

At the same time, there is a practical result. Our insurance premiums are reduced. Therefore, self-interest is served. Is the compassionate content of our carefully thought-out safety procedures any less compassionate because the self-interest of our company is well served by it? Absolutely not, if the value of the compassion is measured by its public good.

The Asbestos Scare

To demonstrate the enormous costs imposed upon our society by "junk science," I thought it would be useful to discuss some of the shibboleths which have been erected in the messages beamed our way—impelled by the incessant, hysterical, publicity seeking doomsayers that are "scaring us to death."

Let's take asbestos for a starter. It can be a dangerous material, but only in fairly well-defined situations. How dangerous is it? Is it a hazard that should be feared by ordinary people encountering it under normal living conditions? Absolutely not. But, that's not the way it's viewed by the public at large. The almost universal belief that asbestos is a deadly material to be avoided at all costs is a national cancer (I use that scare word purposefully). The need for psychological chemotherapy, to continue the metaphor, is urgent.

What proof do I have for that flat statement I have made? Simply, that I am unaware of any reported death from asbestosis (that's the name of the lung condition caused by inhaling asbestos fibers) as the result of a lifetime of exposure to asbestos in ordinary daily life. I mean, not only asbestos encapsulated in walls of buildings, but asbestos in the millions of square feet of asphalt tile used in kitchens over the past forty years. I mean also brake linings, which, until recently, contained asbestos as their most important ingredient. Every time someone stepped on the brakes, fibers of asbestos were spewed into the air. I wonder how many millions of fibers of asbestos have been discharged into the air we have breathed over the past fifty years. The general public has not been completely insulated from asbestos exposure for half a century, yet suddenly any asbestos in schools and the workplace is assumed to cause cancer.

In reality, the only known cases of asbestosis have occurred with exposure to asbestos in workplaces, and, at that, only after many years of exposure. In other words, only those who worked with asbestos for a livelihood for decades are at any risk—and usually only those who did not use simple protective masks.

Here is the authoritative summary issued by Harvard University's Kennedy School of Government in 1989:

> Deaths from asbestosis are observed only among individuals that have been occupationally exposed to high levels of asbestos. Present levels of asbestos in workplaces utilizing current control procedures are not expected to produce any measurable impairment. Further, if asbestosis occurs, due to recent and much lower levels of asbestos exposures in workplaces, it has a slow progression and rarely results in serious disability or increased mortality. *Consequently, there does not seem to be any evidence that asbestosis is a concern as a result of environmental exposure.* (emphasis added)

Look back at the table of Lifesaving Costs. According to this table, if the money spent to save one life from the danger of occasional exposure to asbestos were used instead for pneumonia vaccinations, for example, we could save about twelve thousand lives. The right choice seems obvious, but it might not be necessary to make a choice at all. There is a thoughtful way we can do both, and that is to use a surgical scalpel instead of a twelve-pound sledgehammer. To understand how to do that, we need to understand where all of this scare hysteria came from.

The potential hazard of asbestos was originally discovered when some shipyard insulation workers died from lung cancer, after thirty to forty years of daily exposure to asbestos pipe insulation. There seemed to be a plausible connection between their lung cancer and the irritation of asbestos fibers in their lungs. Asbestos, the cheapest and best insulation material, is used to reduce heat loss from hot steam lines and to prevent people from getting scalded by contacting those hot pipes. It is used extensively in most ships and in chemical plants of the type our company designs. Starting during World War II, when ship production zoomed, there was little awareness of the lethal effect of getting asbestos fibers in the lungs over a long period of time. Very few insulators (the workers who sawed and cut asbestos pipe covering) bothered to use simple breathing masks (there's that "macho" thing again). It was out of this group that asbestosis began to appear many years later.

Asbestos is a natural fibrous mineral found in deposits all over the world. There are three types, two of which cause asbestosis after relatively short exposure. The third type, chrysotile, can only cause problems when inhaled over decades. About 95 percent of the asbestos used in the United States is of this relatively benign variety. To illustrate the last point, chrysotile asbestos has been mined in Globe, Arizona, since 1926, and only one death from lung cancer was recorded in those exposed to that mineral on a daily basis over the intervening years. However, the terminal case of lung cancer occurred in a man who was also a heavy smoker!

That interested me, so I asked one of the health physicists who works for our company what he knew about this. He told me that an analysis of the deaths from asbestosis after long-time exposure in the workplace had shown that the death rate was ten times as high for smokers as for nonsmokers. So, there's one way to reduce the cost of saving lives from even the most intensive exposure to asbestos— only hire nonsmokers to work with asbestos! The likelihood of getting asbestosis would be decreased tenfold.

The second way to reduce costs for saving lives from exposure to asbestos is to follow proper safety practices in both the mining and application of asbestos. Our company has been intimately involved in asbestos removal. The safety equipment that is available today is enormously effective. If it had been used by asbestos workers for the past forty years, I doubt that anyone would have suffered from asbestosis.

If all of the scare stories about incidental exposure to asbestos were ignored, and we concentrated all of our efforts in two areas (the prohibition of the use of the two bad varieties of asbestos and the introduction of safety features for those who are continuously exposed to raw asbestos), then the cost per life saved would go down to thousands of dollars or even less, rather than millions. If we exercise discrimination in protecting against asbestosis, then we can have sensible regulations and save more lives. Canadian laws to diminish danger from asbestos follow this model.

The Asbestos Hazard Emergency Response Act (AHERA) went into effect in 1987. It mandates that school buildings— public and private—must be inspected for asbestos. For those containing asbestos, an abatement plan was required by October 1988. (There was no requirement that the presence of a hazardous environment be shown. It was falsely assumed that the mere presence of asbestos was hazardous.)

Here are some negative consequences of current asbestos programs:

• Many asbestos removal programs will put more fiber into the air than if the asbestos were left in place.

• Negative consequences include closure of many schools that cannot afford rip-out.

• Insulation, once provided by asbestos, is now being provided by substitutes. Studies indicate that for workers applying insulation, these manmade fibers may be as hazardous as asbestos.

• The estimated direct cost of asbestos removal is between $100 and $200 billion. The indirect costs, such as shutting down buildings, disrupting production, and laying off workers, could cost several times the $200 billion. As Natalie and Gerald Sirkin state in their article "Asbestos,"

> These immense sums will be spent to raise levels of airborne asbestos and create risks of illness and death where none now exist. The organized opportunists

and ignoramuses—the National Education Association, the Sierra Club, Nader's public-interest group,
and the rest—have worked through the ignoramuses
and cowards of Congress to bestow this deadly blessing upon us. (*Rational Readings on Environmental Concerns*, ed. Jay H. Lehr [New York: Van Nostrand
Reinhold, 1992], 119–122)

Although harsh, these words are an almost automatic
reaction to the doomsaying fingers of guilt and fear pointed
at us. Can anyone avoid clutches of fear when we use two
highly emotional words, *children* and *cancer*, when referring
to asbestos? As a result, New York City taxpayers will spend
$7 billion to remove asbestos from one hundred schools.

I have direct observations to add to that article. Our
company, sensing an opportunity, decided to look into asbestos remediation as a business venture. We have become
nationally recognized experts in environmental evaluation
and restoration, and it seemed a logical application of our
know-how. We were caught up in the hysteria and could
envision an enormous market. I once did a back-of-the-enve-
lope calculation that showed if every office building in the
country were remediated for asbestos, the cost to the economy
could be over $400 billion!

We finally bid on and won a contract to remediate a
large office building in Boston, Massachusetts. I believe the
contract was for about $20 million. That project was a night-
mare for us and especially for the owner. He had the awful
logistical problem of scheduling the ending of leases and
releasing our crews to move in on each floor. We had to cope
with start-and-stop work, but the overwhelming nightmare
was in the regulatory requirements. We had to put our
workers in "moon suits" so they could strip the walls down
to bare steel. The removed asbestos was taken down in sealed
containers (at night).

The legal hassle that ensued over the disposal of this
supposedly dangerous chemical was debilitating. We sub-
contracted with a company to haul the asbestos to a certified

disposal pit. There was a lot of legal wrangling as to when "care and custody" passed to the haulers. We could visualize all kinds of law suits if a truck overturned and spilled the asbestos on the streets. We insisted that the hauler accept care and custody from the time he picked the bins up at our site. The fact that no real hazard would be created was not at issue. Finally, the problems got to be so complex that the owner and our company agreed to cancel the contract when it was about 80 percent complete. We didn't lose any money on the project, but we didn't make any either. We were impelled to reexamine our commitment to asbestos remediation and decided it was not for us. No matter how unjustified, the potential litigation we faced was enormous, while the real hazard was insignificant.

The greatest burden upon society resulting from the gross exaggeration of the risks of asbestos has been in the enormous legal costs involved. The classic case is that of the Johns-Manville Company, at one time the primary producer of asbestos. When the furor over asbestos hit the press, the company was inundated with claims. Contingent fee lawyers jumped on the bandwagon to extract their guilt money from this company. The potential claims were so great that in 1982 the company filed for protection under Chapter 11 of the bankruptcy laws. After months and years of wrangling, a trust fund of about $2.2 billion was established to deal with all the claims. Since this fund was established in 1988, the number of claims filed have exceeded those originally contemplated, and they are still coming in. With 200,000 new claims it now appears that claims will far exceed the amount reserved. It is unknown how much will go to legal fees. The lawyers will get rich, but I'm not sure about the claimants.

Recently, several suits have been filed making a unique claim. Workers exposed to asbestos filed suit claiming damages. Though they had not developed asbestosis, they claimed that the fear of contracting it was causing distress. This wildly fanciful "stress" claim, based upon exposure to asbestos, exemplifies the harm of junk science.

Reaction to hysterical fear can lead to hastily enacted

legislation that stays on the books, even when subsequently discredited. I am not aware that there is any methodology to review and rescind or modify such bad laws based upon bad science. And yet, we'll go on spending billions of dollars because those dumb regulations are on the books. The only other way out is for us to become scofflaws!

Acid Rain

Another issue supported by junk science is "acid rain," a subject that precipitated an international confrontation between Canada and the United States. When it was discovered that certain lakes in the northeastern U.S. and southern Canada were quite acidic, causing fish to die and the lakes to become virtually sterile, the radical greens blamed this upon sulfur dioxide emissions from the smokestacks of industrial America. It was pure speculation. "Business" is a very convenient whipping boy. There was so much controversy over the cause of acid rain that Congress authorized a National Acid Precipitation Assessment Project. An assemblage of distinguished scientists spent $600 million and produced a voluminous study with which no one could really quarrel. Their conclusion: No cause and effect between sulfur dioxide emissions from stacks and subsequent pollution was discovered. Indeed, the real cause was simply a leaching of acid from natural acidic soils around the lakes. The lakes had always had varying levels of acidity.

Despite these results, Congress proceeded to pass the most stringent, pervasive, sulfur dioxide stack control laws ever, costing American industry billions of dollars annually. There are indications that recently, the EPA has reduced their activity and responded to the studies.

What impels Congress to ignore their own expert studies? The activists who promote these things are, after all, a very small minority, but their influence is deemed to be very broad. With the help of the media message so adroitly manipulated by them, most polls show clear support for these faulty projections of doom. Thus, Congress is coerced into believing that they will lose votes if they don't do the activists' bidding—and don't forget that enormous war chest that the environmental lobby controls.

Am I against regulating the sulfur dioxide emissions in stack gases? Not at all! I believe in minimizing sulfur emissions, but remember the asymptotic curve or Judge Breyer's "tunnel vision." Is it worth it to go to these extremes of sulfur removal when a $600 million study showed that acid rain is a myth?

Global Junk Science

Ozone is a catchy word. It's ominous sounding, though few know what it is. I have used ozone for its marvelous oxidizing power. There is a method of purifying water that involves using ozone, instead of chlorine, to kill bacteria.

Ozone is sometimes a villain. It is the ozone in the air that oxidizes the hydrocarbon emissions from automobiles, thus causing smog. But, for another group of zealots, ozone in the so-called ozone layer is billed as a "savior," and anything that presumably destroys it is considered bad. Which is it—friend or foe?

The ozone layer in our upper atmosphere had gone unnoticed until two scientists, named Rowland and Molina, postulated that chlorofluorocarbons (CFC's) had the potential to rise to the stratosphere where they might decompose in the sunlight, releasing chlorine atoms, which would thin the ozone layer. So what? Supposedly, the thinning of the ozone layer will increase the ultraviolet radiation reaching the earth. Exposure to ultraviolet light (UV rays) can cause skin cancer; therefore, an increase in UV radiation might cause a rise in skin cancer. There's that scare word again: Cancer.

This hypothesis has been examined by a whole host of atmospheric scientists, including Ronald Bailey, Alston Chase, Hugh W. Ellsaesser, and my favorite one, S. Fred Singer. The titles of their articles tell much about their views: "The Hole Story: The Science Behind the Scare," "My Adventures in the Ozone Layer," and "An Atmosphere of Paradox, From Acid Rain to Ozone."

Here are the problems with the Rowland-Molina hypothesis, as distilled from the writings of these scientists:

Ozone levels vary considerably from natural causes alone. In fact, sunspot activity can have a measurable and demonstrable effect on the ozone layer.

The relationship between sunspot activity and the rise and fall of ozone has a much better statistical correlation than does the postulated CFC relationship. There was minimal sunspot activity in 1986-87. Since then, ozone levels have risen despite peak use of CFC's

Few CFC's actually reach the stratosphere, so any damage hypothesis based upon the amount of CFC's in our atmosphere has a questionable correlation with how much will get into the stratosphere.

Volcanoes release fifty times more ozone-destroying chlorine than the worst postulated for CFC's. It appears likely that more reduction in the ozone layer could be postulated from natural causes than from CFC's.

Ultraviolet radiation is not noticeably increasing, despite the increased use of CFC's. Besides, the amount of increase postulated by the Rowland-Molina thesis is not demonstrably harmful. The clincher is that the amount pessimistically projected by them to come from CFC's is only a small percentage of the natural variations of UV radiation, in geographic location alone. For instance, the amount of UV reaching the ground in Florida is twice that reaching the ground in Minnesota.

Rowland and Molina postulated a 7 to 13 percent decrease in ozone from CFC decomposition over one hundred years. Based upon the UV gradient from Minnesota to Florida, a 5 percent decrease in ozone (which practically no credible scientist thinks would happen), would increase UV exposure by an amount that would occur by simply moving sixty miles south in the direction of Florida! In other words, the postulated increase in UV from using CFC's reaching the earth is much less than for a person moving from Minnesota in a southerly direction.

Yet, CFC's have been mandated out of use by 1995. The cost to this country is incalculable. I know of two chemical companies who have spent close to half a billion dollars developing new refrigerants to supplant CFC's. But, that's not all. Literally millions of refrigerators and air conditioning units will have to be scrapped. The costs are mind boggling. These laws, based upon this dubious science, are not proposed; they are on the books and are being enforced.

I am persuaded that using the Rowland-Molina data to postulate harmful effects is seriously flawed. At worst, it should be simply a caution to wait before committing substantial resources. But, no; Congress and the bureaucracy were panicked into passing a sweeping law. It is interesting that the Montreal Declaration, as reported in the 10 October 1991 edition of the *New York Times,* was signed by Sherwood Rowland. This document is a most incendiary, distorted presentation of pseudoscience and has been criticized heavily by most scientists.

Fred Singer reports that "about $135 billion worth of equipment uses CFC's in the U.S. alone, and much of this equipment will have to be replaced or modified to work well with the CFC substitutes. Eventually, that will involve one hundred million home refrigerators, the air conditioners in 90 million cars, and central air conditioners in 100,000 large buildings. Good Luck!" Specifically, retooling to manufacture household refrigerators will require $200 to $300 billion annually, until the year 2000. Two years ago, the cost of CFC-12 was fifty cents per pound; today it is ten dollars and by 1996, it will be twenty-five dollars, if you can find it.

Fred Singer is a careful scientist, and I do not think he would purposely exaggerate, but even if the figure was only a quarter of what he says, the implications are mind-boggling. The amounts of money spent as a result of this foolish law, based upon junk science, would be enough to balance our budget and even go a long way toward reducing our national debt. I ask, what kind of judgment goes into passing these laws so cavalierly? What kind of a hold do these activists have on our lawmakers, that they can blithely ignore the enormous costs of laws so casually passed? I place most of the blame upon the shoulders of well-meaning and, indeed, patriotic liberal congressmen who blindly endorse any proposal that bears the label of compassion (even though

falsely). I ascribe additional responsibility to the perception
that the compassion of conservatives is suspect. But, of course,
that's what I'm writing about. Compassionate liberal congressmen of good intentions and undoubted patriotism,
please take heed, for these Cassandras of junk science will
lead to the destruction of your compassionate vision. They
are much more destructive of your compassionate goals than
anything you can project upon conservatives. Liberals, may
you be delivered from your so-called friends.

In promoting the concept of a risk-free society, how do
we select the most important risks to be avoided? All too
often, decisions are not made rationally, but primarily on
how scarily the scenario can be portrayed. Global warming
is one of these cases.

The activists have discovered a way to elevate themselves above the mundane level. Since anything that's "global" must be awesomely overwhelming, they now want to
save the globe. How's that for compassionate validation?

Global warming has, by repetitive use, taken on a catastrophic, Jovian thunder from the heavens that makes us all
quiver. Is global warming a newly discovered phenomenon
created by man? No! Even the most vociferous of the
scaremongers claim only that human activity will add to
global warming. Global warming is a natural phenomenon
to which we literally owe our lives. Without natural global
warming, this planet would be thirty-five degrees colder,
bitterly cold at night and hot during the day. Global warming is mostly (some estimate 75 percent to 80 percent) caused
by natural phenomena, such as cloud cover, temperature
gradients, the heat absorption of the seas, etc. The question
raised is whether so-called greenhouse gases, notably carbon dioxide, significantly add to global warming. And, if
they do, is the calculated increase more or less than the
natural variation which would occur without the "greenhouse" gases? Please notice the pejorative use of "greenhouse" gases now in common use, though I doubt whether
any significant number of people could say what they are or
why they might be harmful. This is a standard manipulation
of words, i.e., describing something by using the assumed

effect as an adjective. If a newspaper were reporting a crime suspect, they would normally use the term *alleged* as a modifier. But, in this case they do not say the "alleged" greenhouse gases. So, we have been seduced into accepting as an established fact that certain gases (whose names may have been forgotten) cause some mysterious thing called a greenhouse effect.

It all started in 1988, which was a particularly warm year. Despite the fact that similar temperature variations had occurred many times in history, suddenly this phenomenon became headline-grabbing news! A climatologist by the name of Jim Hansen at NASA's Goddard Space Institute testified at a Senate hearing that he was convinced that the warm temperatures that year were a result of the greenhouse effect. He postulated that carbon dioxide coming from industrial activity (where else?) was causing the atmosphere to reflect heat from the earth back to the ground, thus raising temperatures (that's what is now known as the greenhouse effect). When Hansen expressed a "high degree of confidence" that the unusual rise in temperature in 1988 was related to this greenhouse effect, it made big, scary headlines, implanting it in popular thought. As a result, few people today have any doubt that there is a greenhouse effect and that it does cause global warming. The underlying implication is that the result will be bad for humanity. Yet, every one of those popularly held opinions is open to serious question.

In his book, *Sound and Fury: The Science and Politics of Global Warming*, which was published in 1992, Patrick J. Michaels debunks these ideas. S. Fred Singer, a climatologist with impeccable credentials, has not only called all of these notions into serious question but has presented a scary assessment of the costs that will be incurred if the apocalyptic vision of global warming is the cause of unwise and costly legislation.

Other noted climatologists took issue with Hansen's predictions. First of all, the basic data upon which he postulated his scary headlines were questioned. There are many other records of global temperatures that indicate that NASA's data were perhaps 30 percent too high. The cause of this variation may be in the way each of the groups measured those temperatures. So, the basic effect that Hansen was scaring us with may have been grossly incorrect. Then, and this error is obvious to anyone (except, perhaps, to those in Congress), he took the average temperatures for the first ten years of the fifty-year period and compared them with the average temperature of the last ten years, completely ignoring what happened in between! Selecting only those data which support your thesis is pretty unscientific. As a matter of fact, historical data shows that increases and decreases of temperatures from year to year are wider than the ones Hansen used to scare us to death. Furthermore, the computer program which projected global warming was tested against history by Hansen's critics. It shows absolutely no correlation with any global warming over the past fifty years—and these were the years in which carbon dioxide emissions increased dramatically.

Might global warming increase as a result of human activity? It might, of course, but will it be significant? The answer to that seems to be no. Even if Hansen's concern about the increase in carbon dioxide were so, the effect on global temperatures would still be minimal because any such warming is not linear with carbon dioxide concentration. In other words, if the carbon dioxide doubles in quantity, the projected temperature rise does not double; the effect would be much less.

Let's look at global warming, even to the extent that Hansen erroneously predicted. Would it be catastrophic? In all likelihood, it wouldn't be. The possibility that the polar ice caps will melt and raise the sea levels catastrophically has been dismissed by almost all serious scientists. And, the global warming which occurs naturally is actually a great blessing to us since we couldn't grow crops for food without it. An increase in global warming, even taking Hansen's faulty projections, might actually result in longer growing seasons, warmer nights, and bountiful agricultural production that would defy Malthusian theory and eliminate hunger from the world.

   Those who spread fear of global warming make a double speculation: First, that global warming is inevitable; and second, that it will happen just because we put too much carbon dioxide in the air. The final speculation is that, if it happens, then mankind will be impacted adversely. How many suppositions are we required to validate? Even if one of these assumptions is fulfilled, the others also have to be fulfilled for us to take this case seriously. Have the laws of probability been repealed by the zealots?

   The best attack on the predictors of doom was prepared by Thomas Gale Moore of the Hoover Institute in 1995. The title summarizes Moore's compelling argument: "Global Warming: A Boon to Humans and Other Animals,"

   However, do not underestimate the power of the activists who promote the scare scenario of global warming. How they ever organized, planned, and got worldwide support and World Bank funding for the Earth Summit held recently in Rio de Janeiro, is beyond me. The politics behind this are interesting.

   The United States is way ahead of all other nations in the amount of environmental cleanup accomplished and the stringency of our environmental laws. The only area in which we are laggard is in so-called carbon emissions, i.e., carbon dioxide. There was apparently a conference between environmentalists and South American diplomats prior to the Rio conference. At this meeting (according to Greg Easterbrook in an article appearing in the *New Republic* in July 1992), the group "relentlessly hammered Washington about the greenhouse effect because that is where the United States seems to be the wolf and all the others gentle elves."

   Somehow, the whole conference was devoted to global warming, though that subject should only have warranted peripheral attention. Yet, that was the only issue upon which the United States could be declared the "bad guy" (envy raises its ugly head again!). All of the other environmental factors which clearly affect lives today were largely ignored. Was it because the United States clearly leads the world in environmental responsibility? What a spectacle to see heads of states pledging tens of billions of dollars to prevent such an elusive threat as the greenhouse effect, when the United Nations says that over 3.2 million children die each year from impure drinking water. President Bush resisted being pushed into endorsing efforts to attack global warming, recognizing that the data were inconclusive. However, the pressure is still on in Washington. And, unless global warming can be discredited, the pressure on the politicians is only going to increase, especially with Vice President Gore's environmental bias. We may soon be pouring billions into this elusive chimera of environmental doom.

What are the potential costs? Reducing carbon dioxide by only 20 percent will cost close to $100 billion over the next ten years, and electricity prices will double, according to the Department of Energy. Compassionate ones, please worry about the regressive nature of electricity prices and the poor who will bear a disproportionate cost of this zealotry!

From all reports of the Rio conference, it was a cacophony of U.S. bashing. There were repeated demands upon the "rich" nations to help the poor, underdeveloped South American nations. These were naked, undisguised pleas to transfer wealth from the United States to help the poor unfortunates in the South (undisguised envy again). How is this transfer of wealth to be accomplished? Not by providing pure drinking water systems, which would clearly save many lives, but by endorsing a worldwide major expenditure to reduce carbon dioxide emissions!

It is ironic that in finding the key spot in which the United States could be made to look vulnerable, namely carbon dioxide emissions, the meeting took on this surrealist aura. Do those who promote this hysteria over global warming realize what they are doing to the poor peasants of South America? When some sensible politicians or bureaucrats recognize that three million lives are being lost each year because of unsafe drinking water, what will happen? They'll go to the "rich nations" and say, "Please help us by putting in safe drinking water systems." The answer that comes back might be, "Sorry, we are putting all these tens of billions of dollars into reducing carbon dioxide emissions so that we can avoid the global warming you were so worried about."

What is so damaging and costly is the so-called precautionary principle. This holds that environmental policy should be guided by what *may* happen, "that science should embrace the principle that the environment must not be left to show harm before action is taken" (from Greenpeace U.K., quoted in the *Financial Times*, 6 September 1993). There are many similar statements cited by atmospheric scientist Ronald Bailey, all adding up to the institutionalizing of this dangerous doublespeak. I ask, aren't there enough proven dangers to erase, without this desperate reaching? Again and again, it is not the actual dangers that attract these activists' attention, but the emotional content of those they champion. Some have suggested rather cynically that the Sierra Club and others must deal in apocalyptic projections of doom, otherwise how could they get enormous financial support from the public? Advocating the construction of safe drinking water plants in South America would hardly arouse much fear in people's hearts, nor would it generate $400 million in annual support.

I'm willing to concede that perhaps the critics of all of this junk science may be trying to scare us with the enormity of the costs involved. But, even if their estimates are wrong by a factor of two or four, we would be right in asking, "Why spend even that?"

The Environmental Protection Agency (EPA) has not grown exponentially by muting the frantic exaggerations of the activists seeking a risk-free society.

Why should we divert desperately needed funds to save us from "what could happen," when there are so many things that *are* happening? Promoters of this junk science, do you have real compassion? Is your need for recognition of the goodness of your compassion so strong that you can only attach yourselves to apocalyptic visions of world doom? Would you not be content to urge advanced countries like the U.S. and organizations like the World Bank to provide sanitary drinking water for the poor in undeveloped countries? You may not get headlines, but you would surely save lives. Is that not an adequate goal for compassion? If not, and the sensationalistic, headline-grabbing calamities, backed by junk science, are the choice for your compassionate energy and our resources, then I submit that your compassion may be severely tainted. By self-aggrandizement, perhaps? Or moral greed? Or a need to attract membership and financial support to pay your salaries? If that sounds cynical, I mean it to be!

10. Social Engineering: Mythical Compassion

I know of no safe repository for the ultimate powers of society but the people themselves; and if we think them not enlightened enough to exercise their control with a wholesome discretion, the remedy is not to take it from them, but to increase their discretion by education.

—Thomas Jefferson

The term *social engineering* is an insidious and deceptive use of language—an oxymoron. The idea that the discipline and quantitative constraints of engineering can be applied to social legislation is misleading. Implying that the engineering model can be used to shape social legislation that works (which is the primary criterion for engineers) is ludicrous.

The assumption that human behavior, or more precisely human happiness and welfare, can be reduced to a mathematical or engineering construct denigrates the wonderful diversity of human beings.

The liberal theorists try to legislate compassion. Faced with the repeated failures of the liberal programs in practice, I wonder if the term *social engineering* was coined to impart validation to what is, at best, an intuitive and risky venture. Most social legislation impelled by liberal compassion fails because of the imperfection of the people who implement the programs. Compounding the problem is the unpredictability of the people for whom these nostrums are concocted.

I find it particularly ironic that the term *engineering* should be used when none of the methodology of engineering is employed. The one engineering principle most often violated in social programs is the obligation to recognize and acknowledge when the proposed process does not work. Why aren't so-called social engineering actions treated in the same way as engineering proposals are—recognizing when they have not worked and, thus, learning from experience? Arrogance born of an assumed purity of motive is the probable answer. GM's arrogance was based upon market success, and they were brought to their knees by that same market. The virtue of the liberals' compassion is unquestioned and unchallenged, so their arrogance is also understandable. But, that leads them to underestimate the people they want to help and to overestimate the ability of the people to whom they entrust the implementation of their vision. The purity of their motives blinds the liberal theorists to the impurity of the methodology. We conservatives have purity of vision equal to theirs, but we are more aware of our fallibility. We try to devise methods that acknowledge and accommodate experience, for we have learned that all of us strike out often.

There are many social engineering efforts that have demonstrably failed. I have chosen just a few to illustrate the flawed methodology.

First, take rent control, the centerpiece of the Tom Hayden school of liberalism. Can anyone deny the compassionate purpose of rent control? Here is the proposition clearly stated by John Atlas, president of the National Housing Institute (what an intriguing and benign label!): "Rent control *simply* limits *unbridled rent gouging* and real estate speculation while allowing apartment owners a *reasonable profit*." All the emphasis is mine because these words produce an imagery that needs to be exposed—the tyranny of words in action. Let's take them one by one:

The word *simply* says, "See how easy this is? No problem—just freeze rents by passing a law and set up a bureaucracy to see that the law is not broken!"

Perhaps Mr. Atlas should examine the rent control laws in New York City. They are a most complex and tortuous labyrinth of arcane language that renters and landlords endlessly exploit. Rent control laws are anything but simple. The concept is, of course, very simple, but people who are affected—the renters, the landlords, and the bureaucracy who enforce the laws—are anything but simple (neither simple as human beings nor simple-minded). So, as each weakness in this supposedly simple law is exposed by renters and landlords seeking their self-interest (remember Adam Smith?), the successive Band-Aids turn a simple concept into an incredibly complex one in practice.

Unbridled Rent Gouging: These prejudiced, value-laden words are used to set up the "bad guy." But, who is going to restrain this bad guy? Pure-hearted, compassionate people like Mr. Atlas. How? Through the power of government, of course! But, Mr. Atlas forgets how many real estate speculators are sitting in the wings, saying, "I want a piece of that action! I want to have some of that 'unbridled rent gouging.' I'll invest my money in apartments for the poor and I'll draw people away from the gouger by charging only a little less." No, Mr. Atlas says, a bureaucracy can do it better! Has he toured the virtual war zone of the Bronx where block after block of abandoned apartments testify to the government's inability to control prices? How many times does this fallacy need to be highlighted?

Mr. Atlas does not recognize that his use of the term "unbridled rent gouging" invalidates, rather than supports, the need for government intervention, for what is more attractive to those other greedy landlords out there than to try to get some of those gouging rents? Nothing attracts competition more than somebody else making "obscene profits."

And, what happens when competition sets in? As night follows day, prices become more reasonable and gouging decreases. For the arrogant elitists who want to spread their compassionate wings wide, it is too easy to go from the particular to the general. Is there rent gouging where free markets prevail? Of course. But, what is the incidence? How often does it happen? Is it transitory, until the poor renter finds that there is another landlord who will gouge him less? Is it so prevalent that all people need the protection of rent controls? Every experience to date says the answer to that question is an unequivocal no.

Finally, let's consider *reasonable profit*. Does Mr. Atlas really think that a government entity can determine a "fair or reasonable profit"? The first question is, fair to whom? The renter or the landlord? With his obvious bias, Atlas would undoubtedly come down on the side of the renter. The result: The Bronx war zone and a limitation on the supply of housing for the poor.

More specifically, Atlas argues, "Rent control helped slow down gentrification and curbed displacement of the poor and working class families." It appears that he has concluded that "gentrification" is bad. When I go to some of the old neighborhoods where I was raised in Brooklyn, I am pleased to see them gentrified. Would Atlas prefer that they be abandoned or allowed to deteriorate because the landlord was dissatisfied with the "reasonable" profit set by a bureaucrat? Would he allow the properties to deteriorate for the sake of providing low rents for the poor? Isn't gentrification a welcome upgrading of a neighborhood or a city? From a social value standpoint, would a city prefer to have slums so there will be cheap rent for the poor? Isn't gentrification a positive value rather than a negative one, as Atlas implies?

For those who notice my choice of words, I readily acknowledge that I am using a word of tyranny when I call the alternative "slum" rather than "low cost." But, the fact is, that in too many cases, "low cost" housing is also a "slum," and the choice of which word to use depends upon the chooser.

There is another alternative method to provide shelter for the poor, again involving massive government action, and that is publicly financed subsidized housing. Any reasonable study of this extremely costly expression of a compassionate government would result in a bleak view. Not all, but a large number of the "projects," as the inhabitants call them, are run-down cesspools of criminal activity and wanton destruction. As a result, very few social activists today defend public housing as a way to help the poor.

The Department of Housing and Urban Development (HUD), the government agency which has an enormous budget to build subsidized housing for the poor, has been damned right and left for graft and corruption. The entire agency is built upon a structure that invites nothing but waste, fraud, and abuse.

Even though the agency has been headed by such distinguished public servants as George Romney, Patricia Harris, Carla Hills, and Jack Kemp, the enormous bureaucracy of this monster of compassion grown corrosive and ponderous defies any rational control. The examples of failed housing projects are legion. The most famous is Pruitt-Igoe in St. Louis—built in 1957 at a cost of $57 million ($300 million in today's dollars). Supposed to be a model of compassionate social planning, the project became infested with criminals and vandals. As the decent residents fled, the buildings were virtually abandoned, and in 1972 the whole project was demolished. The land is empty today, a testament to the inherent weakness in liberal social vision. Even Henry Cisneros, the present secretary of HUD, admits that HUD has, in many cases, exacerbated the declining quality of life in urban America.

The only move that makes sense today is for the tenants who are abused so badly to take over ownership from the government. By advocating ownership, I am reaffirming the value of private property. Do the liberal theorists who acknowledge no other instrument than government to put their compassion into practice understand how wrongly they have chosen? The new owners, usually led by angry mothers, say, "We own this place, not some bureaucrat downtown." Then they say, "Crack dealers out! No more guns! Gangs out." Ownership is the defining difference. Throughout all of the underprivileged areas, it has been proven over and over again. People do not burn down or let property that they own be destroyed.

Thus, the fierce defense of property rights by conservatives is validated. It is not often recognized that property rights and human rights are inseparable. The right to own property was the key right awarded when a slave was freed. Transforming a slave from "property" to a "person" was the ultimate conferring of dignity.

Perhaps the most tragic consequence of rent control is the large-scale urban displacement that it causes. Where are the poor to go when they have been displaced? In an uncontrolled rental climate, the owners of those thousands of abandoned apartments in the Bronx would have maintained them enough so they could become a supply for those who could not afford the gentrified prices.

To the arrogant elitists, it is incomprehensible that compassionately motivated proposals to limit rental payments for the poor could work so perversely. But they do. Could Mr. Atlas or Tom Hayden have predicted that such a well-intentioned law as rent control would produce a new class of property owners who were perfectly capable of being as exploitive as the original property owners they considered "unbridled rent gougers"? Rent-control laws give the residents of rent-controlled apartments the power to become "gougers." So, as a result of trying to curb the power of one set of gougers (the landlords), we now have two sets of gougers: The original landlords, and the tenants who occupy the rent-controlled apartments. Since rent-controlled apartments are priced below the stock of apartments available, the differential rent is now "owned" by the tenant—to be exploited in any way that his greed dictates. Is the resident of a rent-controlled apartment less greedy than the property owner? Study the New York situation and you'll get an answer.

Even the repulsive image of the "rent-gouging landlord" is a demagogic bogeyman. Cassandra Moore of the Cato Institute found, for instance, that 60 percent of the landlords in New York own only one building and a majority have incomes of less than forty thousand dollars per year. Once again, the tyranny of words serves the liberal activists very well. The activists are using a few isolated cases of a flawed free-market system to declare the system obsolete and to invest a government with more wisdom than it has ever been capable of exhibiting. In fact, experience has shown that by controlling rent prices, they replace a slightly flawed free market system with a massively flawed legal and bureaucratic system.

I know both apartment owners and tenants in rent-controlled apartments in New York, and the games they play are bizarre and Machiavellian. The renters play two games with the landlords to keep their low-rent apartments. One is the code violation game. There is a regular, but arduous, time-consuming procedure that landlords have to go through to get rent increases authorized by the complex bureaucracy. It involves reams of paperwork and bureaucratic game-playing. But, these rent increases cannot be implemented if there is any city code violation in the apartment. Certainly, gross code violations should be punished, but something as simple as a missing light bulb can be cited as a code violation and, therefore, a reason to delay the implementation of a rent increase. The tenants can simply create violations and keep creating them. This game can go on for months or even years.

The property owners are not without their own game in this travesty called rent control. Those who commandeer the power of government to control rents not only underestimate the poor; they also underestimate the landlords. Contrary to the normal workings of the marketplace, the landlord, under rent control, has a positive incentive to get rid of tenants—absolutely the reverse of normal economic motivation. Rental laws always have "vacancy allowances." In an attempt to mitigate their anti-landlord stance, the ordinance reluctantly recognizes that there are costs associated with vacancies. Therefore, the ordinances allow the landlord to raise the controlled rent if a tenant moves out. Ergo, the landlord does everything he can to get a tenant to move, including the ugliest kinds of harassment. Name every dirty trick in the book and some landlord has thought of it.

The bureaucracy, recognizing the inequity of the landlord's angry retaliation against those who deprive him of his property rights, counterattacks: The elaborate "antieviction" laws introduce a new round of consequences.

The exploited tenants are somewhat protected by these laws, but what about the guy on the top floor who blasts his stereo all night long, or the crack dealer, or the house of prostitution? It is not necessary to keep enacting law after law to correct the inequities resulting from earlier laws. Instead of this bureaucratic strangulation, there is a simpler way to mitigate the occasional glitches in the free market system—the competition of the marketplace.

Does the free market system produce injustices? Of course it does, but those inequities are redressed fairly quickly—especially in these days of instant communication and ease of mobility. Many liberals seem not to recognize the dynamic nature of our economy. The kind of monopoly of Ida Tarbel's or Upton Sinclair's day (only seventy-five years ago) no longer exists. The John Kenneth Galbraiths of the liberal movement are so out of touch they are tilting at windmills that have long ago crumbled—by technology, not by liberal disapproval. This leads back to the question I've raised before. Are the liberals the advanced modern thinkers they portray themselves to be, or are they hopelessly behind the times?

Besides the nightmare of regulation and reregulation, there have been other disastrous consequences of the "reduction to practice" of these well-intentioned expressions of liberal compassion. Above all, isn't the dignity given to people by the assumption that they can largely control their lives and resist exploitation, an enormous benefit of letting them operate in a free market? Or, is it preferable to make them dependent upon the goodwill of the activists and the bureaucracy?

With all the pain and the enormous cost—both in financial and human terms—rent control laws do not even produce the desired results. Does rent control increase the supply of housing for the poor? Are the poor people the primary beneficiaries of rent control? In fact, rent control laws actually result in fewer apartments for rent than in an uncontrolled environment. A nonpartisan budget commission in New York concluded that tenants with incomes of $75,000 per year or more enjoy an average rent subsidy of $345 per month, whereas the rent subsidy for tenants with incomes of $10,000 to $19,000 per year get a subsidy of only $176 per month.

Michael St. John did a study of the rent control laws in Berkeley and Santa Monica, California (the favorite playgrounds of the arrogant elitists of the liberal movement). In both cities the practical result of the rent control laws was to get rid of the poor. Apparently, they could not find enough cheap rent-controlled homes and moved to neighboring towns.

Many studies have shown that rent control laws in practice do three things: 1) Promote inefficient use of housing stocks; 2) discourage new private construction; and 3) create disincentives for existing apartment owners, thus decreasing the availability of rental units.

Does all economic history have to be ignored? Does anyone doubt that the lowest prices are obtained when supply exceeds demand? In Los Angeles today, one can rent recently built office space for less than half the cost of replacement. Why? Because greedy landlords were attracted by the high profits during a brief period of shortage. Los Angeles has benefited from these low rents for four years and landlord after greedy landlord has gone broke (including the much-feared Japanese, who were "going to own us!"). Could the government have mandated such low rents? Would it have been acceptable to bankrupt so many landlords? The market did what no government is able to do; it treated greed more harshly than any government fiat!

From this, and all of the things economists have learned about how competition works, it seems clear that the fastest way to reduce rents in a city is to let it be known that there are rent gougers out there. Very quickly, there will be an oversupply of housing as other landlords flock into the area. Competition will bring prices down faster than a law can be passed and a bureaucracy can be created.

Rent control laws take private property out of the hands of the owner by dictating its worth (as established by the allowable rents). How does this differ from the condemnation of property for public use, as often occurs when highways are built, for example? The right of "eminent domain" is established in law, but the government must provide "fair" reimbursement for the property so seized. And, how is "fair" determined? In court case after court case, the market value for the "highest and best use" is the price to be paid. Dictating the value of property by fixing the allowable return on it is no different than determining the value of land to be condemned for a highway. Therefore, should the city council or the state legislature vote on the value as they do with rent control laws? Why not let them vote on what the value of condemned land is, rather than use "market price"? Is this not also a violation of the Fifth Amendment?

Can any government entity determine what is fair (a nonreferent word) better than a willing buyer and a willing seller in the marketplace? Arrogant government bureaucracies are treating people so arbitrarily that they may attract a test of constitutionality under the Fifth Amendment.

I can just imagine the reflexive liberal reaction to the suggestion that property rights are as important as human rights. But, property rights, I maintain, are the very foundation of human rights. You simply can't have one without the other. The right to own property is the hallmark of the difference between slavery and freedom. This has been the case for more than two millennia, dating back to the days of Rome and before. The thousand-year serfdom of the Russian people, whether under kings and queens or under Socialist bureaucracy, was characterized by the denial of property rights to all but a few. Human rights and property rights are inseparable.

Rent control laws are an abomination. They clearly do not help the poor. The immorality and disrespect for law created by them is far worse than any sins projected for the free market system. In a world where civility and simple good manners are constantly being degraded, it is reprehensible to impose laws which exacerbate the tensions and stresses between people. Why, then, are they not discarded when they've been shown to be failures? It's that same old reluctance to abandon exquisite theory that has not worked.

Another social engineering icon is the minimum wage. Nothing can activate the compassionate juices of liberals and conservatives alike more than the thought of people being paid wages below that which they need to live on—"slave wages," as they are pejoratively classified. This bona fide compassion for the underpaid led to the proposal of another simplistic solution: A mandated minimum wage.

Who should set the minimum wage? In these days of "government knows all," it was decided that the government should, of course! But, that ignores a fundamental law of supply and demand—which is the real determinant of prices. According to the liberals, we should ignore the law of supply and demand when it allows less than a living wage. But, what is a "living wage"? The problem now becomes much more complex as we reduce the admired compassion to practice. Should the wage earner eat meat once a week or three times a week? Should he own a TV—or a car? How many hours a week should he work in order to feed his family? Forty hours has been enshrined. How about those who work seventy-two hours a week to avoid poverty? What is an appropriate minimum wage in North Dakota? In New York City? The complexity is endless.

There is really a demonstrably superior judge to answer all these questions: Free markets and free choice. There is also a by-product to free choice in a free market—dignity.

Even the elite recognize what a difficult task it is to reconcile all the thousands of factors that determine what the minimum wage should be. But, there is a simple way out: Submit it to the political process—just foist it upon Congress and they will declare it as "the will of the people."

What results is a politically determined minimum wage that simply does not have any relationship to a "real" minimum wage. Instead, it is determined by the number of votes it will—or will not—get. What do the unions want? What do the owners of hamburger stands want? Does a wage thus determined have any rationale? No! And by the way, is it right for farm workers in North Dakota? How about people working in a mine—or an automobile plant? It doesn't answer any of the questions I ask. All it does is pass the political test. "Poor wage earner, you are not smart enough to protect yourself against exploitation, so we'll take a vote on it for you!" How degrading!

O.K., now we have a minimum wage arbitrarily established by Congress through a purely political process. Next, we enact a law that says that everyone who works will get this minimum wage, right? Exactly, but what about those who don't work or who can't get work because the minimum wage is so high? Don't worry, they can go on welfare! The government, by paying that welfare, then subsidizes the minimum wage that business cannot afford. What does this amount to? If the businessman cannot afford to hire the person at the artificially high minimum wage, the government simply taxes the businessman in order to pay welfare! The minimum wage law is thus an imposed cost on society that also expands dependency.

Actually, there has been a great deal of study, all of it compelling, that a minimum wage law is a disincentive to employment. As early as 1946, George Stigler wrote a classic paper for the American Economic Review arguing that raising minimum wages would result in the dismissal of unproductive workers.

When I started work at the age of twelve, I worked twelve hours a day on weekends selling soda pop in a park near my home for three dollars a day. Later, as I learned to be a "soda jerker," I got a little more pay and earned tips, all of which helped pay part of my living costs at home. By the time I was in college, I had graduated to third cook at a country club. If I hadn't become an engineer, I might have become a chef and opened my own restaurant. If a minimum wage existed when I was young, I might not have gotten either of those jobs, one of which provided a training process that could have resulted in my owning a restaurant.

If the present overbearing government was active then, I would have surrendered and said, "Please keep us from starving!" Perhaps I'd have even been on welfare if it had existed. Actually, my mother would have never allowed that, even if she had to work eighteen hours a day. In Arabic she would have said, *"Eyb"* (translated, "shame!"). This illustrates that a person's worth is determined in many ways, only one of which is wages. For centuries, apprentices worked inhumane hours for a place to sleep and some food, in order to learn a trade. Perhaps they enriched their employers, but in return they learned a trade that gave them a lifetime of earning power. Setting a minimum wage creates a hurdle to learning that should be determined by the youngster's wishes and needs—not by a government's false compassion.

One could argue, properly, that minimum wages force industries to become more efficient. But, they accomplish this by introducing labor saving machinery, which eliminates existing jobs. Even at that, the social good of a more efficient industry might outweigh the attendant job loss. But, is it beneficial to force that increase in efficiency artificially? Answering that question requires that we examine what happens when we mechanize. We may, in fact, create jobs as a result of being more efficient, but what kinds of jobs? Necessarily they must require more skill (to operate those machines), so we may be creating a scenario that cruelly freezes out people of low skills, instead of letting the employer and employee decide what is a fair pay.

That side effect was examined thoroughly by Dr. Walter E. Williams of George Mason University. In a 1982 book, *The State Against Blacks*, he argued that raising the minimum wage would result in "adverse effects for those workers who are most disadvantaged in terms of marketable skills"—in particular minorities and youths. He cites example after example of the adverse effect of minimum wage laws upon just those people it was intended to help—the minorities, youngsters, and those with few skills. And, I add to that, it denies them the opportunity to learn a skill that may insure a lifetime of productive, rewarding work.

Look at the derogatory image of the young and the poor that this attitude implies. "Arbitrarily raising wages," Williams concludes, "makes as much sense, and accomplishes as much as doctors curing patients by merely declaring that they are cured." Those laudable motives of compassion and those theoretical concepts that seem so pure do not withstand the test of real people in a real world and in real time.

Though the exquisite theory is laudable, the final discipline must follow the scientific method. Does it work? A scientist's theories are rejected so many times in the laboratory that he has no psychological problem in accepting that judgment. He learns and moves on. But, the compassionate liberal theorist, rarely understanding the scientific method, is not so conditioned. The evidence of the laboratory or the marketplace is repeatedly ignored or rejected. "It can't be my compassionate and noble theory that is wrong!" he says. "It is the people who carry it out or do not share my vision who are at fault." Some view the failure even more desperately: "Those people for whom I am so compassionate, and for whom I've devised my nostrums, do not behave the way they should. They persist in pursuing their self-interest in ways that defy my theories."

There is a subtle point that should be considered in putting a theory to test. Even if it does work in practice, that does not mean it should automatically be used, for there may be more than one procedure or method that works. Therefore, we reintroduce the necessity of choice or discrimination. I can illustrate that from my own experience.

During World War II, Dr. Fleming of Great Britain discovered penicillin. Drs. Florey and Chain developed a laboratory method for making and purifying it, and they came to Merck & Company in the U.S. to ask them to devise a commercial process to make it in large quantities. I was assigned that task and quickly developed a practical way to make it, using the fundamental fermentation process Florey had used in the laboratory. I found out how to do it using large-scale equipment.

The army medical corps, anxious to get this wonder drug, urged Merck to build a large production plant based upon the fermentation process design I had helped develop. At the meeting considering the proposal, the head of Merck's synthetic organic chemical research group stated that he felt he was very close to synthesizing penicillin by chemical re-

actions, rather than by the bulky and expensive fermentation methods that I had worked out. He urged delay in
responding to the army's request. Other pharmaceutical companies jumped and built much larger plants, even though
Merck had a clear head start. The Merck scientists were not
able to synthesize penicillin in any reasonable time. Many
years later, a synthetic process was finally developed. The
process did work and could be reduced to practice. But, it
was never used commercially because it was simply too expensive! Fifty years later, penicillin is still produced by a
(much improved) fermentation process. The basic mistake
the chemists at Merck made was not so much in confidently
predicting that they could synthesize penicillin, but that when
they did so, it was necessarily going to be a cheaper process.
Not only must an idea be able to be reduced to practice, but
it also must be the best idea. It must compete with other
good ideas.

In the case of the social engineering legislation that I
have discussed, the compassionate liberals could claim their
ideas had been reduced to practice. Some of them have, but
then I have to ask, "How well do they work and what are
the alternatives?" To me, and to all conservatives, they don't
work nearly as well as the tried and true free market system
of competition. Admittedly, there is no social process that
works perfectly. But, which works better? There are no doubts
in the conservative's mind. All we ask is that the free market
system be evaluated objectively against the social engineering methodology.

The year 1994 is the fiftieth year since Friedrich Hayek
wrote *The Road to Serfdom*. This was the seminal work sounding the conservative caution against the gradual erosion of
our liberty by socialism. Avoiding oversimplification of the
word *Socialism*, the content of what Hayek talked about were
derivatives of Socialist theory, which have become part of
our modern-day liberal political methodology. Many in the
liberal community would, quite properly, deny that they are
Socialists. They would acknowledge, on the other hand, that
they have adopted those parts of the Socialist agenda that
they believe are compassionate.

To the extent that the liberal community has borrowed the methodology, the big government, the command and control mechanism, and the bureaucratic intervention, they also borrowed the faults of that system. Remember Michael Novak's remark that "compassion is the lure of the left!" It is a mistake for the liberals to think that they can borrow piecemeal from the Socialist model and leave behind the imperfections. So, Hayek's *Road to Serfdom* is still very much the definitive work on the dangers we face. But, the real weakness of Socialist theory is the impurity of the compassion that it actually delivers. Hayek says that these supposedly compassionate methods lead unerringly to a "serfdom" that was never contemplated by the well-meaning supporters of collective action, as opposed to individualism.

Individualism, the great force of the nineteenth century, was dealt a blow with the absolutely senseless slaughter of World War I. Individualism failed completely with the Depression in the thirties. Thus rose Franklin Roosevelt's plan for government to take over for a flawed capitalist system. Despite Hayek's warnings, collectivist solutions have risen, and the serfdom he predicted is now becoming evident to all but the old-fashioned liberals who repeat FDR's prescriptions over and over again, even as they see them fail. Yet, there is real hope that there will be a resurgence of individualism.

This resurgence will not be fueled by conservative theory or by books by Hayek, William F. Buckley, or Rush Limbaugh. The underpinning of this revolution in social thought will be technology, the ultimate expression of reduction to practice.

I have discussed, in several places, the restructuring of business enterprises and how it is making us more competitive. The centerpiece of restructuring is in management that is much flatter and less hierarchical. Flatter management means that decision-making is moved down to the lowest level. That means more democracy in the workplace, and the essence of democracy is individualism! The enormous improvement in information flow makes this revolution possible. Noel Watson, CEO of our company, can sit at his computer and know the complete details of how a project is going in our Cork, Ireland, office in an instant. That's how he can empower the several hundred people in that office to make decisions quickly and decisively. It no longer takes days or weeks for a hierarchy to report in—by which time the data is history. "Management by history" was the way I stated it when criticizing what the business schools were teaching twenty years ago.

Malcolm S. Forbes, Jr., articulated this eloquently in a tribute to Hayek which appeared in *Policy Review Magazine* (Summer 1994):

> Technology is now an agent of individualism. The microchip, which is expanding the reach of the human brain the way machines expanded the reach of the human muscle in the last century, is flattening hierarchies the way electricity physically flattened factories when it replaced steam power in the early part of this century. We simply don't need as many layers of management to process information as we did before. The corporate sector has been undergoing this process for years; the public sector will soon be hit with it, too.
>
> The microchip is the enemy of the tyrant. Not so long ago, money had to be transported physically by, say, putting bars of gold in ship bottoms or in wagons. Governments could literally prohibit their citizens from moving their wealth outside of their jurisdictions. Today the blip of a computer can transport hundreds of billions of dollars in less than a second.
>
> Dictators can enslave the body, but they can no longer capture the true source of wealth, the human mind.

So, the free market in ideas interacts with the free market in technical brains, and the twenty-first century may become the age of a new freedom for man.

Finally, a word about the greed that is used over and over again to justify the social engineering agenda. Let's grant that greed exists and that it tends to create a harmful imbalance. Newton's third law dictates that the intensity or extent of the greed will generate an opposing force of equal intensity.

But, is greed confined to matters concerning money or property? Certainly, greed for power is obvious in the political sphere. But, what about greed in the realm of ideas? I referred to this as "moral greed" in chapter 2 in a way that says it all. And, let's not forget that Newton's law will prevail. Excessive moral greed will induce a reaction to it!

These unscholarly thoughts will, I hope, add some little bit to the force of opposition to the moral greed which threatens to consume us and, most unfortunately, demeans those upon whom its corrosive compassion is showered.

Part Three

Toward Solutions

11. Morality in Business

Agriculture, manufacture, commerce and navigation, the four pillars of our prosperity, are most thriving when left most free to individual enterprise.

—Thomas Jefferson

When choosing examples of the tyranny of words, I wondered which is the smallest word that causes the maximum distortion. The adjective *big*, is a clear winner.

Take the simple word *business* and add the adjective big. The compound word *big business* has suddenly been invested with wide-ranging emotional stereotypes—most of them not very admirable. That little word *big* can arouse more anger, resentment, and pure bile than Ebenezer Scrooge. Big and business are locked together so often that even the noun *business* is now beginning to carry almost as much baggage as the compound word. Those who mistrust the free market system validate their prejudice with the term *big business*, and I ask, "How big is 'big'?"

Perhaps the coupling is driven by a latent anti-capitalistic sentiment. Business, after all, is how capitalism is finally expressed. But, liberals shy away from indicting the millions of small shopkeepers with the perceived sins of capitalism. The use of *big* has little to do with size, but much to do with the questionable prejudgment that businesses are basically immoral. John Kenneth Galbraith is a prototype of those who make the unsupportable claim that capitalism is all right for small businesses but not for large ones.

Adam Smith observed that much human action is characterized by the pursuit of self-interest. For many liberals, this is at odds with their idealized view of man. Since selfishness (a more pejorative word) is, in their eyes, an evil flaw in a person's make-up, the statement that the self-interest of individuals can lead to a better society is, for them, suspect. Somehow, self-interest is regarded as tarnishing idealism. Again, the tyranny of words intrudes, and for those who have a bias against our free market system, self-interest translates into the more pejorative word *greed.*

It is ironic that liberals are so distrustful of business. After all, liberal compassion is supposedly for the benefit of the "little people." Yet, it is around those very same people, as consumers, that the business world revolves. Small, independent business owners are the heart and soul of capitalism. After decades of traveling around this country, I have never lost my wonder and admiration as I pass row after row of shops in every town. Watched over by an owner or manager and, at most, a few clerks, these are the real testimonials to the free market. And, these same "little people" are the customers of business, big or little, whom the capitalist woos every day.

Big conveys similar bias when hung on other carriers, too. A favorite hook for conservatives is government. *Big Government* implies a ponderous, slow-acting bureaucracy that is inefficient and even slothful. Yet, there are millions of government workers who are conscientious and hard-working and who care about doing a good job. We conservatives are not completely free of word manipulation ourselves. However, there is a deeper and more distressing inference being signaled by those who use the term *big business* to project an unsavory image—that of immorality. Perhaps this stems from an instinctive feeling that capitalism must be immoral since it is based upon self-interest. But, those who think this way show very little understanding of the moral good that can arise from self-interest. They should remember that though compassion may have a selfish component, this does not invalidate its social good. Business, with its thrust of self-interest, often results in enormous social good.

Standards of morality in a culture like ours vary considerably. Nevertheless, the immoral image projected by the word *big* is unmistakable, even conceding the uncertain meaning of "morality." And, morality is something that every community cherishes, no matter how it is defined.

I find it very difficult to understand the constant reference to business as an impersonal, monolithic entity. Today, about twenty million people in the United States work for some form of government, according to the National Taxpayers Union. But, the rest of the employed work for "business." Are those who ridicule business unwilling to admit that we create jobs more efficiently than government does?

If I flashed the term *big business* or even *businessmen* on a screen and asked the public to free associate, many of the responses spilling out would be negative: Acquisitive, advancement at the expense of colleagues, driven, greedy, inhumane, insensitive, materiality over art, ruthless, ulcer-ridden, unhappy, overachievers, profits above people, and immorality. On television or in the movies, and even in daily life, I hardly recall a use of the term *big business* that isn't associated with acts of malfeasance, brutal power, dishonesty, chicanery, and other immorality. The worst part, however, is the thoughtless and sometimes deliberate implication that big business itself is the *cause* of immoral acts. The tortured reasoning runs as follows: "Money is the root of all evil," therefore, the pursuit of money—the almighty dollar, the "bottom line"—is inherently a corrupt action.

The false assumption is that even a moral person will, in a business setting, alter his values. In the case of the shoe repair shop, an immoral act by its owner is clearly a personal immorality. But, when a business becomes "big," its inherent culture—according to the popular myth—fosters immorality. This flawed thought process holds that corporations are formed to make money and that the need to make money encourages a culture of dishonesty. Why? Because of the presumption that one can make more money by being dishonest than by being honest! Based upon my fifty-year business career, I know that is simply untrue.

222   Joseph J. Jacobs

Associating the term *big business* with immorality demeans the good people who toil in our free market system. This image almost always is projected by those who have had little or no experience in business. I've never heard a businessman take this position.

I've been struck by the paradox of the media portraying big business in a negative light when, in fact, the publishing and movie industries are themselves "big business." Are the writers getting back at their bosses? Are they using their "artistic integrity" to express their envy of those for whom they work? For the lazy screenwriter, the malevolent image of business is so ingrained that the presentation of villainy is a slam dunk.

Without a doubt, there are immoral people, but the assumption that big business will force a moral person to act immorally is based upon a most cynical, prejudiced, and uninformed view of the free market system and a lack of experience in how businesses actually operate.

It is rarely recognized that compassion is an essential ingredient of a successful business, not in the form of liberal indulgence, but rather, as a high standard of quality that earns the customer's trust and improves his standard of living. Business is a service to others—period. If it fails that, it fails everything.

I ask the simple question, "When I get in my car to go to work in the morning, do I leave my moral values behind? When I walk into my office, do I suddenly adopt different standards of morality than I do outside that office?" Absolutely not. That would be evil. It would be stupid and unrewarding. Yet, that is the myth that persists.

I am not claiming that immoral acts are not committed in a corporate setting, but I insist that the immorality is not promoted by the setting. It is the act of an immoral individual against society and against the interests of business. It is a sin against the public, as well as against God.

When I was a soda jerker working my way through school, "knocking down the cash register" was the slang term for the ugly, immoral act of putting cash in your pocket instead of in the cash register. Today, businesses of any reasonable size have elaborate internal audit procedures because they recognize that people are not perfect, that they can be tempted, and that some may at times do the wrong thing for some personal gain. Out of "corporate self-interest," companies go to great lengths to prevent cheating. This benefits a company's honest employees, its shareholders, and its customers. Self-interest, as James Madison wrote, must be a sentinel to the public good.

Any business, big or little, is a collection of people, and it cannot be less moral than the morality of the people who make it up. It has been my observation that businesses, on the whole, tend to be *more* moral than the individuals who comprise them, and I think this can be explained. As Congressman Dick Armey stated recently in a magazine article, "The market punishes immorality. If one is indifferent to the needs of his fellow citizens in a capitalist economy, he will find himself in poverty."

The free market system is based upon choice. Does anyone really believe that people will choose to do business with a company that cheats, in quantity, quality, or price?

The headlines you read are not proof that businesses are immoral, but only that an individual immorality has been exposed, usually by a routine oversight audit. Dishonesty in other arenas, such as education, government, and even religion, is only rarely attributed to the low standards of the particular structure in which it occurs. Why imply that big business creates a special environment in which dishonesty is condoned?

Take the same headlines from which we generalize this false impression and look at them from a different standpoint. Aren't those very headlines a powerful deterrent to immoral business practices? Immoral businesses inevitably fail because they are subject to constant public evaluation by both their customers and their employees. Intelligent self-interest requires vigilance. Were Charles Keating and Ivan Boesky smart? No! Were they successful? No!

I am not suggesting that the pursuit of profits cannot lead to conflict with ethical or moral standards. But, business is no more guilty of creating this conflict than any other human endeavor. Ambitious pursuit of any goal will produce such conflicts. Are environmental extremists free of such destructive ambition? How many hoaxes have occurred in science when the pursuit of fame or professional acknowledgment has tempted some to immorality? And, what about ambition in the field of literature, or art, or music? From other headlines, many of us recognize that there may be as many acts of malfeasance and fraud in our universities as in our businesses. Even in the media, fraud and failure of responsibility occur. To give the impression that the pursuit of profits exerts more pressure or has an unbalanced leverage on morality does not meet the test of experience. Is the lusting for power in a bureaucracy or the pursuit of votes in the political arena less tempting? Yet, big business is uniquely singled out as morally inferior.

In fact, small businesses have more opportunity to operate dishonestly. The small business operator essentially has only his own conscience to answer to—and his customers' approval. Smaller businesses are more likely to receive their incomes in cash. The amount of lost taxes in the underground economy is enormous. Of course, most small businesses probably are run in a legal and highly ethical manner, and so are most large ones. Large businesses go to extraordinary lengths to prevent dishonesty.

For a number of years, I was on the board of the Del Webb Corporation, owners of the Sahara Hotels in Las Vegas, Reno, and Lake Tahoe—gambling casinos! There's a business that can foster immorality as no other does. And, indeed, those casinos run by the "mob" were run immorally—but only because they were owned and operated by immoral people to whom "skimming" was a minor aberration compared to their workaday world of murder, mayhem, and mugging.

The Del Webb Corporation, on the other hand, was publicly held and was run straight as an arrow—often to the bemusement of the mobsters. To run such a business amid the decadence, immorality, and low ethical standards of the gambling industry took extraordinary measures. The "eye in the sky" above the blackjack tables; the layers of independent observers overseeing the handling of the cash; the check-ing and cross-checking of receipts; and the elaborate cost and income reporting to detect even minor aberrations were eye-opening to me.

Even in the midst of a decadent environment, the moral-ity of a business is the morality of the people who comprise it.

In academia, there has been a rising interest in evaluat-ing the public image of the free market system and its pro-genitor, business. Stanley Rothman, director of the Center for the Study of Social and Political Change at Smith Col-lege, finds that key elite (there's that noun *elite* again) in academia and in government are systematically hostile to the free market system. In *The Media Elite*, Rothman and his colleagues cite polling techniques which point to an amaz-ing confluence of liberal view points that are held more passionately by the media than the population as a whole.

In another work, the same author polled key television writers, producers, etc. They are part of what he has termed the "New Class." He surveyed over six hundred television programs and found that businessmen, with little exception, are depicted as having most undesirable characteristics. In these programs, a disproportionate number of violent crimes were committed by businessmen, as compared to other people, including criminals. The portrayal of businessmen on television supports the view that business serves no use-ful social function.

I do not easily accept conspiracy theories. What, then, motivates the "New Class" to display us as ogres? Do they secretly resent their dependence upon us to solve the hard, mundane problems of the world? Their dependence upon our financial support makes them search for our feet of clay. Is their portrayal of us an expression of envy? I suspect that if one were to dig deep enough, this powerful force of envy, that lies deeply hidden, has a strong influence in this false portrayal of business. I don't have the answer. The behavior is clear; its motivations aren't.

James Q. Wilson, the eminent social scientist from UCLA, writes in his ground-breaking book, *The Moral Sense*:

The daily discourse of ordinary people is filled with direct and oblique references to morality. They talk constantly about being or not being nice, or dependable; about not having good character; about friendship, loyalty and moderation or fickleness, sincerity and addictions. Ordinary men wish to make moral judgments.

While they hold firm moral views, most people know that other people express their own morals differently. Many intellectuals take advantage of this tolerance and this reluctance of Americans to impose their own values on others. They deny the existence of values and preach a kind of relativism. What this accomplishes is to choke off any discussion of what are "good values," by denying that values have any value. It is an attempt to avoid dealing with the complexity of man.

In rejecting that cynical view, Wilson says:

But before drawing so bleak a conclusion, the reader should ask why bloodletting and savagery are news. The first reason is that they are unusual; the second is that they are so shocking. Though in the heat of battle or the embrace of ideology many of us will become indifferent to suffering, in our calm and disinterested moments we discover in ourselves an intuitive and powerful aversion to inhumanity—a moral sense.

What Wilson is saying is that those who reject the concept of "values" fail the test of patent law—reduction to practice.

In the business world, morality has a pragmatic basis—it pays. It must, of course, compete with the other, less desirable sources or drives, such as envy, greed, etc., but to deny the existence of morality as a social force would condemn us to a cruelly destructive world. Without an underlying moral sense, business could not function. It is difficult for some to accept that Adam Smith's self-interest leads to morality as a social good.

There is another point that *I* do not believe Wilson makes, at least not directly. There is an innate human sense or drive to avoid chaos. That sense has made us evolve from the primeval slime to a slowly evolving civilization. Attempting to make order out of chaos is, after all, exactly what defines us as civilized creatures. Morality is the underlying instinct which guides us in making a just order out of disorder.

It should be noted that this impulse to avoid chaos is at odds with another cherished condition—freedom. But, that is the everlasting challenge for a civilized society—properly balancing freedom and order. What made Americans during our earliest days voluntarily come together to restrict their preciously won freedom? Wasn't it an innate moral sense that told them that totally unrestrained freedom could lead to anarchy—and immorality? I believe that was the impelling force that led us to control our freedom voluntarily in a way that de Toqueville admired so much. Morality serves our self-interest because it insulates us from the anarchy that will destroy us.

Recently, I had the privilege of spending some time with Michael Novak, after he had received the cherished Templeton Prize for Progressive Religion. I have long been an admirer, and when he enthusiastically encouraged me to write this book, I was greatly pleased.

Not unexpectedly, I got some wonderful ideas from him. He has recently published a book entitled *The Catholic Ethic and the Spirit of Capitalism*. In it, he takes on the historical tendency of Catholic thought to distrust capitalism. He shows how Pope John Paul II and others have come to see the value of capitalism as a positive ethical force. I was most intrigued by a piece he wrote in *Crisis* magazine, of which he is editor. He lists the "seven plus seven" corporate responsibilities as follows:

1. To satisfy customers with goods and services of real value.

2. Make a reasonable return on the funds entrusted to the business corporation by its investors.

3. To create new wealth.

4. To create new jobs.

5. To defeat envy through generating upward mobility and putting empirical ground under the conviction that hard work and talent are fairly rewarded.

6. To promote invention, ingenuity, and in general, "progress in the arts and useful sciences."

7. To diversify the interests of the Republic.

In item seven, I believe Novak is arguing that to overcome "the tyranny of the majority," a nation needs many diverse commercial interests in competition with each other, limiting and checking one another, so that no one interest becomes too large.

The most interesting thing Novak does is to couple those seven functional components with seven moral responsibilities of business leaders, which he deems to be inseparable. Those moral responsibilities are:

1. To establish within the culture of the firm a sense of community and respect for the dignity of persons.

2. To protect the political soil of liberty.

3. To exemplify respect for law.

4. To win the allegiance of the majority.

5. To overcome the principle of envy.

6. To communicate often and fully with their investors, shareholders, pensioners, customers, and employees.

7. To contribute to making the surrounding society, its own habitat, a better place.

It is not surprising that Novak, an ethicist, should couple positive values with the burden of responsibilities.

These eloquently express the conclusions of my own experience. I find it a refreshing confluence of a philosophic view with a pragmatic one that should be most encouraging to thoughtful business people, whether conservative or liberal in their political views.

Even with this, however, we cannot ignore the reality of public opinion. Why is there enormous support among the general population (most of whom work for "big business") for the idea that businesses are inherently immoral? Is there a deeply suppressed need to take comfort from those dark views of business and businessmen? This is a paradox, really—a legion of people who themselves work in business, depend upon business for their livelihood, and are themselves businessmen in the sense of working for companies of many sizes; yet who accept the dark view of businessmen. Perhaps there is an answer.

As the founder of a business which has grown to a substantial size, I have participated in thousands of decisions to select those who would be given increasing responsibility. For everyone selected, there was at least one and usually more who were not selected. I have been exposed repeatedly to the psychological dynamics of those who don't make it in this selection process.

Those of us who are involved in making decisions about who gets which promotion have no illusions that our conclusions are at all clear-cut. Most such decisions involve a lot of uncertainty and even anguish for those who make them. We know we are affecting people's lives, their self-esteem, and their ambition. And, if *we* have that uncertainty, it's not surprising that the loser should suspect that he was unfairly treated. It is unrealistic to expect the one who has been bypassed to say passively, "The other guy was simply better than I."

What does a man say to his wife and friends when he has been bypassed for a vice presidency? It is not easy to say simply, "The man selected was better qualified." This is especially ironic, considering that those who made the selection had no such unequivocal view. It then becomes convenient to fall back on the negative images of business and businessmen so seductively projected in the media. There is an "out" to all of those who have not achieved quite the success they unrealistically dreamed about. Isn't it easier to use the images of immorality projected, than to face the reality that the successful colleague simply worked harder or performed better? How many of these disaffected people are willing to say, "I made a choice not to invest all that time and effort to advance in my job; I did my best, and I will abide by the results"? The few who do are the truly admirable. But, most find that too difficult.

Maslow, the psychologist, says that the desire to win is stronger in successful people. Not that they don't enjoy the fruits of winning, but the game is the thing. For most of those who have less of this desire to win or to succeed, it is difficult to acknowledge the reality of their lower expectations of themselves, for our culture demands otherwise. It is thus easier to characterize a more successful colleague as a ruthless, aggressive, self-promoting, fawn of the boss. So, the falsely projected image of business is accepted and even promoted by some because it helps justify the disparity between their secret dreams and harsh reality. The next self-justifying thought is "The guy who gets ahead does so by being insensitive and stepping on other people along the way. I am above stooping to such tactics!"

I accept that there are insensitive, ruthless, selfish businessmen, but they are clearly an exception. Leaders cannot gather loyal teams around them to fuel a great enterprise without sensitivity to the feelings of their colleagues. Fear of failure is a factor, of course, but most successful businessmen I know are superb at recognizing and satisfying the ego needs of their colleagues as long as it does not prove detrimental to the enterprise itself. Sensitivity is their greatest tool in attaining their leadership (using positive reinforcement, as the behaviorists say).

Sometimes, the epithet "ruthless" really is a complaint against the high standards of performance set by the leader. Those standards are what make a business—and a businessman—successful. The public good is well served by the hard decisions and high standards of the business leader.

Let's take on another myth—"profits above people." Do critics who talk that way ever consider what an absolutely stomach-churning job it is to fire someone for incompetence or to pass over a friend or a really nice person for promotion? I deny that selfishness is the motivating drive, for what would be easier than overlooking the incompetence of "Good old George"? Wouldn't it be kind and generous to give him the job he aspires to, though he may fail? But, what of the jobs and the well-being of the families of those hundreds, and perhaps thousands, of other people who depend upon the success of the enterprise they work for? Dare a businessman imperil *their* futures by making the easy decision—by being Mr. Nice Guy? Compassion is a virtue, but not all compassion is equally virtuous. A choice must be made. There is no escape.

I have confessed elsewhere to a multitude of failures in my business life. The most painful memories, however, are not just of my own failures, but of those failures I caused. How many times have I given people increased responsibility hoping, or even believing, that they would rise to the challenge of their new jobs? And, how many failed at those jobs? Even one would be too many, but there have been more than that, and each one has left an indelible feeling of guilt in me. To see a person crushed by failure, caused by my misjudgment of his capabilities, is heart-wrenching.

Businessmen cannot indulge in the infantile fantasy that no one fails and that ineffectual nice guys must always go forward and must be protected from their failures (the myth of a risk-free society!). No wonder the businessman who makes these tough decisions needs frequent relief in the world of art, music, movies, plays, TV, and evocations of childhood fantasy. In that play world, there are no tough, stomach-churning decisions for the "good guys"—only the need to resist the "bad guys."

The ingredients for maximum success in business (and in any other organizational structure) is presented by Blake & Mouton, behavioral scientists. In "Concern for People" and "Concern for Production," they select two of the most important factors in business success. One is epitomized by "Mr. Nice Guy" and the other by the hard-driving manager or "drill sergeant." On a scale of one to ten, the best business leader scores about nine on each scale. This correlates exactly with my own observations. I might say parenthetically that those who have an excess of concern for people and yet, do not demand high standards, are not really being kind. They prevent the objects of their concern from attaining their maximum potential and thus from attaining the maximum self-respect and pride.

Remember that a by-product of the striving and hard work of businessmen is employment. It has been amply demonstrated that a dollar placed in the hands of American businessmen will produce more jobs, even after paying the stockholders' dividends, than when placed into the hands of a government bureaucracy. The activities of these business-men also produce, for the disadvantaged, the by-products of self-respect and self-esteem because they provide jobs in-stead of the dole. One cannot insure success but one can provide an opportunity to succeed.

Businessmen are not paragons of virtue. They suffer the same weaknesses as everyone else, but they do not deserve the image that has been foisted upon them for years. The myth is largely perpetrated by those who toil with words, images, and fantasy. Failure occurs often in business. The real world does not make success easy. No fantasies—just reality. "Meeting the payroll" may be a most banal term, but it may also be an exceedingly difficult challenge that pro-vides a moral fiber for our society.

Making Tough Choices

In business and in the workplace, the purity of the sense of compassion is put to the test and reduced to practice every day. There is an unlimited number of potential objects for our compassion, but because of the finite resources in a business (the "balance sheet"), we are forced to choose which compassionate actions we take.

Let me cite a number of examples. One of the first things the builder of an enterprise must recognize is the human needs of those who join with him to advance that enterprise. The reality one must deal with, however, is the inequality of ability among people. Even that is a dangerous generality, for the complexity of the variables going into evaluation of ability is enormous. From the idiot savant to the most brilliant of people, the gradation of ability in each narrow sector makes evaluation of ability a most difficult and uncertain task. The genius may possess no social skills and have impaired self-esteem. The best-loved human being may be unequal to the task of taking risk. Man is not only imperfect, but being so complex, his skills can reach heights in some areas, yet be nonexistent in others.

Most of us have great difficulty in forming an objective view of ourselves and our abilities. But, the real world, by the constant testing of human interaction, tends to tell us the truth. The truly happy and contented man is one who accepts that reality and reconciles it with his dreams, with no loss of self-esteem. Those who do are rare and blessed people. But, for most of us, our vision of what we might be, or wish to be, is often very different from what we can be or what the world judges us to be.

Firing a person deemed to be incompetent is clearly an unpleasant act. But, my compassion for the welfare of the other people in the organization who will be adversely affected by the man's incompetence deserves greater weight than my compassion for him, and I have had to make a clear and painful choice. I acknowledge that I have not been compassionate to him, although, even here there have been some cases where the shock of being fired has made a man take a realistic view of his abilities, and he later thanked me for helping him to know himself better. Again, I must choose for whom I shall express my compassion.

Next, but less obvious, is the choice to increase the responsibility of one man in the organization and not another. Someone has to make that judgment in order to protect the people who are dependent upon the enterprise for their livelihood. To the extent that my judgment is bad, I will fail, and perhaps the enterprise will fail. Can I avoid being in that position? I can, but only if I reject the responsibility of leading a business.

There is a third case where I decide to give someone increased responsibility because he is loyal, hard-working, conscientious, trustworthy, likable, and has many other desirable attributes. I do this, though I have these niggling doubts that the new job may be above his capability or talent. He fails; therefore, I have failed. I have failed him when I thought I was being compassionate, and I have failed my associates. On the other hand, sometimes, happily, the man grows into his responsibility and performs well. I have had enough right guesses to continue taking the chance, and enough bad guesses to keep me worried every time this kind of decision must be made. If into this miasma of uncertainty one introduces race, color, or minority status, then the problems with affirmative action become overwhelming.

Finally, I'd like to share an exaltation of compassion that I've experienced perhaps less than a dozen times in my career. Don was my friend. I worked with him at Merck from 1942 to 1944. Brilliant, handsome, gentle, a great basketball player in college—Don was a man I admired immensely.

After I left Merck to come West, I had only sporadic contact with my friend and former colleague. He left Merck later to take jobs at other companies with increased pay and responsibility. We met one time about twenty years ago, and though he had a job of quite some importance, he confessed to being unhappy in it, though the reasons were unclear. I asked if he would come to work for us as head of our process department, for Don was one of the most brilliant and ingenious engineers I knew. I admired him as a person and as a talent. He came with us and, after a year or two, I began hearing complaints. "A brilliant, wonderful guy but . . ." "The department is in confusion!" "I wish Don would make up his mind."

Finally, I asked him to spend half a day with me. "What's wrong Don?" I asked.

I'll paraphrase the conversation that followed. "Joe, the accepted measure of a person's accomplishment in this society is his title, the number of people who work for him, and along with that, his income. But, I am unhappy at my job." A tribute to our friendship, his trust in me, and my affection for him, our conversation uncovered his frustrations. Don hated judging people, he hated the paperwork, he hated the idea of management placing upon him the responsibility for the performance of the people working for him. He hated having to make choices that would perhaps negatively impact people for whom he had compassion. He didn't like being a manager, though his self-esteem in the community demanded that he be one.

The proud result of that conversation: Don gave up his position and became senior technical consultant, at no reduction in salary. He moved to a small office with nobody reporting to him and only a part-time secretary. He had none of the trappings by which people incorrectly judge success.

Within a short time, there were lines of young engineers outside his office. "Don, I have a tough technical problem here. Do you have any ideas?" He always did, because his technical knowledge and wide experience were encyclopedic.

One time, I was walking by his door, and I heard him saying, "Back in 1943, Joe and I were working on this process and we came up with this solution and it worked. Why don't you try that?" I couldn't have recalled that small incident if my life depended upon it. Don spent almost twenty years at that position with our company, revered and respected by everyone, and he retired recently. My friend Don was, in my view and to those who know him, an eminently successful man.

What a glow I get at having been able to help Don shuck society's definition of success and come to terms with himself and his inner needs. In my opinion, Don attained the greatest success of his career when he became senior technical consultant and only had a part-time secretary. The eager young people sitting at his feet attested to his worth and to his self-esteem. He is now happily retired, though he comes back occasionally when somebody says, "I wonder if Don would know how to solve this technical problem?"

In summary, I think the experiences I relate here not only defend business against an undeserved reputation, but serve to support my main theme that we conservatives and businessmen must be accorded equal claim to the mantle of compassion. We make that claim because we are constant practitioners of compassion and we are good at it. Daily, we face the fact that compassion takes many forms (some of which attain the glorious promise of virtue, and some of which do not). In making the tough choices in our own work, we businessmen make a claim upon real compassion that we will not relinquish. We see every day how misdirected compassion can be destructive.

Can the destructive, negative image of business be turned around? I believe I see a ray of hope. There is a new buzz word in business today, and that is *empowerment*. Most people who use it do not realize what a constructive force this can be.

In the past, because of slow communications and an inherent distrust of the decision-making process at the lower levels, business has evolved into a pyramidal, hierarchical structure. Articulated by Alfred Sloan of GM, and promoted by business schools, the common view was that "business cannot be run like a democracy."

For a number of reasons, that view has been called into question. The microchip has sped up communications exponentially, eliminating the need for a stultifying blizzard of written reports to be circulated through a hierarchy. As a result, much flatter management structures are possible. Business has also begun to question the organization charts required by these vertical structures. What is the purpose of the hierarchical model? To avoid and catch mistakes by the employees. But wait—is the system costing more than mistakes would cost?

In many cases, the answer is yes. But, the most profound observation is that good ideas on the shop floor have been ignored or lost in the complex business structure. Did GM's fourteen layers of management between shop floor and the chairman's office prevent errors? Furthermore, wasn't the cost of those fourteen layers one of the reasons they became noncompetitive? But, the most serious defect was the smothering of ideas coming from below.

Bob Eaton, the new chairman of Chrysler, addressed this new style of management. In talking about the worker teams who are empowered to plan, design, and budget for the introduction of new Chrysler models, he says, "Now, if management became involved with them, inevitably we would give our opinions, and we would get our imprint upon it. It would become Chrysler's vehicle or Bob Eaton's vehicle. But because we stay out of it, it becomes their vehicle and they work much harder, with much more pride, and the success or failure is theirs."

I stress the word failure because to me, the possibility of failure is the essential ingredient of conservative compassion, since it is the primary basis of self-esteem and is so often missing in liberal compassion. What this means is that business has discovered that democracy works better than dictatorship. Business, out of self-interest, I'm quick to point out, has discovered a newfound respect for the common man. The inevitable result of empowerment is ownership, and that sense of ownership profoundly affects the pride, self-image, and identification of most people in the business.

The blurring of the line between the bosses and the workers is a mostly healthy dose of democracy introduced into business. If the trend continues, I suspect it will eventually deprive those who malign business and capitalism of much of their constituency. I am much heartened by this trend for more democracy in business. It is a reaffirmation that Adam Smith's self-interest eventually leads to public good.

12. Energy, the Staff of Life

Subject opinion to coercion: who shall we make your inquisitors? Fallible men were governed by bad passions, by private as well as public reason.

—Thomas Jefferson

Bread is the traditional "staff of life." But, what does bread do in preventing us from starving? It provides energy—energy to power the muscles, energy for the brain, energy to propel a society, energy to improve the quality of life, and energy to give us leisure. Without energy there is no life. Energy is the sun upon which life depends, and the sun itself is the source of all energy. That is a factual statement as well as an allegorical one.

Much of the astounding improvement in the quality of life which has taken place since the industrial revolution has been fueled by the increased production and use of energy. Our profligate use of energy, however, is attacked by some as an evil burden on society. Which is it, the very center of our quality of life or the evil drug to which we have become addicted?

Analyzing the Costs

(Richard) Buckminster Fuller did an inventory of all the earth's resources and concluded that they were adequate to feed the known world population if only they could be distributed properly. The word *if* is a big one, since distribution is a matter of cost—whether expressed in dollar terms or in the expenditure of energy. As uncomfortable as the word *cost* is to those social theorists who study an idealized society, it is a reality which intrudes into every theory when reduced to practice.

Academic liberals tend to dismiss cost as a factor to be taken into account when evaluating their theories. Thus, the old chestnut "Those who can, do, and those who can't, teach" perhaps takes on a more profound meaning than normally intended. If one accepts that there are not limitless resources, then cost is the simple numerical method for measuring the amount of resources consumed. The word *do* in the aphorism is shorthand for "reducing to practice" and represents the ultimate test of those theories in the real world. Particularly in the field of energy utilization, cost is a reality that stares idealism in the face.

If compassion is focused on the people, and especially the poor, energy is an absolute basic requirement. First, of course, energy is needed in the form of food and then as a source of heat. Finally, it augments muscle power in the creation of all the other necessities, such as clothing, shelter, and ultimately leisure.

Compassion should be directed to delivering the maximum amount of energy at the lowest cost. Although that is not easily accepted by liberal theoreticians, it is, in fact, a most powerful, compassionate statement. Since the cost of energy is a much higher percentage of the cost of living for the poor than for the affluent, lowering the cost of energy shows special compassion for the poor.

The regressive nature of increasing the cost of energy is illustrated by data comparing the percentage of income used for all forms of energy by the average family in different income brackets. For the lowest 20 percent of income, energy is a startling 40 percent of income. For the highest 20 percent of income, it is only 10 percent. These figures could be exaggerated because they represent an attempt to measure the energy content of everything we consume. On the other hand, direct outlay for fuel, heat, light, etc., clearly has about twice the impact on the poor's budget than on that of the affluent.

The inescapable fact is that true compassion requires that energy be produced at the lowest possible cost—including the negative cost of environmental damage. Many of our extremist environmental laws do not meet this requirement. Sadly, the environmental benefits of many of those laws are enjoyed to a much greater extent by the middle class and the affluent—a reverse regressivity. It's surprising how few passionate environmentalists realize how elitist their prescriptions usually are.

To the extent that minimizing those environmental by-products adds to the cost of energy, then the impact on the quality of life may, in fact, be to diminish it. Every cent spent on subsidizing so-called clean sources of energy ultimately is funded by taxing the people and taxing them regressively. Is the average 10.8 cents per gallon extra cost of gasoline imposed by the requirements of The Clean Air Act of 1990 any less a tax than the 4.2 cents per gallon imposed so reluctantly by the Congress in 1993? The liberals do not understand that by embracing every environmental cause, they are often oppressing their traditional constituency—the poor!

It was sadly laughable to watch Congress cavalierly interpreting science by not only setting standards for the emissions produced from the gasoline, but essentially acting as the scientific authority for the petroleum industry. They not only set standards but prescribed the components of the gasoline which would presumably produce the desired emissions.

Lawmakers conspicuously avoided the pain of explaining to the public that this measure would add more than ten cents to the price of a gallon of gasoline. Such is the power of the activists and the lack of courage in Congress to call a tax a tax.

I shall not argue the desirability of reducing the side effects of the production and the use of energy, but no one can avoid the responsibility for recognizing that it has a cost, and that this cost reduces its availability in a world of limited resources. The quick and thoughtless response to that is often, "Good, we use too much energy anyway!" Maybe you do and maybe I do, but how about that homeless fellow burning boxes in an alley to keep warm or that family on welfare trying to stay warm or cook their food? When is the negative impact of these measures on the poor clearly set forth in any public debate?

Because of the undesirable side effects of producing this tide of energy, the search for alternate or renewable or cleaner forms of energy has been enshrined as an unquestioned social goal.

A simple question: Is there any useful endeavor in our social system that does not have some undesirable by-products? What about the man who tills the fields to produce food? He winds up with sore muscles, falls into exhausted sleep, and has no free time to read books or enjoy symphonies. We eliminated those by-products of manual labor by making an abundance of energy available. Is it not a utopian dream, comparable to the concept of a risk-free society, that there is any social good that does not have a price?

The extreme environmentalists consider only the cost in terms of environmental damage. The endangered species activists express it in terms of the destruction of whatever species they select in order to express their compassionate need; the naturalist considers it in terms of despoiling pristine beauty, and so on. Each of these is measured on an indeterminate scale of emotional intensity that is different for each of us.

But, about the only known quantitative way of measuring this cost is in dollars! I can hear the screams of indignation. "Typical conservative reaction—enslaved by the almighty dollar, etc., etc." Look at it, though. No one will disagree that each of these goals of reducing the undesirable side effects does have a cost. Cost is a quantitative term. Unfortunately, passion cannot be quantified. Unless the effect can be measured, any reasonable person must ask, "Compared to what?" Monetary cost is society's way of comparing value. Historians have ascribed the creation of money, whether sea shells or gold coins, to a need to create a method of expressing value quantitatively. And, some have even described money as the ultimate quantitative measure of human energy!

Alternative Forms of Energy

Let us go over some of those forms of energy which have been touted as desirable alternatives to fossil fuels.

Solar Energy

Solar energy is one of the most romantic of these. The idea of harvesting energy from that warm, beautiful center of our universe is appealing because "all energy is derived from the sun!" but devising a new mechanism to convert the sun's energy is an awesome task for the scientific community. Billions have been spent upon these schemes with no noticeable success.

I have had much experience with solar energy devices, as I've described previously. But, this was but a drop in the large dollar pool of money spent on this chimera touted as "virtuous" by impractical ideologues. Major oil companies, recognizing their "civic responsibility," have spent enormous sums on such projects, ultimately to abandon them—sums, I might add, extracted from their stockholders. This is yet another hidden tax upon our economy clothed in the golden cloak of compassion.

Other than the fundamental issues of nature versus contrivance, there are many pragmatic reasons why solar energy through artificial collective systems should be viewed with skepticism as a serious alternative major power source. Solar energy can only be used when the sun shines. Query: Would it be more productive to spend the resources to bring water to the desert to produce food from that solar energy, than to spend those resources to produce power? Solar power obtained through artificial devices is very unlikely to become practical except in unusual circumstances. Pursuing this avenue with the hope that scientists will make some magic breakthrough is not something I would bet on.

More than ten years ago, the U.S. Department of Energy (DOE) established the Solar Energy Research Group. It expanded so rapidly that in the early 1980s a large, elaborate building was constructed near Denver, Colorado, housing hundreds of research scientists. Despite the fact that an economically sound solar energy conversion device has never been found; despite the fact that no commercial enterprise of any size has found it a viable business, despite the hundreds of millions of dollars spent by industry, the government's research goes on—and expands!

Since it was formed, the Solar Energy Research Laboratory has gone through a subtle name change. It is now Solar and Renewable Energy Laboratory. In fiscal 1994, their total budget was $347 million. Their projected budget for fiscal 1995 is $397 million. Bureaucracies do not die—they mutate and grow.

Can we afford increasing budgets on projects of such low expectation when the DOE is facing a $200 to $300 billion cost to clean up the severe pollution that exists in many of the DOE facilities, such as Oak Ridge, Tennessee; Hanford, Washington; and others? What is it about government money that makes it immune to the forces of reason, the economic imperatives that guide industry? It's that same old myth that somehow Washington has a bag of money that's different than yours or mine. In fact, it *is* yours and mine.

Completely overlooked by the solar energy enthusiasts is the fact that nature—wonderful nature—has produced the most efficient and by far the best converter of solar energy ever devised: The tree! This fact was finally recognized within the DOE, but they had to invent a pseudoscientific buzz word—*Biomass Energy Production,* which simply means growing wood in some form or other and burning it. Consider this. The tree is a renewable form of energy. It takes the energy from the sun through its leaves, minerals from the soil, and water, when it's available, and stores these in its wood. And, wonder of wonders for all those who are fearfully immobilized by the prospect of global warming, that pseudoscientific scare, the tree consumes carbon dioxide and gives off oxygen. If you burn the tree in order to produce energy, there is a sublime balance. It is a zero sum game; there is no net increase of either carbon dioxide or decrease of oxygen in the ecosystem.

But, who would dare propose such an environmentally sound solar energy system? Destroy the habitat of the spotted owl? Cut down those beautiful forests? They should be preserved for our children—to fall down and oxidize slowly from disease or old age and benefit no one. What about sustainability? Certainly, lumber company after lumber company has demonstrated that trees are a renewable resource. Most companies treat them as a crop—with a ten-year cycle in the Southeast and a thirty-year cycle in the Northwest.

Ethanol

Another often touted renewable alternate fuel is ethanol, which is made from corn or other carbohydrates by fermentation—the same alcohol as in bourbon. Great idea, except that it takes more energy to manufacture the ethanol than is contained in the final product! But, the farm lobby is so strong that they extracted substantial subsidies for the use of ethanol as an "oxygen carrier" to be added to hydrocarbon fuels to improve the emissions. Without subsidy, I doubt whether ethanol could compete in a free market with other alternative oxygen carriers. That subsidy is again a hidden tax, and it's regressive. But, recently it has been mandated— a purely political act to appease the farm lobby.

Nuclear Power

What about atomic energy? The term evokes images of atomic bombs, mass destruction, and awesome loss of life— Nagasaki and Hiroshima! But, we need energy, and we want it to be "clean energy." I state unequivocally that, compared to other methods of producing energy, nuclear power is probably the cleanest known to man. Notice that I have made an interesting word transition here, "nuclear" energy has much less associated imagery to an atomic bomb than does "atomic energy."

Two stories: Walter Murphy, an alumnus of Brooklyn Poly, my university, was the editor of *Industrial and Engineering Chemistry*. After World War II, he was invited, along with other journalists, to join a group of the first civilians witnessing an atomic weapon being exploded on the island of Eniwetok. Along with a couple of friends, we met him on his return. Over drinks he was unusually somber in contrast to his normal ebullient and witty Irish charm. We were dying of curiosity. "Fellows," he said, "I have become a charter member of the 'League of Frightened Men!' " He was visibly shaken as he told us about what he had witnessed. That's the vision almost everyone carries today when the word *atomic* is used. It dominates the imagery whenever the subject of the peaceful use of nuclear energy is considered.

Another story: In 1942 when I went to work at Merck, I found that most of us there had been rejected by the armed forces for various reasons; I was legally blind without my glasses. We brought sandwiches for lunch and played bridge, or had bull sessions and told tall stories. The air was charged with danger and patriotism, as we worked on many secret projects.

During one session, someone asked if anyone knew anything about the Kellex Corporation, a newly formed company that was using large "help wanted" ad displays and hiring engineers at a record clip. They were advertising not just for chemical engineers, but for atomic physicists, metallurgists, and a whole series of other specialties.

I casually mentioned at one of these sessions that I knew of a fabricating company that was building millions of dollars worth of exotic chemical processing equipment for a very secret project designed by Kellex. The equipment was being shipped to some mysterious place in Tennessee where "they" were rumored to have built a whole city behind a barbed wire enclosure. Each of us chimed in with other anecdotes, and our curiosity was aroused.

We compared notes on advertisements we'd seen and rumors we'd heard; we speculated and tested various ideas. Finally, one of the fellows said, "I'll bet they are working on U-235!" Everything fell into place. Someone recalled that physicists had, years before, isolated the uranium isotope with the atomic weight of 235. Existing in ordinary uranium in small percentages, it was "fissionable" and capable of generating enormous amounts of energy.

Then someone also remembered that Niels Bohr, the great Danish physicist, had made the statement that if one could control and sustain the fission of U-235, one pound of that material could supply enough energy to drive a battleship around the world. That was it! The U.S. government was attempting to recover U-235 from uranium so the navy could use it to power the ships, replacing tons of fuel oil.

I was teaching in the graduate school at Poly in the evenings. One of my students worked for Kellex, whose ads had piqued our curiosity. When I ran into him one evening, I mischievously said to him, "Hi Fred, how's the U-235 going?" His face blanched and he blurted out, "How did you know?" "Oh I just guessed" was my flippant reply as I left him visibly shaken.

The next morning, I received an urgent call from the Merck head office asking me to come over immediately because two gentlemen wanted to see me. I met these ominous looking people in a private office, and they flashed their identification as U.S. Army Secret Service. They shot out, "What do you know about U-235?" Trembling with fear and apprehension, I repeated the story and how it had developed. After much quizzing, they finally admonished me not to ever mention U-235 again or speculate about it at all. All the participants in our group were then summoned over and one by one sent back with the same stern warnings.

There are two points to this story. One is the wonder of how a few people with no special training in atomic fission could stitch together a secret like this from a jumble of isolated facts, a few rumors, and curiosity. That's espionage in its elemental form—no cloak and dagger stuff at all. The CIA employs thousands of people. Not more than a few percent of them act out the romantic, dangerous role you see in the movies. The rest do, in an organized way, what we did in those conversations at lunch. It's really astonishing what a well-kept secret the Manhattan Project was.

The other point, which is more related to what we are discussing, is that our country's specific use for the U-235, though horrible, did hasten the end of the war. We amateurs, on the other hand, thought of U-235 not as a weapon, but as a remarkably efficient and lightweight source of power and energy. Indeed, it took great mechanical ingenuity for the men and women at Los Alamos to use that fission energy in such a way as to result in the awesome destructive power of the atomic bomb. The cost of developing it as a simple, cheap power source would have been much less. Niels Bohr was on the right track.

We learned later that our speculation about the use of U-235 to produce power was indeed studied in those early days, but the bomb was deemed to be more urgent. Nuclear power was conceived to be the ideal propulsion for a submarine and, indeed, it was and is. Nuclear power changes the submarine into a true underwater vessel eliminating the need for enormous gulps of air before going underwater again for short stays.

It's ironic that Albert Einstein, the epitome of the peaceful, impractical dreamer, should be the one who convinced President Roosevelt that the power of the atom should be used to kill people rather than as a new source of propulsive power, as Bohr had predicted.

After Winston Churchill's famed speech at Fulton, Missouri, where he recognized the start of the cold war by Stalin, our monopoly of the atom bomb was our singular answer. The Atomic Energy Commission (AEC) became an enormous bureaucratic force. But, there were many engineers and scientists who hailed the other power of U-235. Cheap, limitless power to improve our standard of living was in sight, and yet, our country embarked upon a headlong rush to build more atomic weapons. The nuclear bomb overshadowed the glory of the electricity, heat, and power that could be produced so cheaply and relatively effortlessly. It's rather ironic that what Professor Fermi did under the University of Chicago grandstands was to build a rudimentary nuclear power reactor in the first sustained and controlled nuclear fission. He did not build a bomb!

Do I deplore building of the bomb? It certainly hastened the end of a brutal war and that's a plus, but it had a serious side effect. The bomb was so horrible that it scared people away from using nuclear power to provide cheap, non-polluting power.

Is nuclear power safe, given the events at Three Mile Island? *Nuclear meltdown* has been the scare term of the antinuclear forces, and Three Mile Island seemed to prove the doomsayers right.

In fact, the accident at Three Mile Island proved the doomsayers to be absolutely *wrong*. There was a partial "nuclear meltdown" at Three Mile Island, but it was completely contained in the pressure vessel surrounding the plant. And, the safety systems, even though they were early designs, still contained the accident.

Remember, Three Mile Island was one of the earliest nuclear power plants. It was designed when safety systems were still in the early stages of development. Yet, it survived the most unimaginable combination of design faults, construction errors, and poorly trained operating personnel. It would be difficult for any designer or operator of such a complicated plant to imagine or project the odds of such an unconnected set of conditions coming together at one time. Yet—and this is the whole point—*there were absolutely no fatalities*. There has been no evidence of radiation sickness and no visible destruction of any kind except within the plant. With all the things going wrong—faulty valves, bad welding, operators opening the incorrect valves, and on and on—the safety system and redundancy built into this early plant still worked. They worked in spite of all the dumb things that happened.

But, the alarmists say, "What about the long-range effects which will not show up for forty years or more?" The politics of "projected fear" is one of the most immoral and reprehensible tools of the advocates of the "risk-free society." When they (the emotional antinukes) found that Three Mile Island did not produce the cataclysmic disaster they had predicted, they weakly fell back on that most fatuous of all arguments: "Well we don't know that it won't produce radiation sickness thirty or forty years from now! Therefore, let's not take a chance." The teeth-chattering fear of the seekers of a risk-free society immobilizes us.

Today, Three Mile Island is synonymous with disaster. But, it should be screamed from the house tops what a great example it was of how much care was put into guarding against human error. The fail-safe features in the design were tested to the limit, and they worked! Because of hysteria, nuclear power is becoming infeasible due to the cost imposed by monumental overdesign and the enormous bureaucratic and political roadblocks thrown up by the antinuclear forces.

It might be useful at this point to use Tom Hayden to illustrate liberal ambivalence toward nuclear power. The positions he often takes are good examples of liberal compassion turned corrosive.

Hayden, a radical in college, got public notoriety with the Port Huron Statement in 1962, articulated by a coterie of left-wing activists he headed. What he said then was "With nuclear energy, whole cities can easily be powered, yet the dominant nation-states seem more likely to unleash destruction greater than that incurred in all wars of human history." Later in that same document, it was recommended that

> every nation must build an adequate infrastructure (transportation, communication, land resources, waterways) for future industrial growth; there must be industries suited to the rapid development of differing raw materials and other resources; education must begin on a continuing basis for everyone in the society, especially including engineering and technical training; technical assistance from outside sources must be adequate to meet present and long-term needs; atomic power plants must spring up to make electrical energy available.

By the late 1970s, after he married Jane Fonda, he adopted her ferocious antinuclear stand. In the fall of 1979, they embarked on a fifty-city tour to promote "economic democracy," a euphemistic cover-up for pure Socialist doctrine. During this tour, antinuclear speeches were featured. In a magazine interview, he said, "I want to affect the politics of the next President, to make solar power versus nuclear power and economic democracy versus corporate power the issues in the United States." This statement exemplifies how zealots or arrogant elitists of Hayden's stripe can take the core of well-motivated liberal compassion and turn it into a political fire bomb by word manipulation. Substitute *free market system* for *corporate power* and *socialism* for *economic democracy* and the issue is joined properly. Then, compare the use of our scarce resources to produce solar power versus atomic power. How many of these resources will be taken from the disadvantaged to pay for the substantially higher cost of solar power? This is a distorted model of liberal compassion that demeans the essential core of liberal thought.

What about Chernobyl? This was an old-fashioned carbon pile reactor. We had a similar, but much safer, one known as the "N" reactor at Hanford, Washington. That has been shut down, but the Chernobyl design was one we would never use here. It has a positive temperature factor, i.e., elevated temperatures tend to accelerate meltdown, whereas all of ours have a negative temperature factor. It is known that the International Nuclear Energy Commission tried in vain to convince Russia not to build Chernobyl, but they ignored all warnings.

There isn't any method of producing power without risk. Indeed the number of fatalities resulting from building and operating fossil fuel power plants (by far the major source of power in the U.S.) is a matter of record. Add to this the environmental impact from burning the coal (and the loss in life from mining the coal), and the damage to society is obvious. Yet, death from nuclear exposure seems somehow crueler than death from falling at a construction site. Compare the safety record of existing nuclear power plants against alternate power sources and there is absolutely no contest. I state unequivocally that nuclear power is the safest source of power available. And, don't forget, it would not contribute at all to global warming, which should comfort another group of zealots.

What about cost? Here's where the apostles of the no-risk society have harmed us irreparably with a sneaky punch below the belt. Under the guise of protecting us from unknown and, as far as I'm concerned, totally unreasonable dangers, they burden us with excessive regulation costs. The costs of the permitting process, the bureaucratic inertia, and inciting and exploiting the fears of nearby neighbors are astounding. Many experts have estimated that nuclear power plants could be built at less than half the current costs—and be just as safe—if it weren't for excessive regulation.

The only way around the bureaucratic maze is to develop a single standardized design incorporating all the desirable safety features. The French have done this, and they produce more than 70 percent of their energy from atomic power.

Even with a standardized design, there is no way of anticipating the added cost of NIMBY, the commonly used acronym for "Not in My Back Yard!" The forces of no-risk exploit this fear of anything nuclear. They shamelessly use the courts and the media to force their unreasonable fears upon us.

Finally, I'd like to respond to the naysayers who ask about the disposal of spent fuel rods. The technology is in place and has been used commercially in France and England to reprocess these rods to recover plutonium (another good source of atomic energy), unused uranium, and highly radioactive residue. Why don't we build such plants? One reason is that it is an additional, and somewhat difficult to control, source of plutonium which makes a dandy atomic bomb. During the cold war, this was a worry, but should be less so now. Another impediment is the endless debate about what to do with the high-reactive residue. Our company, along with many others, has been studying this problem for the DOE for many years, and a multitude of solutions have been devised.

One system that is already in use in England and France casts these radioactive wastes in molten glass inside of heavy stainless steel drums. When the glass is solidified, these drums are stored deep underground. This could be done here in volcanic tuff in Nevada (at a site already selected). These same drums also could be stored more than two thousand feet underground in caverns surrounded by hundreds of feet of dense solid salt (the WIPP project). It's interesting that use of the WIPP project facility is being delayed by states concerned about the transporting of the drums of nuclear waste to the storage site. Out of fear, they have refused to allow the rail cars carrying the waste to pass through their states.

Very few people know that the Allied Chemical Company, encouraged by the government, built a nuclear fuel reprocessing plant in Barnwell, South Carolina, in the late seventies. This plant, costing hundreds of millions of dollars is idle and unused today—it was never even started up. For some inexplicable reason, President Carter signed an order canceling the start-up just as it was ready to go.

The anti-nuclear forces are fervent and determined. Fired by their holy mission, they attack all of the steps in the nuclear cycle because disrupting one step stops the whole process. What happens now to the depleted nuclear rods used in a power plant? They are stored in large "swimming pools" waiting for a decision to be made on how they should be handled. Frankly, that method of storage scares me. Why not reprocess the fuel at Barnwell? I've never heard a satisfactory answer to that. The technology already in use seems very reasonable and certainly is far superior to storing the rods in swimming pools. So, why the delay? The regulatory agencies, at the urging of the antinuclear crowd, have stipulated that these methods of storage must be shown to be effective for ten thousand years. Why ten thousand years and not one thousand years or even five hundred, when that would clearly be better than the existing swimming pools? I don't know the answer to that. As far as I can tell, the requirement is arbitrary, but it serves the activists' needs for a major stumbling block. Is there anyone who can predict what kind of natural disasters will happen over the next ten thousand years?

Here's a story that will illustrate the absurdity of the extremes of risk avoidance that have been imposed. A team of scientists were assigned to devise a method for being certain that future generations would know that dangerous nuclear wastes were stored at one of these sites. Would any language, signs, symbols or barriers exist one hundred thousand years from now? Would anyone understand them? What new language might be in use? I shudder to think of the tax dollars and valuable technical brains wasted studying such absurdities. Meanwhile, rods are piling up dangerously in swimming pools and are not being reprocessed or stored in some manner that will only be safe for even one thousand years. This is the myth of the risk-free society freezing us into immobility and depriving us of the benefits of cheap, safe power, with minimal environmental hazard.

What is sad is the lack of recognition other good energy projects have received. Many have been halted in their tracks by the risk-avoiders and the manipulators of NIMBY. I remember one that is the epitome of misplaced compassion.

In the late seventies, the OPEC cartel raised the cost of crude oil above thirty dollars per barrel (from two dollars to five dollars before then). President Carter, in a rousing speech, called for the development of alternate sources of hydrocarbon fuels. He dubbed the massive engineering effort he proposed as "The Moral Equivalent of War."

Billions were poured into alternative routes to crude oil— oil sands, coal conversion (as South Africa had done), the extraction of oil from extensive deposits of Western oil shale, and many other schemes.

Industries were turned inside out based upon confident predictions that crude oil would ultimately reach five dollars or more per barrel. The engineering and construction industry virtually doubled in size as these massive projects were taken on. The effort collapsed in the early eighties (a very tough time for our company—but that's another story) when the monopoly was broken, as all monopolies eventually are, and the price of crude dropped precipitously. What happened? The free market system triumphed again with the discovery of substantial quantities of oil, notably in the North Sea. The higher price of oil and the projected future prices made it worthwhile to explore for oil in very difficult areas. The costs to produce oil in these places, though more than Saudi Arabia's, were still way below the artificial prices established by OPEC. All the elaborate schemes and the billions of dollars invested in the alternate fuels effort in the U.S. went down the drain. Carter's "Moral Equivalent of War" was now tagged with the derisive acronym "MEOW."

During this crisis time, Southern California Edison, which owned power plants that operated on fuel oil or natural gas, came up with a brilliant concept. They decided to build a giant coal-fired plant on the Kaporowitz Plateau, a vast desert wasteland near where California, Nevada, and Utah intersect. There were sizable coal deposits in the hills several miles from the proposed plant site. Their plan included mining the coal, delivering it by conveyor to the plant, and returning the ash to fill in depressions left by the mining process. Because of the size and close proximity of the coal, Southern California Edison could have produced power for the people of Los Angeles at an extremely low cost.

The public relations attack on this brilliant plan was so unrelenting, bitter, and devastating that the utility finally had to abandon the project completely.

Why was it attacked? The plant was some twenty-five miles or so from the beautiful Bryce and Zion National Parks. Though it was agreed that winds in that area would, most of the year, disperse any particulate matter coming from the stacks (which were to have elaborate stack cleaning devices), there would nevertheless be a few days a year when these winds would not be there. On those few days, the obscuration of the views of the scenery would be reduced by 5 percent—or less.

Who was the popular leader of the attack upon this project? Robert Redford, who had a house in that area, was the much publicized defender of NIMBY. Just as out of a movie, he was the pure-hearted hero galloping forth on his mission of mercy, white teeth gleaming and blond locks flowing as he attacked the monsters of "big business." He could not stop clouds or storms or wind-whipped sand from obscuring the view, but he could stop Southern California Edison and did, almost single-handedly. Fifteen years later, the utility has had to build more power plants in the Los Angeles basin, where the winds rarely disperse the particulate matter and we have smog. The cost of electricity has increased substantially.

Had Robert Redford or his adoring followers thought through their zeal, they would have concluded, as I do, that their actions adversely affected the poor in the ghettos of Los Angeles. Instead, these activists single-mindedly satisfied their moral greed by giving the elite sightseers of the Bryce and Zion areas relief from minor obstruction of their view a few days a year. Unfortunately, they also increased the price of electricity to the poor in the process.

As much as anything, this chapter illustrates, in stark terms, how compassion, when "reduced to practice," can produce bad results. In the presumably compassionate drive for alternate energy, we use up very precious resources that might be better spent elsewhere. The direct result is a regressive and unfair burden placed upon the poor.

In attempting to make sense out of this welter of technology, we should take what the engineers call the "systems approach." If someone lives in the country near a running stream, perhaps it makes economic sense for him to put in a small water wheel to generate power. If he is out in the desert with no utility transmission lines nearby, it might make sense for him to use solar cells. Wind power would make sense in other places. Indeed, windmills were common on many farms until the government subsidized rural electrification and built central power plants.

What irony that the same government should now subsidize a return to windmills. A systems approach with free market choice is the only sensible solution to this quagmire.

13. The Freudian Slip

Sometimes it is said that man cannot be trusted with the government of himself. Can he then, be trusted with the government of others.

—Thomas Jefferson

The *American Bar Association Journal* recently cited a case in which a defense lawyer insisted that indulging in pornography was a form of intoxication, and thus reason to mitigate the sentence an Indiana man received for rape and murder. He claimed that his client suffered from sexual sadism because of pornography, rendering him unable to gauge the wrongfulness of his conduct.

The following case was reported in the 6 June 1994 issue of *Time* magazine:

> Moosa Hanoukai . . . bludgeoned his wife Manijeh to death. When the businessman did not contest the facts, prosecutors assumed they had an easy second degree murder conviction. But Hanoukai's attorney said his client was a victim of husband battering and 25 years of abuse. Because of the stringencies of an Iranian-Jewish culture, Hanoukai felt trapped and killed Manijeh because he was not allowed to divorce her.

The jury found Hanoukai guilty only of voluntary manslaughter. Instead of fifteen years to life, he may serve a prison term as brief as four and a half years.

Another lawyer in Milwaukee coined the term *cultural psychosis* to explain why an inner-city teen-ager killed another for her leather coat.

257

The criminal justice system is "on the verge of a crisis of credibility," says Los Angeles District Attorney Gil Garcetti. He admits that in the Menendez brothers' cases, he and his team underestimated "the emotional pull" the abuse defense had on the jurors.

Damion Williams, who attacked truck driver Reginald Denny, used the "black rage" defense and was acquitted of attempted murder, despite the graphic video taken of the attack. He was convicted only of the much lesser charge of felony mayhem.

From these revealing stories, the crushing conclusion is that there has been an alarming change in our values. What has happened? The fundamental force at work here is a faulty Freudian psychology.

Looking at the whole of modern social thought and the bulk of the prescriptions generated by the liberal intellectuals, it is apparent that Freudian precepts form the basis for much of our modern political actions. Freudianism has been adopted as the basic psychological and behavioral guide from which many of the modern laws have been derived. It is especially true of those laws which are used to implement compassion.

Our social structure contains not just distortions of Freud's work, but outright misreading of it. "Neo-Freudian" doctrine corrupts our political system and our educational methodology. It promotes the myth of a risk-free society and corrupts compassion. The most serious distortion, however, is in the cult of the "victim."

There is a trend in modern social justice to absolve people of responsibility for their crimes against society. The flawed neo-Freudian theory holds that outside forces, either in the family or the community, are ultimately responsible for anti-social behavior.

In his last published work, *Civilization And Its Discontents*, Sigmund Freud said, "All that I have exposed in the forces of the unconscious as motivation for individuals must not be used to excuse pathological acts against others."

Admirable compassion turns destructive if we assume that people have little control over what happens to them.

The morally devastating paternalism of compassion, carried too far, spawns the "victim" thesis. Indeed, Freud's "talk therapy" had as its purpose the identification of the forces affecting a person's behavior in order for the patient to be able to exercise control and to assume responsibility for his own behavior. A successful therapy strived to free a patient from *becoming* a victim of those external forces.

Despite those who are currently debunking Freud and his works, I believe he will still be recognized as having effected a revolution in the study of mental and emotional health. Though many of his theories enjoy only scattered scientific support, and some were pure flights of fancy, he nevertheless gave us great intuitive insight into the forces that mold people's behavior. In explaining the outside forces that influence people, his primary drive was to explain to his patients the sources of their unhappiness or anti-social behavior. There was an implicit assumption that the patient would then alter his behavior. Freud's studies were essentially of abnormal psychology, i.e., aberrational behavior. He studied unhappy and troubled people and tried to help them understand their unhappiness and to free them of an unhealthy reaction to their environment. He sought to help people not to be victimized.

Since the era of Freud and his disciples, another psychology has gained stature. Led by Abraham Maslow, these psychologists have studied the activities of happy, motivated, and successful people. Maslow's recognition of the "self-actualization" process and how it impels successful and socially acceptable behavior is the exact opposite of the study of abnormal and unhappy people, which was Freud's arena. In the starkest terms, Freud studied the psychology of despair, of failure, of disconnection from society, and of morbidity, whereas Maslow, et al., studied success, victory, realism, and happiness.

Freud observed and catalogued the dark sides of our psyche. Maslow celebrated the positive and bright sides of our psyche. The faith that Maslow expresses in the ability of people to be "self-actualizing" is, unfortunately, rarely reflected in any social legislation that we enact. That is a major complaint of conservatives, who put Maslow's view of man at the core of their formulae for compassionate programs. They realize that there are many more people with self-actualizing attributes than the liberals acknowledge.

It appears contradictory that liberal-inspired social engineering should use the neo-Freudian model. The liberals' unrestrained vision and their belief in the perfectibility of man should conflict with the essentially dark Freudian view.

Perhaps the compassionate impulse that is so essential to liberal self-esteem produces this anomaly, for one of the requirements for expressing that compassion is to have an object, or person, or group of people who need that compassion. The deeper the need, the greater the emotional satisfaction derived by the one performing the compassionate act. The emotional need to feel good about one's self is well served by defining the imperfect, the dependent, the victim, the miscreant, and the helpless as one's constituency. That makes the liberal's social prescription more urgent. The worth of these programs to the compassionate liberals is thereby increased, and their own sense of worthiness is reinforced. How can one be compassionate toward a Maslowian "self-actualizer"? But, isn't the encouragement of the self-actualizer instinct in our citizens just as worthy a goal? We believe there are many more self-actualizers than liberals realize. Ours is a much more optimistic view of our people.

Furthermore, the conservatives recognize that only a small percentage of people are either one or the other—unhappy and dependent or, in contrast, self-actualizing and independent. All of us have elements of both within us. Much religious and philosophic thought has embraced this dichotomy of man.

Since the conservatives' vision of compassionate formulae is always tempered by our sense that the marketplace (i.e., the "people") may know more than the elite do, we have difficulty in competing with the liberals' vision of the inherent superiority of their compassion. Theirs is a theoretical construct, and ours is claimed to be superior only in the reduction to practice. Do the liberals know their "market"?

Are they misjudging it just as GM did? Is their market the pathological model of neo-Freudian vision, or is it something else? In fact, the market consists mostly of people who have instincts for both dependence and independence. The question is, which impulse should be appealed to, or reinforced, in designing social policy? The weakness of the liberal vision may be its view that its constituency is constructed only on the neo-Freudian model of pathology, i.e., the primacy of the unconscious, uncontrolled desire, dependency, victimization, and lack of responsibility for our own actions. As a result, their beautifully constructed visions are designed to serve an unreal and incompletely defined constituency.

By developing their prescriptions primarily for those who "need" to be cared for, they create a burgeoning constituency of people "in need." People are seduced into believing that dependency brings them immediate rewards, rather than understanding that the desire to be independent sometimes offers more valuable, though perhaps delayed, rewards. If "great big government" is saying, "You will be rewarded if you are dependent," who can resist? Even those who have an urge to be free are tempted.

The Controlling Elite

So much energy and intellectual debate have centered on the nature-versus-nurture argument as to liken it to deciding how many angels can dance on the head of a pin. Freudian precepts led to the extreme positions of behaviorists such as B. F. Skinner, who posited that a child is born as a blank slate upon which external forces, i.e., the social environment, make their imprint. I once saw him on a TV interview, seriously suggesting that if he were given a just-born child in an isolated room he could, by applying the proper stimuli, raise a model citizen. I remember thinking at the time, "What arrogance! Pray tell, Professor Skinner, what omnipotent, perfect person of unchallenged values will decide what those proper stimuli are? You? And furthermore, whose specification of the perfect citizen will be used? Yours?" There flashed before me the vision of the Brave New World of Aldous Huxley and its chilling portrayal of the ultimate genetically engineered and centrally controlled society.

The extremes of Skinner's behaviorism have since been discredited, and most thoughtful people will acknowledge that both heredity and environment influence a person's behavior. Arguing about which is more important or trying to apportion the influence of each of them is fruitless. More than likely, their relative influence is different in each person, depending upon the strengths of the acquired characteristics or the intensity of the environmental influences. Conclusions based upon averages of any classification can be terribly misleading when applied to a particular situation. Thus, Charles Murray's book *The Bell Curve* has been repeatedly misunderstood by those who attack him.

It occurs to me that the allegorical novel *Brave New World* and its author reinforce these prints. It's ironic that Aldous Huxley, an intellectual leader of the Left in Hollywood, should write a novel so devastating to the vision of the controlled society, which grew from the Socialist model. The grandson of the famous English biologist Thomas Huxley, Aldous, the author, was at the center of the liberal intelligentsia in the Hollywood of the 1930s. Well before George Orwell's chilling novel *1984*, he depicted the ultimate horror of state control of human behavior.

The civilization Huxley portrayed started with the creation of human beings *in vitro*—in a glass jar. This was a far-out, fanciful idea at the time, but today's genetic engineering advances suggest that the idea is not that far-fetched. The people so produced were programmed for specific niches in society, from laborers to managers to intellectuals. They lived in a society that was completely controlled, and their every action was dictated by a pervasive hierarchy. The novel's protagonists are a couple who did not come out as programmed, who were biological aberrations or "sports."

Their conflict with the ultimate command-and-control society is the basis of the book's plot. Socialist and Marxist advocates did not see in this story the foreshadowing of the destruction of their own ideological dreams. They thought of it only as an indictment of the Fascist dictatorship of

Hitler. Little did they realize that their Marxist ideology would, in Russian hands, turn into a mirror image of fascism, for the great Russian experiment was to create a "Brave New World," modeled upon Socialist political doctrine. Thus, the compassionate ones shall shelter the less well endowed people through some form of "command and control," carried out according to formulas devised by the intellectual elite.

Huxley did not recognize, as many sociologists have since then, that the "dictatorship of the proletariat" is, in practice, not much different from the dictatorship of a "man on horseback"; both oppress those they claim to free. "The Brave New World" was as much an accurate portrayal of the Socialist society as that of a Fascist dictatorship.

The transformation of compassionately driven programs into "entitlements" probably has a neo-Freudian origin. If someone is a "victim," with no control over, or responsibility for, his actions, then he is incapable of "earning" the rewards to which he would then be "entitled." If a person has been conditioned by his environment to be devoid of self-reliance, then the "creators" of the environment take on the responsibility for providing the very need which they have themselves created.

Without a doubt, there are people who are virtually helpless under particular circumstances. However, the false neo-Freudian perception that such helplessness pervades the population leads to serious excesses.

The enormous increase in the cost of many supposedly compassionate programs coincided with the time when the term "entitlements" was used to describe them. One of the reasons I am concerned about what may seem to be a minor shift in terminology is that it reflects the existence of a hidden component of compassion. I've seen, time after time, the undercurrent of resentment in those who receive charity, i.e., those to whom we are compassionate. It is not socially acceptable to exhibit anything but gratitude for compassionate acts. But, deeply sublimated (a Freudian term!) is a resentment at the dependency which is created.

This resentment, in fact, has an important role to play

because it can serve a useful purpose; to provide a stimulus to escape from the sense of obligation and the dependency created when people receive compassion in the form of "charity." However, when these compassionate programs are labeled as entitlements, the sense that they are "earned" or "deserved" lessens the need to escape from a sense of obligation.

The doctrine of the "victim" validates the need for compassion. At the same time, it deprives the object of that compassion any measure of control over his condition. By using the victim model, the liberal programs simply reinforce their lack of respect for their constituency.

By not accepting that there are innate moral values in people, liberal compassion very often corrupts the people who receive it. If people are morally neutral, they have no natural force to free them from the influence of their surroundings. It takes a moral sense, as James Wilson points out, to avoid being victimized by one's social environment. Michael Novak more sublimely calls it a belief in God.

The habit of generalizing from specific examples is common with liberals. When programs designed for the truly helpless are extended to those people who can partially help themselves, the latter are converted to a "class" of people who now absolutely must have our help. Are we not thus creating a new form of slavery? Will anyone deny that we have institutionalized welfare dependency?

The conservatives want to limit their compassion to the narrowest segment and to give the people as much say in establishing their need as is practical. Because we believe that most people have a social dimension that includes a moral sense, conservative compassion will seek to reinforce that moral sense.

If social actions make it rewarding to be dependent, then that is the characteristic that will be reinforced. People quickly find that it "pays" to be dependent. The principles of negative and positive reinforcement are basic to behavioral modification. Most liberal legislation reflects the reinforcement of dependency.

Compassion implies an inequality which leads to the

elitist view: "I (or we) know what's best for them." Is the conservative moral posture any better than the liberal? Not necessarily. But, since we start with a higher regard for the people, we are less arrogant about imposing our solutions upon them too broadly.

Liberal social programs are corrupted by two forces. First, the proponent of the social action wants to cast as large a shadow as possible. Once enacted into law, the bureaucracy has its own internal need to grow. They are judged primarily by the numbers of people in their group and the number of people covered by their regulatory umbrella. They have an understandable need to extend their power and control. And, there is no downside risk! How many bureaucracies have failed and gone out of business?

Social Security is a prime example of a compassionately driven program in which good intentions have been corrupted and expanded exponentially. The Social Security system began in 1935 during the Great Depression. It was initially designed to be a government-supported pension plan that would provide retirement benefits for those who did not have company retirement programs or who were incapable of saving enough money for their old age. However, it has now become an entitlement for everyone who works and many who don't. It has been described as a middle-class welfare system.

As originally conceived, the government was to take 1 percent of the first three thousand dollars of each employee's salary as a payroll tax and another 1 percent from employers. The most each person would pay into Social Security would be thirty dollars a year, with the employer matching that for a total of sixty dollars. The government would then invest the money in interest-bearing accounts or government bonds and pay benefits based on the earning power of the funds each individual paid in (along with the employer's contributions).

In 1937, however, before the first benefit check was paid, a commission inexplicably recommended two very far-reaching changes, which were adopted in 1939. The first change expanded the types of people who could receive benefits and did away with the insurance aspect, i.e., the investment of the premium to earn additional income to pay future benefits. It was little recognized at the time how devastating these changes would turn out to be. Keynesian economists apparently dominated that commission, and they feared that the huge pool of savings generated by Social Security would depress the economy (something we hardly fear today!). So, the system became "pay-as-you-go"—current retirees get their money from taxes collected each year. The surplus collections were merely expropriated for use in the general fund. The myth persists to this day that this is an "insurance" program, but it is not!

The second change made spouses, widows, and children of retirees eligible for Social Security benefits. Those "survivors" benefits show that Social Security more closely resembles a welfare program than a pension plan, because the family of the working man is covered, not just the worker. Today, with the disabled and others, virtually every citizen has Social Security benefits. Social Security payments have escalated until today they represent almost 15 percent of payroll.

In 1972—just as inflation started to rage—Congress started indexing benefits to the cost of living, and that let the tiger loose. If the premiums had been invested as they should have been, the earning power of the premiums would have protected against inflation.

In 1950, there were sixteen working adults paying Social Security taxes for each retired person. By 1970, the figure had dropped to three workers for every retiree. Now, it is projected that this ratio will worsen so that by the year 2020 or so, there will only be two workers for every retiree. To maintain benefits, some economists project that payroll taxes may have to exceed 30 percent. Contrast that with the original premium of 2 percent!

I can't resist quoting from a column by Paul Magnusson in a recent issue of *Business Week*. In it, Magnusson deflated a recent pledge by President Clinton to tell "everyone every year what is in his Social Security account." In a letter to his seven-year-old daughter, Magnusson showed that Clinton was either misleading people or perhaps didn't even know that there was no such thing.

Dear Elizabeth,

Pay attention, Sweetheart, because this gets compli-cated. Even the President gets it wrong. I'm very sorry, but there's no money in your Social Security account and never will be. That's because no one has her own Social Security account. Instead, people send 7.6% of their pay to Washington, their bosses match it, and it's spent right away paying Social Security and medi-cal benefits to older folks. And what's left over is spent on other important things, such as aircraft carriers, national parks, and foreign travel for members of Congress.

Meanwhile, the Treasury Dept., which pays all the government's bills, replaces the money it borrows with IOU's. Of course, the Treasury Dept. has to pay inter-est. So it just sends more IOU's to the Trust Fund. That's how the Trust Fund is really "invested"—in IOU's, to be paid by future taxpayers. That's you!

All this will change in 2013, when you turn 26. That's when the first wave of Baby Boomers—including me—starts retiring. Since there are so many of us, there won't be enough money coming in from payroll taxes to pay for our retirement. So you'll have to start pay-ing back the IOUs through your regular income tax. Then you'll pay for my retirement through your regu-lar Social Security payroll tax. Whew! Your tax rates will have to be pretty high! I hope you'll feel my generation spent your money wisely.

Love,
Dad

To demonstrate how far the Social Security system has strayed from its original intent, I cite my own case.

The week after my seventieth birthday, there appeared in the mail a check for something like $2,600 from the Social Security office. I was notified that, having reached seventy, my wife and I were to receive monthly checks from that time on. I was unaware that I was entitled to these payments, nor had I requested them. They continue to come to this day, increased by COLA to about $3,000 per month.

Did I need this retirement benefit? Absolutely not. I am well paid by our company. Since I don't need the Social Security payment should I return it? Absolutely not. The government in all likelihood would waste it on some frivolous scheme. I'd rather give it to the Jacobs Family Foundation, where I know it will be spent wisely.

The irony is that private pension funds are administered by a particularly rigid bureaucratic group enforcing the Employee Retirement Income Security Act (ERISA). They force companies to publicize and account for underfunding. Since their benchmark "projected" earnings on pension funds are very conservative, they have forced companies like GM to take enormous hits on their balance sheets to account for future underfunded liabilities. Even though GM is earning considerably more from their pension funds than the ERISA yardsticks, they are still forced to use the government mandated rates by bureaucratic fiat. I wonder how the government can be made to face up to the unfunded liabilities of the Social Security system and to declare the system bankrupt.

Why have I diverted into this discourse on Social Security? Because it is an example of the intrusion of psychological doctrine into social engineering. Now that Social Security payments are virtually universal, the concept of "victim" has been expanded to encompass everyone, whether they are real victims or not. From a relatively small group who could properly be classed as "victims" of the Great Depression, the program has now expanded to cover literally everybody—and most people still have the delusion that they are paying "insurance premiums." By government action, my wife and I have been classified as "victims" who are unable to provide for our retirement!

The victimization paradigm is only one example of the influence of neo-Freudian thought on our social system. There are other effects that may actually be more important.

Moral relativism is a modern, cultist, pseudointellectual

belief that saps our moral fiber. Many have come to question the concept that morality is the basis for guiding one's behavior in a society. The premise has been denigrated and demeaned for many by the claim that it has no basis in science. Most importantly, moral relativism is a second-order derivative of the paradigm of the victim: If there is no moral dimension to the so-called victim, then he has no standards or resources which allow him to *resist* becoming a victim. This is, of course, the role that religion traditionally played, before the secular rejection of a moral sense spawned the cult of the "victim."

In *The Moral Sense*, James Q. Wilson takes the amoral or morally neutral crowd head-on. He argues for the existence of a moral sense from pragmatic observation of the way people act, rather than from a religious stance, and he supports it with a wealth of recent behavioral studies that confirm that morality is innate and has evolved over millennia.

Wilson's point is that moral neutrality is, in effect, an endorsement, or at least an acceptance of, immorality, for if one cannot define or articulate moral values, then one certainly cannot define *immorality*. And, if you can't define it, how can you deplore it?

Why is the moral sense important? Because it is the very foundation of the need to be compassionate, which is a virtue to be prized.

Many liberals will be caught in a dilemma here. They allege the moral superiority of their compassion, yet at the same time they often deny the existence of a moral sense, or they ignore its existence in their constituency. Their conferring of special virtue to their compassion thus becomes suspect.

To lay it out more clearly, the liberal dominance of all of the compassionate programs, from welfare to environmentalism, has two glaring weaknesses. The first is the faulty neo-Freudian assumption that most people are victims. From that, it is inferred that if they are victims, they have no control of their lives. And, if they have no control of their lives, then "We, the elitists (read: Government, the state, the bureaucracy) shall protect them and insulate them from those who victimize them." Completely disregarded are the internal strengths that people have and their need to be free.

If moral relativism is accepted, then these compassionate programs have no moral content—and that is the second weakness. They are mechanistic and concentrate on material values, deliberately avoiding moral dimensions with the excuse that these are subjective. Not having any moral content, they thus make the recipients mere chattel in the crudest way—not unlike slaves in the service of a benevolent plantation owner.

As Wilson, Sowell, and many other writers have pointed out, the programs that have the best results in getting disadvantaged youngsters out of the cycle of crime, drugs, teenage pregnancy, and despair, are those that enforce discipline, responsibility, and accountability. It is only when these youngsters finally believe that they have control of their lives and that rewards come only when they are earned by them, that they start to become—and are "entitled" to be—productive citizens. We conservatives call it "tough love." In society, as in the family, self-respect or self-esteem is earned, not given.

What liberals fail to understand is that most human beings are not only capable of taking care of themselves, they are also quite resilient. When they have an opportunity to learn just how capable and resilient they are, they develop self-reliance—a prerequisite for personal responsibility in a free society.

Neo-Freudianism in the Courtroom

I have so far avoided taking on the legal profession as that, I fear, would be a book in itself. It is probably true that the arena in which neo-Freudianism has become most solidly entrenched is in our courts. This is due, in part, to the "contingency fee," which puts the lawyer's self-interest ahead of his client's. As lawyers search harder and deeper for "facts" to support their cases, they are led into the pseudoscientific world of psychology, in which there are as many so-called experts as there are opinions. The Menendez case is a stark example. Another is the case of a college instructor who sexually harassed a female student. When fired, he claimed discrimination because he suffered from impulse control disorder.

How is that for psychobabble? The case was appealed to the U.S. Supreme Court, which ruled against him. A banal story to illustrate a serious subject.

The federal law barring discrimination against persons with disabilities (originally meant to be "physical" disabilities) has spawned all sorts of absurdities. A decision to reimburse drug addicts whose addiction was considered to be a "disability" was featured in a "60 Minutes" program. Apparently, large payments are given to an addict's "guardian" (sometimes the local liquor store owner!) to spend upon, guess what?

What is the motivating force behind these cases? Compassion, of course! But, is the heart-thumping, virtuous, emotional surge that one associates with compassion not denigrated and sullied by these bizarre examples of "reduction to practice"?

Despite the triviality of some of these actions, there are others that have more serious consequences. Take the rapidly hardening position that stress is an identifiable factor in causing injury to people and thus is used to support their workmen's compensation claims. The financial consequences of accepting the thesis that a fuzzy, neo-Freudian, nonphysical force can cause injury can be devastating. It is not that there aren't known physical effects from stress, but the whole concept is fraught with problems.

Job stress has become a *cause célèbre* in workmen's compensation claims, especially in California. In this state, psychiatric or so-called mental stress claims have increased by 700 percent over the past ten years.

Let's look at it with some attempt at logic. Does any given job cause stress? If it does, does everyone who performs that job suffer an equal amount of stress? Probably not, but if they do, does it cause disability in everyone? Certainly not. Then does the job create the stress and, creating the stress, does it disable all people who do that job? Certainly not. It seems fairly clear that it is how a particular person reacts to stress that counts, i.e., it's a deficiency or weakness or a pathology of the person, rather than the job, which acts upon that person. Usually, most people who do that job are not disabled by it—which further defines it as an individual's problem. Must we psychoanalyze every applicant for a job to be certain that he can do it without stress? Job stress claims are the absolute ultimate in the victimology that is corroding our national psyche.

We had a stress claim case in our company some years ago that sticks in my mind. A bright chap in his fifties, running one of our technical divisions, had a heart attack. He recovered after an angioplasty. A lawyer persuaded him to make a workmen's compensation claim for a "stress induced" heart attack, which I believe was awarded administratively.

When he returned to work, we gave him a lesser job in his old department to relieve him of the stress of running the department. Poor fellow, he had to accept a humiliating demotion because of his stress claim. Even sadder, less than a year later he suffered a second heart attack and died. The reduced stress in his lesser position did not save him from that sad end. The fact is that a significant percentage of angioplasties collapse in time, and that's what probably caused his death.

The final monument to the cult of the victim in our social system is our handling of criminals, and the incessant debate of whether to punish or treat them. Unfortunately, psychiatry has only been marginally successful in preventing crimes against one's self, but it has been even less successful in inhibiting crimes against others. James Wilson says that there is a criminal personality—that a fairly constant segment of the population (about 10 percent) commits most of the crimes.

Should crimes against society be punished? The answers of experts in the field are all over the map, but probably the real answer lies in Judeo-Christian ethic. The "eye for an eye or tooth for a tooth" prescription goes back to the Old Testament, giving rise to the position, "Let the punishment fit the crime." Some scholars have pointed out that even that statement has been misinterpreted. It may actually have been supporting a *limitation* on punishment.

This problem of whether to punish or not may actually become more acute as we develop psychotropic drugs. We are finding increasingly that many mental illnesses or behavioral problems are caused by malfunctioning chemical reactions in the body and the brain. If the shadowy cause and effect of psychological theory is replaced by a more rigorous chemical reaction paradigm, will that be the ultimate excuse for sins against society? Perhaps, but I believe that the central core of the Judeo-Christian ethic will still prevail and those subjective standards will be maintained.

There is another, perhaps more pragmatic, reason why there must be punishment for crimes against society. It is the only practical way of affirming that we abhor such crimes, and it is a semi-quantitative way of saying how serious those crimes are. Words will not do, nor will appealing to a moral sense, which is so minimal in the criminal pathology. Psychologists say that treatment, whether behavioral or chemical, will rarely be accepted without the impelling force of the alternative, which is punishment. They also say that "diagnosis does not exonerate." I have discussed this subject with Dr. Lewis R. Baxter, Jr., the UCLA neuro-psychiatrist. Here is what he says:

> I agree that what pop psychology "neo-Freudians" have done—on many levels—would make old Sigmund spin in his grave. Yes, like all behavior, criminal behavior must have a brain substrate that mediates its expression. This says nothing about cause— and certainly many of the "neo-Freudian" ideas of the "causative" effects of early life experience have been refuted by modern studies. . . . This does not mean that there should not be societal consequences to unacceptable behavior! If you're not going to execute such persons, or lock them up for life—and I certainly do not support such "disposal"—the goals of a penal

system should be both to deter and to reform. In either case, all we know about behavior says that there should be adverse consequences for unwanted behaviors, just as there must be, and usually are, incentives for positive acts.

Modern behavioral work shows that consequences shape future behavior. Our own work may be the first in humans to demonstrate changes in brain function as a result of behavioral modification, but there are many earlier studies in animals, and also demonstrations in humans of how the brain changes function with simple learning.

The problem of people with "impulse control disorders" is that such persons do not properly evaluate the full consequences of their actions before acting. Remember, however, that the goal of any psychiatric treatment of criminal persons, indeed of anyone, should not be "mind control." Rather, the goal should be to allow individuals the functional capacity of mind to correctly evaluate the consequences of actions, and thus be truly "responsible." Whether through medication or talk therapy—for the criminal or anyone else—this is what psychiatry should promote.

If the current trend continues toward a chemically based behavioral model rather than a neo-Freudian one, it may substantially change the face of compassion. Indeed, I hazard the guess that compassion in such an era might turn out to be less destructive than it is with the Freudian model.

Finally, I summarize my views this way:

1. Social legislation should not concentrate on serving the negative pathology of people, but should take into account reinforcement of the positive.

2. Such legislation should be restricted in scope. It is not compassionate to include as many people as possible, because this induces and rewards dependent behavior.

3. People are denigrated by the false image of themselves as helpless victims.

4. Though there is a criminal pathology, it is restricted to a small percentage of the people.

5. Most people have an innate moral sense. Social legislation should aim to reinforce those moral values and "self-actualization."

6. The cult of the victim creates victims. All too often, social legislation is based only upon the abnormal pathology of Freud.

7. The ultimate goal of social legislation should be to free people of guilt, dependency, and the denigration of themselves as victims. It should let people earn self-respect or self-esteem, for then they are truly free or "liberated."

8. Compassion is preferably an action of alert and responsible individuals. It is not an obligation of government.

9. Compassion is a wonderful and yet dangerous emotion. It should be "reduced to practice" with the utmost care.

14. The Tyranny of Words: Redux

Men are disposed to live honestly, if the means of doing so are open to them.

—Thomas Jefferson

The process of writing this book has clarified my mission. My modest hope was that the liberals would grant to us conservatives a compassion equal to theirs. However, now I have a more profound worry.

Disregarding all political labels, a clear majority of thoughtful people in this country share what I call the "Great American Liberal Dream." It is most certainly different from the liberal agenda of today. The adjective *American* gives special meaning as a modifier of *liberal*, not only because we are an especially compassionate people, but because we are also impelled by a deep impulse to be free of too much order. American liberalism is like no other.

The order that men submitted to in America was voluntarily accepted by free men—albeit with great trepidation. In Europe, on the other hand, freedom had to be wrested away from the oppression of the existing forces of order. We went the other way: From complete freedom to voluntary order. This difference between freedom wrested from the forces of order and a degree of order voluntarily agreed to by free men is profound.

Our industrialization was an outgrowth of the freedom we gained after the American Revolution. We came here to be free, and we built an industrial and agrarian culture based upon individualism. Once free of European order, the only order we submitted to, when we had to, was primarily at the local level. With our innate moral sense, we recognized how easily freedom could degenerate to anarchy.

The traditional American liberalism that came from our immigrant origins reached a watershed during the period of the Great Depression and the presidency of Franklin D. Roosevelt. When the rugged American individualism that spurred our growth showed weaknesses during those times, and the laissez-faire capitalism could not cope with the enormous dislocation in our society, we sought to relieve suffering and to bring order through government.

Roosevelt, the patrician representative of the new landed gentry, turned to the federal government. He placed the enormous power and resources of Washington at the disposal of the compassionate who wanted to relieve the suffering of the people. The liberal guardians of compassion discovered a resource that they have never relinquished.

Thereafter, the local government that Tocqueville admired suffered a steady erosion. Over the years, traditional American liberalism's mission became perverted. Liberals were deluded into thinking that they were serving compassionate ends by using "order," i.e., the power of government and its seemingly limitless resources, to implement their virtuous schemes.

We all—liberal and conservative—seek the proper blending of freedom and order. The ultimate wisdom is to recognize freedom and order for what they are, regardless of politics, philosophy, or social systems. There is no perfect blending of the two. Though we may long for Hegel's "golden mean," we shall never attain it. Newton's third law says otherwise, for the "golden mean" itself will generate its own opposing force, out of which will arise another, different "golden mean."

If we recognize the dynamic natural instability that is antithetical to social order, the optimum blending of freedom and order is different today than it was yesterday and than it will be tomorrow. It's a moving target, but that does not mean that we should not constantly strive for it.

Where the two opposing political views should merge or intersect is primarily in faith in the people. Those who have lost their faith in the American people and American tradition, whether liberal or conservative, are the ultimate enemies of freedom. I believe that today's liberals have lost their faith in people more completely than the conservatives. They have been blinded by the enormous power of the central government and have shifted their faith to it and away from the people's ability to bring order to their own lives. Unfortunately, many conservatives have also been seduced into accepting the liberal ground rules, despite an occasional cry of "Too much government!" Many are more interested in who controls government than in reducing it.

It is not as surprising as it might seem for conservatives to have enormous faith in the people. In the free market system, which is at the core of our ethic, we are constantly reminded of their collective power.

The submission of free men to the need for order was born out of a sense of brotherhood, of respect for neighbors, of an innate moral sense. They simply knew that unrestrained freedom would result in anarchy and that too much order would result in the servitude that they had rejected by coming here. That is the compelling and defining difference that is uniquely American.

Rereading Tocqueville, it appears that his celebrity is justified. Despite his idealistic view of America, at a time when freedom and order could most easily be accommodated, he said:

> I am convinced, however, that anarchy is not the principal evil that democratic ages have to fear, but the least. For the principle of equality begets two tendencies: the one leads men straight to independence and may suddenly drive them into anarchy; the other conducts them by a longer, more secret, but more certain road to servitude. Nations readily discern the former tendency and are prepared to resist it; they are led away by the latter, without perceiving its drift; hence, it is peculiarly important to point it out.

He anticipated Friedrich Hayek, and he anticipated what is happening today under the false colors of compassion. He predicted the horror of the completely ordered society portrayed so eloquently by Aldous Huxley, Kurt Vonnegut, and George Orwell—ironically, liberals all!

I question the legitimacy of present-day liberals' claims to compassion. Having lost their faith in the people, they push the agenda of government's mission to "aid the disadvantaged" who are deemed to be "helpless," and are thereby made "helpless." They perceive only victims, and they create victims. They perceive evil and, unfortunately, often do evil. That is compassion grown corrosive and unworthy.

What is the solution? Jack Kemp, Bill Bennett, and others are promoting programs of self-government and empowerment. Conservatives are co-opting what had been the central faith of the America liberal dream. Our desire to be free can be entrusted more confidently to our neighbors and brothers. It's clear now why I am not certain if we know who is liberal and who is conservative! Is self-governance, as proposed by Kemp and others, liberal or conservative? It is nothing more or less than a reversion to the kind of democracy that attracted our forebears to our land. Can we go back to the local government that Tocqueville admired? Certainly not in the same way, but we must try.

Incidentally, conservatives are not immune to the tyranny of words. One of our favorite catch phrases is "If the government were only run like a business!" What fatuous nonsense. We have had Hoover Commissions, little Hoover Commissions, and, more recently, the Grace Commission repeating horror story after horror story. You simply cannot run a political entity the same way businesses are run. Public opinion, for instance, tends to be influenced by words: By how values are presented and by the ever-present polls. The voters are not making daily choices where the preferences are expressed as the sum of thousands of data points.

Conservatives should remember that, ironically, the business structure is really not democratic, or at least it has not been until recently. Business has, in fact, been very hierarchical. What has grown up in business then, is a system where order dominates. Dictatorship has always had the reputation of being an efficient system. So, in the name of efficiency, business was constructed as a rigid hierarchy to impose order.

As I noted earlier, however, there is a peaceful revolution going on in business. The prime mover for this revolution is, as always, the market. But, business could not respond to these market forces as it is doing, were it not for a number of technical and pragmatic reasons.

Though probably no less imperious than other entrepreneurs, I have nevertheless always been suspicious of "systems" for control. As our business has expanded, I've been a constant critic of the increased use of these control systems. My reasons for taking this position have always been based on practical considerations. I would ask the Socratic question, "Is the cost of writing out those reports, shuffling pieces of paper around, having ten different people look at them, file them, etc., more than the cost of the error that has been avoided, if there were no such control system?" Under constant pressure to justify the system, our company indeed has less paperwork than most companies our size.

On reflection though, I wonder if I did not do myself an injustice. I could not have argued that way if I did not have a sublime faith that errors made by people, free of imposed order, were less than those ascribed to them by those who opted for increased order. Wasn't I giving free people more credit to perform morally and correctly than those who distrusted them and thus imposed a rigid order?

The marketplace, particularly the global marketplace, has forced all businesses to face this same pragmatic question: Is the cost of the traditional hierarchical management structure justified? The answer has happily been a clearcut no! The result: Restructuring. The "downsizing" has resulted in a massive reduction in middle management, whose primary function was to control and to reduce the cost of human error. But, you cannot reduce or minimize the control system unless you make a parallel commitment to "empower" people, another buzz word in today's business. And, what is empowerment but simply introducing more democracy into business? So, while the political system is opting for more order and more control, the traditionally order-oriented business system has found out, the hard way, that it must introduce more freedom. The irony is striking.

Michael Novak is right to celebrate the importance of business in supporting tradition, values, and providing the means for advancement of society. It is often forgotten that business is the ultimate "pilot plant," or laboratory, for social change because the people in our much-admired free market give us test results very quickly.

American industry is in full cry, doing nothing more or less than opting for more self-governance or empowerment. We call it "pushing decision-making to the lowest level." We call it "flattening organizational structures." It is working in business, and it will work in government if inertia and mistrust of the business model can be overcome. Those who do not accept the social value of the "self-interest" of Adam Smith would do well to note what it has done to make American business more democratic. Can our political system learn from this?

There are three essential elements that make a reversal of the hierarchical structure of business possible. One is the microchip and the revolution in communications that makes it possible to discover and correct aberrations quickly. We no longer need as many layers of management to process information before effective decisions can be made. Hierarchies (and bureaucracies) can be dismantled.

The second point is a corollary of that, namely, that we recognize and accept that there is no control system or system of order that can totally eliminate error or deviation— perfection is unattainable at acceptable cost. In delegating decision-making to the lowest level possible, we accept man's imperfections. Stated in another more positive way, we confirm the intrinsic worthiness of mankind. Free and empowered people are simply smarter than controlled people because they have to be. A person who is free and recognizes that he can fail makes better decisions than one who is protected from failure by a "system."

Business has discovered that empowerment has a more spiritual component. It also has highly emotional consequences. Self-regard is one. For the people, there is the added incentive to prize what "they" own and to repel the predators. This feeling of ownership will attenuate the human weakness that made the rigid order seem necessary before. You do not let your neighbor burn down the home that you own or destroy the enterprise of which you are an owner. Finally, ownership is most profoundly a testament to freedom, for ownership (of property, for instance) distinguishes freedom from dependence, and, therefore, freedom from slavery. More profoundly, people know that there is a price for freedom, and that price is the possibility of failure. Knowing that failure is possible helps human beings make wiser decisions for themselves than the forces of control can make for those who are dependent and have no freedom. With a risk taken and victory attained comes self-esteem.

I proclaim boldly that American business is leading the way to what I term the Conservative American Liberation movement. The essential moral force impelling that liberation will be an elevated sense of compassion for humankind. It is a movement to free people, or to liberate them, from too much order arising from too much management control in business and too much government in our political life. The Conservative American Liberation movement will, hopefully, restructure the political sector, too, as it is restructuring business. It will attack too much governance in government as it is attacking too much governance in business. It is a movement for the enshrinement of the unique society of free men, which is what America should be. It will free us from the order imposed upon us by the arrogant elitists, whether in business or in government.

Impelled by nothing less than the pursuit of self-interest, as well as our innate moral sense, we proclaim that we are served best by free people, by independent people, by responsible people, by people who will choose to limit their own freedom adequately and properly, because of their moral sense. They will do this because it serves their self-interest to do so. The men and women of America are special and unique. They have much to contribute to this world. They need only to be free—to choose freely what order their moral sense requires. That is their destiny and will be the foundation of their glory.

I hope that I have provided ample proof of the corruption of liberal compassion. Can we expect better from the "compassionate conservative"? I believe so. And, to provide the principles which guide our programs, I present herewith:

The Compassionate Conservatives Credo

• We insist that our compassion is at least as worthy as the liberals' and decisively reject discrediting of our programs by questioning the purity of our motives.

• Because we embrace the free market system, we believe that our confidence in the common man is superior to that of the liberals. Our elite is less arrogant than that of the liberals, as we have been repeatedly humbled in the marketplace.

• Because we have seen how well-motivated compassion can become corrosive, we are more cautious and tentative in our prescription, knowing that there can be unforeseen secondary effects. We seek nothing less than "empowerment" of the people.

• As a consequence of our respect for our citizens, we will prescribe programs that give maximum control to individual choice.

• Our programs will acknowledge that our resources at any one time are limited, requiring an educated citizenry to make choices.

• While liberals pay lip service to "self-esteem," their programs often breed dependency, and we shall avoid that trap. We will devise programs which always encompass an element of risk, for only by succeeding when there is a risk of failure can self-respect be earned.

• We reject the use of the term *entitlements* for human benefits given for those in need.

• Most people in need of help have a mixture of feelings of dependency and the impulse to be independent and free. We believe that the number of totally dependent people is much smaller than the constituency of liberal compassion.

• Our programs will provide maximum rewards, both psychological and material, to those who strive for independence. We will recruit a vast number of disadvantaged to learn the benefits of the free market system.

• More fundamentally, we believe that our present centralized government is archaic and overbearing. Though it served a useful purpose in the thirties, it is hopelessly oppressive today. All government bureaucracies should have "sunset" clauses so their effectiveness can be reassessed periodically.

• We believe the Tenth Amendment should be enshrined as the long range beacon for giving governance back to the people.

• The ultimate goal is to strip central government of control over our lives that should reside with state and local government. The list is long: Education, welfare, health care, housing, environmental needs, labor policy, and many more that have been usurped by Washington.

• Income tax should be returned to its fundamental goal—to raise money to run government—and should be stripped of all social and business special agendas. This argues for some simple form of flat tax.

• We aim to reverse the current situation of the dominant taxing entity being national government. Someday, the primary tax revenue will be city, country, and state taxes.

• We recognize that these changes will take generations to effect, but we will apply the pressure for change, consistently and firmly, because our citizens deserve our unswerving respect and support for them.

• We revere the family and the great strengths it gives us. These include a sense of responsibility, which is the price of freedom, and, above all, a moral sense that clearly distinguishes us from those others who inhabit our planet.

- Finally, with all its faults, this is the greatest country on earth with the greatest people, and that obligates us to always devote enormous effort to make it even better.

Epilogue

But though I am an old man I am but a young gardener.
—Thomas Jefferson

Obviously, the issues I have raised inevitably lead to the question, How can the noble emotion of compassion be reduced to practice without becoming corrosive? It would be fatuous to think there are any easy answers.

My arena for testing these ideas shall be the Jacobs Family Foundation, the implementation of the compact made with our daughters when we agreed, as a family, to give away the major portion of the resources that they would otherwise have inherited.

We formed the foundation in 1989 with an initial gift of Jacobs Engineering Group stock. It currently has assets of about $23 million and could, I suppose, have assets over $100 million when Vi and I die (depending upon how well Jacobs Engineering Group stock behaves).

Sterile wealth (if there is such a thing) has no meaningful social value. I believe that after the first generation, inherited wealth loses the emotional content and the spirit and the values of the people who earned that wealth. There comes a disconnection between the source of the funds and those who control the funds (whether using it for personal comfort or giving it away to satisfy either guilt or a need to be loved). The culture of those in charge becomes not too dissimilar from the culture of the government bureaucracies who dispense funds confiscated from the taxpayers.

My admonition to the family is: "This is our money." I say this not just because of forfeited inheritance rights, but because my family influenced my ability to take advantage of the opportunities in my business career. If I had a selfish, acquisitive wife who needed "things," or who raised a family without pride, modesty, and a feeling of self-worth, I am convinced my accomplishments would have been much less. If I had three daughters who were spoiled, whining dependents who worshipped money, or were perhaps into drugs or wanton behavior, I know my business life would have been adversely affected. I have had none of this to contend with and, thus, can say that our daughters have a clear claim on the material wealth we have acquired. I am a proud man acknowledging that whatever we have achieved, we have achieved as a family.

Our foundation started out in the conventional way, advertising our guidelines and receiving grant proposals, which quickly grew to a flood. Then the intense discussions started as each worthy proposal appealed to us in different ways.

The first few years were troubling. As the grant requests came pouring in, we all were uncomfortable at "playing God." Virtually all of the proposals were meritorious, they were compassionate, and they had social value. But, we had to choose. I confess that I did not lose the opportunity to pontificate on the free market system and the ever present need for choice. We had "limited resources," thus requiring discrimination. In choosing which proposals to support, we had to reject many more programs, also of great merit. We endorsed "winners," and thus we created "losers." For compassionate people, it was troubling.

The other undesirable side effect was the creation of dependency. We in the philanthropy "business" felt like, and were often regarded as, the "automatic teller machine." Grant requests came back year after year for the annual financial "fix." From our standpoint, there was not much emotional reward feeding a bottomless pit. (We are quick to acknowledge that we have emotional needs, too.) We also found that many of the staff of agencies charged with helping the underprivileged were subconsciously supporting their own emotional needs to be loved and admired by their "clients"—

or worse, exploiting their sense of power over them. Commonly, they tended to minimize or overlook the adverse but hidden effects upon those being helped. In turn, they were dependent upon us. They thus helped create dependency in their constituency, and in turn were dependent upon us, the donors. The ambivalent tensions seem to create a special culture in those who work in the nonprofit arena.

Recognizing the uncertainty about whether philanthropy actually delivers its promise, my entrepreneurial instincts asserted themselves. I questioned the conventional wisdom, but also recognized the factors which led to my own deep pride, as well as my family's. After all, isn't *pride* the word that says it all? Wasn't the ultimate objective of philanthropy to help others to get, or regain pride? Money or material things should only be a mechanism for attaining that socially acceptable result—as opposed to dependency. Agapé in its broadest sense should be the guiding principle.

My own pride comes from having benefited enormously from the free market system that I admire so much; the family's comes from their various chosen roles in contributing to society. The key word here is *contributing*. If we could change even a small percentage of people from being dependents of the community to contributors to the community, then pride would result—both for our brothers and sisters and for us.

The doctrinaire liberal view is that the free market system is somehow a necessary evil. My view is that earning one's way is an important source of pride, and that should be our mission. So, another role we decided to adopt in our foundation was that of "teacher"—not a surprising area for the Jacobs family to stress. Fundamentally, the greatest source of pride, and the related self-esteem, is to take risk and court failure, then to overcome the possibility of failure—to succeed.

I suppose the seeds of the methodology we wanted to implement were sown at the time of the terrible riots in South Central Los Angeles. The *Los Angeles Times* solicited opinions from several business people, including me. In the lead quote, I said,

The business community has failed to sponsor or press for creative solutions of self-help that would give hundreds of thousands of destitute people a stake in the free-enterprise system. Rather than a welfare hand-out, many of the poor obviously just want a shot at succeeding. If we believe in the business system, we must be pro-active in bringing this system to disen-franchised people.

After that article appeared, my telephone rang off the hook with calls from businessmen. "Joe, we agree. Let's or-ganize a business group to attack this problem!" Dick Riordan (now mayor of Los Angeles) took the lead, and "Rebuild L.A." was formed. It has only been partially effective, as it had to compete with an entrenched political bureaucracy whose turf was being attacked. That experience suggested that we needed a "pilot plant" to test the methodology.

In dealing with various nonprofits, we were struck by how rarely their methodology takes into account the dignity of the people they serve. Aphorisms abound: "Give a hand-up, not a hand-out"; "Teach a person to fish and he will feed himself," etc., etc. Yet, how rare are the nonprofits that actu-ally implement these ideas.

Take the "teach to fish" aphorism. What does that really say? Instead of supplying a person a fish to eat every day, you teach him to fish. But, isn't that telling him to take a risk—a risk that he will not catch a fish? You express faith in him when you assume that he will learn to fish and feed himself instead of taking a hand-out from you.

The first experimental project is in Pasadena, California, our hometown. This community of 140,000 people is an unusual mixture of wealth, several large businesses, includ-ing Jacobs Engineering Group, and a 54 percent minority population of mostly blacks and Latinos with a sprinkling of other ethnics.

We asked local businesses to participate in a small busi-ness lending project for the disadvantaged. We asked them to help in two ways. First, we asked them to match an out-right grant of two hundred thousand dollars which the Jacobs

Family Foundation had made. This grant was to provide training and infrastructure for the three agencies involved in implementing the program. We also asked the businesses to guarantee loans made by local banks to the agencies. The group, dubbed Greater Pasadena Business Partners, is just getting started. Is it working? Although we are hopeful, the jury is still out. We are discovering a number of unforeseen roadblocks: Cultural problems in a system that is used to living on grant money; a surprising amount of bureaucratic inertia in the banks, with all of their regulatory problems; and impatience on the part of the business community, in addition to constant concern over the responsible handling of their money.

We're getting there, but it's not easy. We are hopeful that when we get the Pasadena model in full swing, we'll have a process that can be replicated.

Another part of our foundation is our "venture fund," which aims to help "start-up" of social service organizations. One may properly ask, "Aren't there enough agencies around which serve the disadvantaged community? Do you need to create new ones?" That is a problem we discussed in detail. We finally concluded that trying to remake the culture of existing agencies can be very difficult, and that we might better help new groups with creative leadership models. We thought that if we could be in on the formation of a new nonprofit, we could shape it and establish an operational process that hopefully would foster dignity for those being helped.

A shining example is Skid Row Access, started by a young man who is the son of a friend of mine. Trained as an architect, he spent five years with an environmental company. Because of a compassionate drive, he went to work as a project manager for a group of churches that owned hotels in skid row. There, he experienced firsthand compassion breeding dependency.

Finally, he formed a partnership with two of his skid row friends who had some skills as wood workers. Backed by his own funds, they started a business and sold various handmade wooden toys. They've grown from a one-hundred-square-foot storage shed to a six-thousand-square-foot facility. They have a long list of products, all made by residents of skid row.

I had a most interesting discussion with this admirable young man. I said, "Chuck, your business is expanding and pretty soon you'll be able to cover your overheads. Who knows? Maybe you'll even be able to pay yourself and your partners a salary. Then what?" The answer: "I hate having to ask foundations like yours for grants, but we could not have come this far without that help. Perhaps we should become a profit-making company instead of a tax-exempt charitable group. What do you think?"

My heart sang! "Chuck, by all means, go for a profit-making organization. Just think what it will mean to those people in skid row to know that they are not only making a living, but that their work is valued enough to be worth more than just a subsistence for them. Isn't there an added source of pride when someone can say he is not only being paid fairly but is also producing a profit for those who had faith in him? They thus have discharged any obligation they may have had.

"If you want to give the profits away to help others in the community, then you will have a self-sustaining model of philanthropy."

I just know in my bones that Chuck will not only make it, but that he will be a shining beacon of uncorrupted compassion.

We had hired a consultant, Jennifer Vanica, to help us work out a new "vision," as she called it, for our family foundation. She was so intrigued with our willingness to challenge the conventional wisdom of private philanthropy that she agreed to give up her consulting activities to become the full-time administrator of our foundation. She and her husband, Ron Cummings, are seasoned veterans of the nonprofit world, and now they are joining with us as we try to remake, or at least influence, the face of private philanthropy.

I cannot shed my entrepreneurial persona. I sense a market need. I sense a challenge to conventional wisdom. With $86 billion in 33,000 family foundations, an enormous amount of money may be being invested in charities or non-profits with imperfect processes. If the clear-cut objective of philanthropy is to help people to be independent, to have self-esteem, to beam with pride—in short to recognize and accept that they are deserving of human dignity—there must be a radical change in methodology.

If we can develop methods for enhancing and measuring the value of philanthropic dollars in cultivating self-esteem and human dignity, we will perhaps reach the goals of the "compassionate conservative."

Are we arrogant in assuming that we can even make a dent in the face of traditional philanthropy? Absolutely! We know it, and we recognize that we are much more likely to fail in the mission we have chosen, than to succeed. But, it will be fun trying.

To go back to my favorite cartoon, like Babe Ruth, we are going to swing for the fences in philanthropy. We may strike out, but who knows? Perhaps we'll "hit a home run." Let's see.

We welcome comments from our readers. Feel free to write to us at the following address:

Editorial Department
Huntington House Publishers
P.O. Box 53788
Lafayette, LA 70505

More Good Books from Huntington House

Handouts and Pickpockets:
Our Government Gone Berserk
by William P. Hoar

In his new book, William P. Hoar, a noted political analyst, echoes the sentiments of millions of Americans who are tired of being victimized by their own government. Hoar documents attacks on tradition in areas as diverse as the family and the military and exposes wasteful and oppressive tax programs. This chronicle of our government's pitiful decline into an overgrown Nanny State is shocking, but more shocking is Hoar's finding that this degeneration was no accident.

ISBN 1-56384-102-9

The Assault: Liberalism's Attack on Religion, Freedom, and Democracy
by Dale A. Berryhill

In *The Liberal Contradiction*, Berryhill showed just how ludicrous it is when civil rights advocates are racists and feminists are sexists. Now he turns to much more disturbing phenomena, revisiting such issues as censorship, civil rights, gay rights, and political correctness in education and offering commentary and punishment, civil liberties, multiculturalism, and religious freedom. Fortunately, the American people are catching on to the hypocrisy. Still, the culture war is far from over.

ISBN 1-56384-077-4

The Media Hates Conservatives: How It Controls the Flow of Information
by Dale A. Berryhill

Here is clear and powerful evidence that the liberal leaning news media brazenly attempted to influence the outcome of the election between President George Bush and Candidate Bill Clinton. Through a careful analysis of television and newspaper coverage, this book confirms a consistent pattern of liberal bias (even to the point of assisting the Clinton campaign). The major media outlets have taken sides in the culture war. Through bias, distortion, and the violation of professional standards, they have opposed the traditional values embraced by conservatives and most Americans, to the detriment of our country.

ISBN 1-56384-060-X

The Liberal Contradiction
by Dale A. Berryhill

Why are liberals who took part in student demonstrations in the 1960s now trying to stop Operation Rescue from using the very same tactics? Liberalism claims to advocate some definite moral positions: racism and sexism are wrong; tolerance is right; harming the environment is wrong; protecting it is right. But, contemporary liberalism is undermining its own moral foundation. It contends that its positions are morally right and the opposites are wrong, while at the same time, it denies that a moral law (right and wrong) exists. This is the **Liberal Contradiction** and it leads to many ludicrous (and laughable) inconsistencies.

ISBN 1-56384-055-3

The Best of HUMAN EVENTS
Fifty Years of Conservative Thought and Action
Edited by James C. Roberts

Before Ronald Reagan, before Barry Goldwater, since the closing days of World War II, HUMAN EVENTS stood against the prevailing winds of the liberal political Zeitgeist. HUMAN EVENTS has published the best of three generations of conservative writers—academics, journalists, philosophers, politicians: Frank Chodorov and Richard Weaver, Henry Hazlitt and Hans Sennholz, William F. Buckley and M. Stanton Evans, Jack Kemp and Dan Quayle. A representative sample of their work, marking fifty years of American political and social history, is here collected in a single volume.

ISBN 1-56384-018-9

Getting Out:
An Escape Manual for Abused Women
by Kathy L. Cawthon

Four million women are physically assaulted by their husbands, ex-husbands, and boyfriends each year. Of these millions of women, nearly 4,000 die. Kathy Cawthon, herself a former victim of abuse, uses her own experience and the expertise of law enforcement personnel to guide the reader through the process of escaping an abusive relationship. *Getting Out* also shows readers how they can become whole and healthy individuals instead of victims, giving them hope for a better life in the future.

ISBN 1-56384-093-6

I Shot an Elephant in My Pajamas—
The Morrie Ryskind Story
by Morrie Ryskind with John H. M. Roberts

The Morrie Ryskind story is a classic American success story. The son of Russian Jewish immigrants, Ryskind went on to attend Columbia University and achieve legendary fame on Broadway and in Hollywood, win the Pulitzer Prize, and become a noted nationally syndicated columnist. Writing with his legendary theatrical collaborators George S. Kaufman and George and Ira Gershwin, their political satires had an enormous impact on the development of the musical comedy. In Hollywood, many classic films and four of the Marx Brothers' sublime romps also bear the signatory stamp of genius—Morrie Ryskind. Forced by his increasingly conservative views to abandon script-writing in Hollywood, Ryskind had the satisfaction near the end of his life to welcome into his home his old friend, the newly elected President of the United States, Ronald Reagan.

ISBN 1-56384-000-6

Combat Ready
How to Fight the Culture War
by Lynn Stanley

The culture war between traditional values and secular humanism is escalating. At stake are our children. The schools, the liberal media, and even the government, through Outcome Based Education, are indoctrinating our children with moral relativism, instead of moral principles. *Combat Ready* not only discloses the extent to which our society has been influenced by this "anything goes" mentality. It offers sound advice about how parents can protect their children and restore our culture to its biblical foundation.

ISBN 1-56384-074-X

Don't Touch That Dial:
The Impact of the Media on Children and the Family
by Barbara Hattemer & Robert Showers

Men and women without any stake in the outcome of the war between the pornographers and our families have come to the qualified, professional agreement that media does have an effect on our children—an effect that is devastatingly significant. Highly respected researchers, psychologists, and sociologists join the realm of pediatricians, district attorneys, parents, teachers, pastors, and community leaders—who have diligently remained true to the fight against filthy media—in their latest comprehensive critique of the modern media establishment (i.e., film, television, print, art, curriculum).

ISBN Quality Trade Paper 1-56384-032-4
ISBN Hardcover 1-56384-035-9

Political Correctness:
The Cloning of the American Mind
by David Thibodaux, Ph.D.

The author, a professor of literature at the University of Southwestern Louisiana, confronts head on the movement that is now being called Political Correctness. Political correctness, says Thibodaux, "is an umbrella under which advocates of civil rights, gay and lesbian rights, feminism, and environmental causes have gathered." To incur the wrath of these groups, one only has to disagree with them on political, moral, or social issues. To express traditionally Western concepts in universities today can result in not only ostracism, but even suspension. (According to a recent "McNeil-Lehrer News Hour" report, one student was suspended for discussing the reality of the moral law with an avowed homosexual. He was reinstated only after he apologized.)

ISBN 1-56384-026-X

Beyond Political Correctness:
Are There Limits to This Lunacy?
by David Thibodaux

Author of the best-selling *Political Correctness: The Cloning of the American Mind,* Dr. David Thibodaux now presents his long awaited sequel—*Beyond Political Correctness: Are There Limits to This Lunacy?* The politically correct movement has now moved beyond college campuses. The movement has succeeded in turning the educational system of this country into a system of indoctrination. Its effect on education was predictable: steadily declining scores on every conceivable test which measures student performance; and, increasing numbers of college freshmen who know a great deal about condoms, homosexuality, and abortion, but whose basic skills in language, math, and science are alarmingly deficient.

ISBN 1-56384-066-9

Global Bondage
The U.N. Plan to Rule the World
by Cliff Kincaid

The U.N. is now openly laying plans for a World Government—to go along with its already functioning World Army. These plans include global taxation and an International Criminal Court that could prosecute American citizens. In *Global Bondage*, journalist Cliff Kincaid blows the lid off the United Nations. He warns that the move toward global government is gaining ground and that it will succeed if steps are not taken to stop it.

ISBN 1-56384-103-7 Tradepaper
ISBN 1-56384-109-6 Hardcover

A Jewish Conservative
Looks at Pagan America
by Don Feder

With eloquence and insight that rival essayists of antiquity, Don Feder's pen finds his targets in the enemies of God, family, and American tradition and morality. Deftly . . . delightfully . . . the master allegorist and Titian with a typewriter brings clarity to the most complex sociological issues and invokes giggles and wry smiles from both followers and foes. Feder is Jewish to the core, and he finds in his Judaism no inconsistency with an American Judeo-Christian ethic. Questions of morality plague school administrators, district court judges, senators, congressmen, parents, and employers; they are wrestling for answers in a "changing world." Feder challenges this generation and directs inquirers to the original books of wisdom: the Torah and the Bible.

ISBN 1-56384-036-7 Trade Paper
ISBN 1-56384-037-5 Hardcover

Homeless in America: The Solution
by Jeremy Reynalds

Author Jeremy Reynalds' current shelter, Joy Junction, located in Albuquerque, New Mexico, has become the state's largest homeless shelter. Beginning with fifty dollars in his pocket and a lot of compassion, Jeremy Reynalds now runs a shelter that has a yearly budget of over $600,000. He receives no government or United Way funding. Anyone who desires to help can, says Reynalds. If you feel a burden to help those less fortunate than you, read this book.

ISBN 1-56384-063-4

Kinsey, Sex and Fraud: The Indoctrination of a People
by Dr. Judith A. Reisman and Edward Eichel

Kinsey, Sex and Fraud describes the research of Alfred Kinsey which shaped Western society's beliefs and understanding of the nature of human sexuality. His unchallenged conclusions are taught at every level of education—elementary, high school, and college—and quoted in textbooks as undisputed truth. The authors clearly demonstrate that Kinsey's research involved illegal experimentations on several hundred children. The survey was carried out on a non-representative group of Americans, including disproportionately large numbers of sex offenders, prostitutes, prison inmates, and exhibitionists.

ISBN 0-910311-20-X

Out of Control—
Who's Watching Our Child
Protection Agencies?
by Brenda Scott

This book of horror stories is true. The deplorable and unauthorized might of Child Protection Services is capable of reaching into and destroying any home in America. No matter how innocent and happy your family may be, you are one accusation away from disaster. Social workers are allowed to violate constitutional rights and often become judge, jury, and executioner. Innocent parents may appear on computer registers and be branded "child abuser" for life. Every year, it is estimated that over 1 million people are falsely accused of child abuse in this country. You could be next, says author and speaker Brenda Scott.

ISBN 1-56384-069-3

Children No More:
How We Lost a Generation
by Brenda Scott

Child abuse, school yard crime, gangland murders, popular lyrics laced with death motifs, twisted couplings posing as love on MTV and daytime soap operas (both accessible by latch-key children), loving parents portrayed as the enemy, condom pushers, drug apologists, philandering leaders . . . is it any wonder heroes and role models are passe? The author grieves the loss of a generation but savors a hope that the next can be saved.

ISBN 1-56384-083-9

New Gods for a New Age
by Richmond Odom

There is a new state religion in this country. The gods of this new religion are Man, Animals, and Earth. Its roots are deeply embedded in Hinduism and other Eastern religions. The author of *New Gods for a New Age* contends that this new religion has become entrenched in our public and political institutions and is being aggressively imposed on all of us. This humanistic-evolutionary world view has carried great destruction in its path which can be seen in college classrooms where Christianity is belittled, in the courtroom where good is called evil and evil is called good, and in government where the self-interest of those who wield political power is served as opposed to the common good.

ISBN 1-56384-062-6

"Soft Porn" Plays Hardball
by Dr. Judith A. Reisman

With amazing clarity, the author demonstrates that pornography imposes on society a view of women and children that encourages violence and sexual abuse. As crimes against women and children increase to alarming proportions, it's of paramount importance that we recognize the cause of this violence. Pornography should be held accountable for the havoc it has wreaked in our homes and our country.

ISBN Trade Paper 0-910311-65-X
ISBN Hardcover 0-910311-92-7

- *Anyone Can Homeschool*—Terry Dorian & Zan Peters Tyler
- *The Assault*—Dale A. Berryhill
- *Beyond Political Correctness*—David Thibodaux
- *The Best of HUMAN EVENTS*—Edited by James C. Roberts
- *Bleeding Hearts and Propaganda*—James R. Spencer
- *Can Families Survive in Pagan America?*—Samuel Dresner
- *Circle of Death*—Richmond Odom
- *Combat Ready*—Lynn Stanley
- *Conservative, American & Jewish*—Jacob Neusner
- *The Dark Side of Freemasonry*—Ed Decker
- *The Demonic Roots of Globalism*—Gary Kah
- *Do Angels Really Exist?*—David O. Dykes
- *En Route to Global Occupation*—Gary Kah
- *Everyday Evangelism*—Ray Comfort
- **Exposing the AIDS Scandal*—Dr. Paul Cameron
- *Freud's War with God*—Jack Wright, Jr.
- *Gays & Guns*—John Eidsmoe
- *Global Bondage*—Cliff Kincaid
- *Goddess Earth*—Samantha Smith
- *Health Begins in Him*—Terry Dorian
- *Heresy Hunters*—Jim Spencer
- *Hidden Dangers of the Rainbow*—Constance Cumbey
- *High-Voltage Christianity*—Michael Brown
- *High on Adventure*—Stephen Arrington
- *Homeless in America*—Jeremy Reynalds
- *How to Homeschool (Yes, You!)*—Julia Toto
- *Hungry for God*—Larry E. Myers
- *I Shot an Elephant in My Pajamas*—Morrie Ryskind w/ John Roberts
- **Inside the New Age Nightmare*—Randall Baer
- *A Jewish Conservative Looks at Pagan America*—Don Feder
- *Journey into Darkness*—Stephen Arrington
- *Kinsey, Sex and Fraud*—Dr. Judith A. Reisman & Edward Eichel
- *The Liberal Contradiction*—Dale A. Berryhill
- *Legalized Gambling*—John Eidsmoe
- *The Media Hates Conservatives*—Dale A. Berryhill
- *New Gods for a New Age*—Richmond Odom
- *One Man, One Woman, One Lifetime*—Rabbi Reuven Bulka
- *Out of Control*—Brenda Scott
- *Outcome-Based Education*—Peg Luksik & Pamela Hoffecker
- *The Parched Soul of America*—Leslie Kay Hedger w/ Dave Reagan
- *Please Tell Me*—Tom McKenney
- *Political Correctness*—David Thibodaux
- *Resurrecting the Third Reich*—Richard Terrell
- *Revival: Its Principles and Personalities*—Winkie Pratney

*Available in Salt Series

Available at bookstores everywhere or order direct from:
Huntington House Publishers • P.O. Box 53788 • Lafayette, LA 70505

Call toll-free 1-800-749-4009.